First World War
and Army of Occupation
War Diary
France, Belgium and Germany

46 DIVISION
Divisional Troops
Divisional Signal Company
1 March 1915 - 30 June 1919

WO95/2678/2

The Naval & Military Press Ltd
www.nmarchive.com
Published in association with The National Archives

Published by

The Naval & Military Press Ltd

Unit 10 Ridgewood Industrial Park,

Uckfield, East Sussex,

TN22 5QE England

Tel: +44 (0) 1825 749494

www.naval-military-press.com

www.nmarchive.com

This diary has been reprinted in facsimile from the original. Any imperfections are inevitably reproduced and the quality may fall short of modern type and cartographic standards.

© **Crown Copyright**
Images reproduced by permission of The National Archives, London, England, 2015.

Contents

Document type	Place/Title	Date From	Date To
Heading	WO95/2678/2 Divisional Signal Company		
Heading	46th Division Divl Engineers 46th Divl Signal Coy R.E. Mar 1915-Jun 1919		
Heading	46th Division 46th Signal Coy Vol I 13-31.7.15		
War Diary	Havre	01/03/1915	05/03/1915
War Diary	Bavinchove	06/03/1915	08/03/1915
War Diary	Pradelles	09/03/1915	09/03/1915
War Diary	Sailly	11/03/1915	13/03/1915
War Diary	Merris	16/03/1915	05/04/1915
War Diary	St Jans Capelle	06/04/1915	23/06/1915
War Diary	Map. Ref Sheet 28 G 21 C 7.6	24/06/1915	28/06/1915
War Diary	G21C7.6	30/06/1915	31/07/1915
Heading	46th Division 46th Signal Coy R.E. Vol II August 15		
War Diary	G21C7.6	01/08/1915	08/08/1915
War Diary	Kruistraat	09/08/1915	09/08/1915
War Diary	G.21c7.6	09/08/1915	31/08/1915
Heading	46th Division 46th Divl. Signal Coy RE Vol III Sept. 15		
War Diary	G21C7.6	01/09/1917	17/09/1917
War Diary	G26C3.4	18/09/1917	30/09/1917
Heading	46th Divl Signal Co. Oct 1915 Vol IV		
War Diary	G26C3.4	01/10/1915	02/10/1915
War Diary	Bethune	03/10/1915	05/10/1915
War Diary	Gosney	06/10/1915	11/10/1915
War Diary	Sailly Labourse	12/10/1915	15/10/1915
War Diary	Gosnay	15/10/1915	26/10/1915
War Diary	Fouquieres	27/10/1915	27/10/1915
Miscellaneous	Orders RE Communications.	11/10/1915	11/10/1915
Diagram etc	Diagram of Communications 46th Division Appendix I		
Diagram etc	46th Divl Core		
War Diary	Fouquieres	28/10/1915	31/10/1915
Heading	46th Div Sigs. Nov. 1915 Vol V		
War Diary	Fouquieres	01/11/1915	05/11/1915
War Diary	Le Strem	05/11/1915	30/11/1915
Heading	46th Div. Signal Coy Dec 1915 Vol VI		
War Diary	Lestrem	01/12/1915	04/12/1915
War Diary	St. Venant	05/12/1915	12/12/1915
War Diary	St Venant P.4c 9.9	13/12/1915	16/12/1915
War Diary	St Venant	17/12/1915	17/12/1915
War Diary	St Venant P4c 9.9	18/12/1915	18/12/1915
War Diary	Lambres N 10d 7.7	19/12/1915	22/12/1915
War Diary	Lambres	23/12/1915	31/12/1915
Heading	46 Div Signal Co Jan 1916 Vol VII		
War Diary	Lambres	01/01/1916	05/01/1916
War Diary	Berguette	06/01/1916	06/01/1916
War Diary	In Train	07/01/1916	08/01/1916
War Diary	Marseilles	09/01/1916	25/01/1916
War Diary	In Train	26/01/1916	27/01/1916
War Diary	Pont Remy	28/01/1916	31/01/1916
Operation(al) Order(s)	46th Div Signal Co Operation Order No. 34	05/01/1916	05/01/1916
Miscellaneous			

Type	Description	Start	End
Miscellaneous	Order For Embarkation 46th Divl Sig Co R.E. (T), By Major EA Louies.		
War Diary	Pont Remy	01/02/1916	21/02/1916
War Diary	Ribeaucourt	21/02/1916	28/02/1916
War Diary	Doullens	29/02/1916	29/02/1916
Heading	46 Signal Coy R.E. Vol IX		
War Diary	Doullens	01/03/1916	06/03/1916
War Diary	Le Couroy	06/03/1916	10/03/1916
War Diary	Le Couroy to Camblain L'abbe	11/03/1916	11/03/1916
War Diary	Camblain L'Abbe	12/03/1916	31/03/1916
Miscellaneous	Memorandum On Signal Communications	02/03/1916	02/03/1916
Miscellaneous	Station Calls For Use In Dangerous Zone		
Diagram etc	French Stations.		
Heading	46 Div Signal Co RE Feb 1916 Vol XVIII		
Heading	46 Signal Coy RE Vol X		
War Diary	Camblain L'Abbe	01/04/1916	22/04/1916
War Diary	Roelle Court	23/04/1916	06/05/1916
War Diary	Pas	06/05/1916	01/06/1916
Operation(al) Order(s)	Operation Orders No. 58 By Major E.A. Louies R.E. Commanding 46th Div Signal Co RE.	05/07/1916	05/07/1916
War Diary	Pas	01/06/1916	29/06/1916
War Diary	Pas St Amand	30/06/1916	30/06/1916
War Diary	St Amand	01/07/1916	02/07/1916
War Diary	Pas	03/07/1916	04/07/1916
War Diary	Bavincourt	04/07/1916	31/07/1916
Miscellaneous	Head Qus 46th Div. Attached is War Diary of this company for month of August 1916	20/09/1916	20/09/1916
War Diary	Bavincourt	01/08/1916	31/08/1916
Miscellaneous	Divisional Signal School. Programme of Work. Appx I	13/08/1916	13/08/1916
Miscellaneous	Divisional Signal School. Programme. 2nd. Week.		
War Diary	Bavincourt	01/09/1916	30/09/1916
Operation(al) Order(s)	46th Divisional Order No. 95	02/09/1916	02/09/1916
Miscellaneous	O/c Signal. 46th Div Cost Night Operations.	03/09/1916	03/09/1916
Miscellaneous	C Form (Duplicate). Messages And Signals.		
Miscellaneous	A Form. Messages And Signals.		
Miscellaneous	Report on raid of 137th Infantry Brigade, Night Of 2nd/3rd Septr.	00/09/1916	00/09/1916
Miscellaneous	Short Description Of Raid. Appendix I		
Miscellaneous	Operation Orders By Major F.J. Trump, Commanding 1/6th Bn. South Staffordshire Regiment. Appendix II	01/09/1916	01/09/1916
Miscellaneous	Operation Orders By Captain H.V. Mander, Commanding 1/6th Batt: South Staffordshire Regt. Raiding Party, dated 2-9-16 Appendix III	02/09/1916	02/09/1916
Miscellaneous	Appendix IV. Officer Commanding, 1/6th South Staffs Regt.		
Operation(al) Order(s)	Appendix V Artillery Programme. Reference 137th Infantry Brigade Operation Order 89	02/09/1916	02/09/1916
Miscellaneous	O/C Signals 46th Div Further report	04/09/1916	04/09/1916
Miscellaneous	A.D.A.S. VII Corps	04/09/1916	04/09/1916
Miscellaneous	O/c Signals 46th Div	06/09/1916	06/09/1916
Miscellaneous	O.C. Signals 46th Division Raid For 5th South Staff. Telephone Communications.	20/09/1916	20/09/1916
Miscellaneous	O/C Rigs 46th Div.	22/09/1916	22/09/1916
Miscellaneous	Report On Communications Arranged For Raid By 8th Sherwoods On Night Of Sept 21/22	22/09/1916	22/09/1916
Diagram etc	Objective.		

Type	Description	Start	End
War Diary	Bavin Court	01/10/1916	31/10/1916
War Diary	Frohen-Le-Grand	01/11/1916	01/11/1916
Miscellaneous	To O.C. Signals 46th Division.	28/10/1916	28/10/1916
Operation(al) Order(s)	Orders No. 54 By Major E.a Lewis D.S.O. R.E.	30/10/1916	30/10/1916
War Diary	Frohen Le Grand	01/11/1916	02/11/1916
War Diary	St Riquier	02/11/1916	22/11/1916
War Diary	Frohen-Le-Grand	23/11/1916	25/11/1916
War Diary	Lucheux	26/11/1916	07/12/1916
War Diary	Henu	07/12/1916	19/02/1917
War Diary	Gouy	20/02/1917	28/02/1917
Miscellaneous	Report On Communication For Raid By 5th North Staff App 71	26/02/1917	26/02/1917
War Diary	Henu	01/01/1917	17/03/1917
War Diary	Chateau De La Haye	18/03/1917	20/03/1917
War Diary	Couin	21/03/1917	24/03/1917
War Diary	Villers Bocage	24/03/1917	25/03/1917
War Diary	Dury	26/03/1917	28/03/1917
War Diary	Norrent Fontes	29/03/1917	12/04/1917
War Diary	Busnes	13/04/1917	16/04/1917
War Diary	La Beuvriere	17/04/1917	19/04/1917
War Diary	Sains-En-Gohelle	20/04/1917	30/06/1917
Operation(al) Order(s)	Arrangements for Signal Communications in connection with Operation under 46th Division Orders 191 and 206	26/06/1917	26/06/1917
Operation(al) Order(s)	Arrangements for Signal Communications in connection with operations under 46th Division Order 182	06/06/1917	06/06/1917
Diagram etc	Diagram of Telephone Lines (Right Brigade)		
Diagram etc	First Corps Wireless Stations Directing Stn ZAA Sub-Directing Stn-ZH		
War Diary	Sains En Gohelle	01/07/1917	03/07/1917
War Diary	Sheet 36B. Chateau O. 10.b	03/07/1917	08/07/1917
War Diary	Boismont Chateau Map Ref O. 10.b	09/07/1917	24/07/1917
War Diary	Sailly La Bourse (Chateau)	25/07/1917	25/07/1917
War Diary	Sailly La Bourse	26/07/1917	31/07/1917
Miscellaneous	O.C. Signals 46th Division Scheme Of Training.	07/07/1917	07/07/1917
Miscellaneous	To O.C. 46th Div Sig Coy R.E. Scheme Of Training.		
Miscellaneous	Training Programme. No. 4 Section, 46th. Divisional Signal Company R.E.	07/07/1917	07/07/1917
Miscellaneous	Training Programme 46th Divisional Signal Coy R.E.		
War Diary	Sailly La Bourse	01/08/1917	31/10/1917
Miscellaneous	O.C. Signals 46th Division Report On Communications 1/6th North Staff Raid.	31/10/1917	31/10/1917
Miscellaneous	Battalion At Am 44	01/11/1917	01/11/1917
War Diary	Sailly La Bourse.	01/11/1917	31/12/1917
Miscellaneous	Reference O.O. No. 33, D/D 29-10-17	30/10/1917	30/10/1917
War Diary	Sailly La Bourse	01/01/1918	22/01/1918
War Diary	La Beuvriere	23/01/1918	09/02/1918
War Diary	Bomy	10/02/1918	03/03/1918
War Diary	Fouquires	04/03/1918	31/03/1918
Heading	46th Divisional Engineers 46th (North Midland) Signal Company R.E. April 1918		
War Diary	Bracquemont	01/04/1918	13/04/1918
War Diary	Bruay	14/04/1918	23/04/1918
War Diary	Gosnay	24/04/1918	31/05/1918
Miscellaneous	46th Division Signal Communications Estimate Of Work Required To Render Lans Battns Safe.		
Miscellaneous	Action In Case Of Attack Signal Arrangements	09/05/1918	09/05/1918

Type	Description	Date From	Date To
Miscellaneous	Signal Orders.	23/05/1918	23/05/1918
Miscellaneous	Headqrs. 46th Divn. Reference 46th Divn. G. 588	25/05/1918	25/05/1918
War Diary	Chateau Les Charmeiux	01/06/1918	02/06/1918
War Diary	Gosnay	02/06/1918	12/09/1918
War Diary	Beaucourt	18/09/1918	18/09/1918
War Diary	Cauvigny Fm	19/09/1918	19/09/1918
War Diary	Vraignes	21/09/1918	30/09/1918
Miscellaneous	46th Divisional Signal Company. General Instructions For Communication In Battle.		
Miscellaneous	Signal Instructions.		
Diagram etc			
War Diary	Vendelles	01/10/1918	01/10/1918
War Diary	La Baraque	02/10/1918	04/10/1918
War Diary	Macny La Fosse	08/10/1918	08/10/1918
War Diary	Fresnoy Le Grand	10/10/1918	31/10/1918
Miscellaneous	Wireless.	02/10/1918	02/10/1918
Miscellaneous	Visual	13/10/1918	13/10/1918
Miscellaneous	Signal Instructions.		
Diagram etc	Diagram A Line Communications 46 Div 16-17 Oct 1918		
Diagram etc	Diagram B Wireless Communications 46 Div 16-17 Oct 1918		
Diagram etc	Diagram C Visual Communications 46 Div 16-17/10/18		
War Diary	Bohain	01/11/1918	01/11/1918
War Diary	Molain	04/11/1918	04/11/1918
War Diary	Larbre De Guise	05/11/1917	05/11/1917
War Diary	Catillon	06/11/1918	06/11/1918
War Diary	Prisches	08/11/1918	08/11/1918
War Diary	Cartignies	09/11/1918	09/11/1918
War Diary	Sains Du Nord	11/11/1918	11/11/1918
War Diary	Landrecies	01/01/1919	09/01/1919
War Diary	Le Cateau	09/01/1919	31/01/1919
War Diary	Caudry	02/04/1919	30/06/1919

W095/2678/2 Divisional Signal Company

46TH DIVISION
DIVL ENGINEERS

46TH DIVL SIGNAL COY R.E.
MAR 1915 - JUN 1919

121/6390

46th Division

46th Signal Coy.

Vol I   1·3 — 31·7·15.

Army Form C. 2118.

WAR DIARY
or
INTELLIGENCE SUMMARY.
(Erase heading not required.)

Instructions regarding War Diaries and Intelligence Summaries are contained in F.S. Regs., Part II. and the Staff Manual respectively. Title pages will be prepared in manuscript.

Hour, Date, Place	Summary of Events and Information	Remarks and references to Appendices
9.30 am March 1/15 HAVRE	Arrived HAVRE. 1 Officer and 57 O.R. left on S.S. TINTORETTO. All on ship. Disembarkation for them in S.S. TINTORETTO. All on ship. One equipment wagon, four mules and one company proceeded to Rest Camp. Two Motor Lorries attached to 16 Squad Co.	
March 2/15 "	Bivouacked at Rest Camp. Remainder of Company.	Equipment received from F.M.C.O.
March 3/15 "		Without equipment today.
10 am March 4/15 "	O.C. took party of 16 men to explore proposed route from ABBEVILLE via AIRAINES, NEUFCHATEL, and HESDIN via NEUFCHATEL.	R.B.M.
11.30 am	Orders received to assume command of Company to entrain at GARE MARITIME HAVRE en route for BAUVIGNE.	
8.30 pm	Entrainment completed.	
8.30 am March 5/15	O.C. and Motor Lorries started for ABBEVILLE where the men were to rest.	LEA
11.30 pm	Arrival of Lorries at ABBEVILLE and BAUVIGNE.	
	Arrival of Company at BAUVIGNE. Billet at RESIERE.	

WAR DIARY
or
INTELLIGENCE SUMMARY.
(Erase heading not required.)

Army Form C. 2118.

Instructions regarding War Diaries and Intelligence Summaries are contained in F.S. Regs., Part II. and the Staff Manual respectively. Title pages will be prepared in manuscript.

Hour, Date, Place	Summary of Events and Information	Remarks and references to Appendices
Mch 6/15 BAVINCOVE	H.Q. established at station. Lieut Jerram R.E. attached to Signal C [illegible]. N.M. Div. while [illegible] Pl. 30 posts. Tests of wires received. Communication established with [illegible] Branch at WAEMAEIS CAESLIE and 2t Bn (S.R.) NOORDPEENE [illegible] with 2nd Army relays etc Woud[illegible]	
Mch 8/15 "	Letts[?] pulled up and communication successfully wp to [illegible] wires in was a workable mass. A hostile despatch rider a LIEUT of CAA [illegible] forward to prisoners to PRADELLES tomorrow	
Mch 9/15 PRADELLES	Marched to new billets. Cables laid to Inf. Brigade at BORRE and MERRIS. Bishops and Army also joined through	
Mch 11/15 SAILLY	Orders to take over lines at SAILLY. Communication established with Langham. SAA. Suffolk Inf. Bde. No to tend men not altogether clear	
Mch 13/15 "	Captain JESSON with main [illegible]	
Mch 14/15 MERRIS	Captain ROBO attached [illegible] to take up billets at MERRIS. Communication established with 2nd Army P Bn Coy.	

P.T.O.

WAR DIARY or INTELLIGENCE SUMMARY

Army Form C. 2118.

(Erase heading not required.)

Instructions regarding War Diaries and Intelligence Summaries are contained in F. S. Regs., Part II. and the Staff Manual respectively. Title pages will be prepared in manuscript.

Hour, Date, Place	Summary of Events and Information	Remarks and references to Appendices
Cont.d Inch 16/15 MERRIS.	Also with Staffs Brigade at OULTERSTEENE, LINES + late TROUAYARD. Notes + details Brigade detrained	
10 am Inch 7/15	Commun. established with D.A. - General Staff	
Inch 8/15 "	Lieut LEWIS attached for instructions with 6th Army with Capt CLARKE and Army attachés to arrive	
Inch 19/15 to Inch 31/15	During this time lends internal work was done. Bipples taking Office management them management cannot not detail	

Army Form C. 2118.

WAR DIARY
—or—
INTELLIGENCE SUMMARY.
(Erase heading not required.)

Instructions regarding War Diaries and Intelligence Summaries are contained in F.S. Regs., Part II. and the Staff Manual respectively. Title pages will be prepared in manuscript.

Hour, Date, Place	Summary of Events and Information	Remarks and references to Appendices
Apr 1/15 to Apr 4/15 MERRIS	Maintenance of Communication	
Apr 5/15 "	Relaid in cable trench-dug to following the line occupied by V. Army.	
Apr 6/15 ST JANS CAPPEL 4.30 am	Communications of V. Army. When an autoft by N.M.Div. Offices close at MERRIS and RELIEF handed over to SIG. M.I. DIV	
Apr 6/15 "	Transferring instruments here as in preparation for new post. Commun. established with 1st 2nd 3rd & 4th Cavalry Regts. 10th Royal Field R.H.A. Telegraph established to O.C.	
Apr 7/15 to Apr 14/15 "	Continuing to make good that [illegible] thro' [illegible] temporary [illegible]	

Army Form C. 2118.

WAR DIARY
or
INTELLIGENCE SUMMARY.
(Erase heading not required.)

Instructions regarding War Diaries and Intelligence Summaries are contained in F.S. Regs., Part II. and the Staff Manual respectively. Title pages will be prepared in manuscript.

Hour, Date, Place	Summary of Events and Information	Remarks and references to Appendices
Apl 13/15 ST JANS CAPELLE	Arrivals working intermixed on present network. Line to Staffs. safely estd. Own lines replenished and brought to position. Commencing working at Poste No 2 getting on lines.	
Apl 14/15 "	Conference with CRA and O.C. Artillery Brigades & R.E., 2nd R.H.A. Drilling keyboards, commencing working.	
Apl 15 "		
Apl 20	Re-changing of poles & withdrawal of telephony communication.	
Apl 21 "		
Apl 22	Putting in power cables for artillery communication.	

Army Form C. 2118.

WAR DIARY
or
INTELLIGENCE SUMMARY.
(Erase heading not required.)

Instructions regarding War Diaries and Intelligence Summaries are contained in F. S. Regs., Part II. and the Staff Manual respectively. Title pages will be prepared in manuscript.

Hour, Date, Place	Summary of Events and Information	Remarks and references to Appendices
9 am Apr 23 St JANS CAPELLE	Commenced a scheme to test Artillery telephonic system on arrival of Batteries & Brigades & Practical work &c	
Apr 24	Artillery war tactics (Conformity Concentration) at CRA Hd Qrs. It is found that this works much more satisfactorily than the previous Concentration	
Apr 25 to Apr 30th	Scheme for Artillery telephonic system continues	

Army Form C. 2118.

WAR DIARY
or
INTELLIGENCE SUMMARY.
(Erase heading not required.)

Hour, Date, Place	Summary of Events and Information	Remarks and references to Appendices
May 1st ST JANS CAPPELLE	Transferred circuit interference between train on 2nd Corps wire well.	
2pm May 2nd "	Conference at KEMMEL with CRA and Brig. ack H.Q. Brig. ading Officers Artillery. Concerned into the R.H.A. Group arrilleted [illegible] and [illegible] which must lead to return lines of communication conversations	
May 3 " to June 4 "	[illegible] points placed as targets (Battery) lines with improvement in [illegible] of methods	
June 5 "	Lieut WHITLEY and Lieut SILITOE attached to Group C for instruction in [illegible]	

Forms/C. 2118/10.

Army Form C. 2118.

WAR DIARY
or
INTELLIGENCE SUMMARY.
(Erase heading not required.)

Instructions regarding War Diaries and Intelligence Summaries are contained in F.S. Regs., Part II. and the Staff Manual respectively. Title pages will be prepared in manuscript.

Hour, Date, Place	Summary of Events and Information	Remarks and references to Appendices
May 15 St JANS-CAPELLE	New telephone class for Artillery telephones commenced	
May 16 to May 22 /15	Receiving cables and substituting same for [illegible]. Picking up dielect cables.	95 miles of dielect cable recovered and unrest appears to suffer tingle to under the same ourfurd carp repair.
May 23 /15	A rumour to camp out with rifles left from to all ranks with or to take part in telephone examined by Staff Que Signal Ing pmuch [illegible] to the papers.	
May 24 to May 31 /15	Repairing cables which have been recovered	

Army Form C. 2118.

WAR DIARY
or
INTELLIGENCE SUMMARY.
(Erase heading not required.)

Instructions regarding War Diaries and Intelligence Summaries are contained in F. S. Regs., Part II. and the Staff Manual respectively. Title pages will be prepared in manuscript.

Hour, Date, Place	Summary of Events and Information	Remarks and references to Appendices
June 1/15 ST JANS CAPELLE	Artillery fought [illegible] under cover not below fire in [illegible] of [illegible] landing in [illegible] &c	
June 10/15	Air [illegible] from CRA to Artillery Bdes. TOC and the Advanced Artillery H.Q.s BRANDHOEK 10 km. [illegible] from [illegible] to [illegible] about 3/4 [illegible] B.d. Office D5 cable [illegible] at between C.RA Chateau and 2nd RFA at BRANDHOEK. Approximately 1½ m.	
June 2/15	[illegible] in establishing of [illegible] for advanced H.Q. P.O. at BRANDHOEK	
June 3/15	New lines from DAG to CRA advanced further. Recovery of [illegible] lines for moving from [illegible]. H.Q.	

Army Form C. 2118.

WAR DIARY
or
INTELLIGENCE SUMMARY.
(Erase heading not required.)

Instructions regarding War Diaries and Intelligence Summaries are contained in F.S. Regs., Part II. and the Staff Manual respectively. Title pages will be prepared in manuscript.

Hour, Date, Place	Summary of Events and Information	Remarks and references to Appendices
June 13 ST JANS CAPELLE	Completed survey for C.R.E. (Estimates) H.D. Weir Stations from at LOCRE and KEMMEL Positions KEMMEL HILL N 28 C.9.5. LOCRE M 23 C 3.1 5 Mile Br (NIEPPE) M L HOU 65A	
June 14 "	Air line section connecting Lt Parsons Ofr No 4 Sec. proceeds on leave. Lt McClure relieves him. All work Butts No 2 Engineerstons tested and found correct.	
June 15 " 10 am 12/30 pm	Capt FISHER attached from 22nd Div for 3 days Advanced H.D. opened for test of communication Advanced H.D. closed. Communic. satisfactory	

Army Form C. 2118.

WAR DIARY
or
INTELLIGENCE SUMMARY.
(Erase heading not required.)

Instructions regarding War Diaries and Intelligence Summaries are contained in F.S. Regs., Part II. and the Staff Manual respectively. Title pages will be prepared in manuscript.

Hour, Date, Place	Summary of Events and Information	Remarks and references to Appendices
June 16 ST JANS ne CAPELLE	Inc. further Active Stuff on hand yet. 139th J. Bde. Mr.b YPRES Stn. 26 M 3.c.6.4. 139th T.M.B. & A in App.	
June 20/15	139th J. Bde. march on night of 20/21 from ZEVECOTEN and OUDEZOM to a point S. of NEAMERTIGHNE leaving LOCRE at 9pm. Reserve Bath. 8th Bn. (4th Div) moved LOCRE.	
23rd	139th J. Bde. removes to ECOLE E. of YPRES, 46.6. Bn. bigrad. section took over from 50th Dy. Sn. Lines completed from CRA to 1st and 4th Bdes. K.B.A.C.	

Army Form C. 2118.

WAR DIARY
or
INTELLIGENCE SUMMARY.
(Erase heading not required.)

Instructions regarding War Diaries and Intelligence Summaries are contained in F.S. Regs., Part II. and the Staff Manual respectively. Title pages will be prepared in manuscript.

Hour, Date, Place	Summary of Events and Information	Remarks and references to Appendices
Jun '16 MAP REF Sheet 28 G.21.C.7.6	Sigs 46th Div closed at ST JANS CAPELLE at 12 noon and opened at Fm marked by Sisters at 12 noon. CRA moved office. Sigs moved similarly at 12am.	
Jun 25 '16 "	Laying phone lines from Wen to Rupert Ge-Ert at KRUISTRAAT and trenches occpd thereof 137, 138 & 139 Brigades. Also trenches Nth of Brigades. Phones to the Right Centre. Laying line from 3rd Exchange to A.D.M.S. Lent TODAY S/L No 2 Que on loan 3rd Bde R.F.A connected up to CRA	
Jun 26 '16 "		
Jun 28 '16 "	Owing to shell fire N.Z of 131th Inf Bde moved from ECOLE to Divnl Advance Report Centre. All lines but though suffering severely communication maintained both Civil & Field (Civ line) D.A.D.O.S	

Army Form C. 2118.

WAR DIARY
or
INTELLIGENCE SUMMARY.
(Erase heading not required.)

Instructions regarding War Diaries and Intelligence Summaries are contained in F.S. Regs., Part II. and the Staff Manual respectively. Title pages will be prepared in manuscript.

Hour, Date, Place	Summary of Events and Information	Remarks and references to Appendices
June 30 GHE 76	Commenced returning DF by Coure Art Line all wire cut by shell fire E of Right Centre	
11:45 pm "		
1:45 am July '16	Wire cut during night repaired and communication by Fulham	
12:5 am July '16	Two shells fired by enemy of H 20 c 7.13 ¼ R on Line from ECOLE to Front line Right Centre	
July 2 '15	Signal Officer instructed in method of B.	
July 3 '16	All leads from own to New Report Office reconnoitred	
July 5 '16	Change LA up HAR to NEW R 14A Rd. R 17 b 5 & 13 R 14 d 2A 1 R 5	

Army Form C. 2118.

WAR DIARY
or
INTELLIGENCE SUMMARY.
(Erase heading not required.)

Instructions regarding War Diaries and Intelligence Summaries are contained in F.S. Regs., Part II. and the Staff Manual respectively. Title pages will be prepared in manuscript.

Hour, Date, Place	Summary of Events and Information	Remarks and references to Appendices
	[illegible handwritten entries]	

Army Form C. 2118.

WAR DIARY
or
INTELLIGENCE SUMMARY.
(Erase heading not required.)

Instructions regarding War Diaries and Intelligence Summaries are contained in F.S. Regs., Part II. and the Staff Manual respectively. Title pages will be prepared in manuscript.

Hour, Date, Place	Summary of Events and Information	Remarks and references to Appendices
July 11/16 GWC 7b	C.O.R. Digwell was taken sick took home. Lt. Gur from station to chief gn. were ran [illegible] by Gen. are further 200 yds of [illegible] infantry.	Sgd.
July 12/16	Round coloured lamps as a [illegible] when [illegible] in Armagh Wood 300. ARMAGH WOOD	Sgd.
July 13/16	[illegible] Enemy have to left further MAPLE COPSE complete [illegible] and [illegible] [illegible] has [illegible] how 13th Bde were £ I 2.4.7.1	Sgd.
July 14/16	Enemy [illegible] in left Battn [illegible] & [illegible] & [illegible] [illegible] A. R. [illegible] to [illegible] [illegible] [illegible] [illegible] [illegible] the know. CRAP 46th 1.30 AM	Sgd.
July 16/16 "	II Corps Commence to [illegible] up with [illegible] [illegible] 13th Bde to running to II Corl. E of ZILLEBEKE (d Command)	

Army Form C. 2118.

WAR DIARY
of
INTELLIGENCE SUMMARY.
(Erase heading not required.)

Instructions regarding War Diaries and Intelligence
Summaries are contained in F.S. Regs., Part II.
and the Staff Manual respectively. Title pages
will be prepared in manuscript.

Hour, Date, Place	Summary of Events and Information	Remarks and references to Appendices
8am July 5th G2IC 76.	Henry Van Ingham came General heavy rain. Communication breaktime on account to after Cuits. All lines restored by [illegible]	
July 15/75 "	18th & 2 Bn move to Hqs B. [Rest]. Remnant of Jaffa Rumshops acquired No 3 Sec	
10am July 27/75 "	Hour with CRA for No 3 brigade in the field. KRUICTERT take over from C Dar. Remnant and rebuilt [illegible]	
July 28 "	Remnant [illegible] after the [illegible] Metalling [illegible] [illegible] [illegible] to [illegible] medical [illegible] on to [illegible]	
July 29/75 July 31/75 "	Abundant communication in NO8 & & Services	

121/6743

46th Division

467th Field Coy RE

August 15.

Army Form C. 2118.

WAR DIARY
~~or~~ INTELLIGENCE SUMMARY.
(Erase heading not required.)

Instructions regarding War Diaries and Intelligence Summaries are contained in F. S. Regs., Part II. and the Staff Manual respectively. Title pages will be prepared in manuscript.

Hour, Date, Place	Summary of Events and Information	Remarks and references to Appendices
August G.H.Q.	Maintenance of lines	—
Aug 2/16	do	—
Aug 3/16	do	—
Aug 4 1915		—

Army Form C. 2118.

WAR DIARY
or
INTELLIGENCE SUMMARY.
(Erase heading not required.)

Instructions regarding War Diaries and Intelligence Summaries are contained in F.S. Regs., Part II. and the Staff Manual respectively. Title pages will be prepared in manuscript.

Hour, Date, Place	Summary of Events and Information	Remarks and references to Appendices
9am Aug 5/15 G.H.Q.7.6	Installing to line transfer exchange Room	
10/30	at Head Report Centre. Conference of Brig Officers at 13th Batt H.Q.	
Aug 6	Working on new and existing lines from G.H.Q. Operations on the No 11 sections and extension (?)	Sub
8am Aug 7/15	Completing arrangements of General lines with exception of Vickers Trench to 13 Batt. Above now carried out.	Sub Aug 15 F.D G H.S.L 7th Batt
12.30pm	G.H.Q. Artery light held Invalid. Getting horses & valise for move.	MASS Corp.S 13th Brigade Signal Section
	TRUVICTRAAT Building supplies last SINTER 30/7/15	

Army Form C. 2118.

WAR DIARY
or
INTELLIGENCE SUMMARY.
(Erase heading not required.)

Instructions regarding War Diaries and Intelligence Summaries are contained in F.S. Regs., Part II. and the Staff Manual respectively. Title pages will be prepared in manuscript.

Hour, Date, Place	Summary of Events and Information	Remarks and references to Appendices
Aug 8/15 G.21.E.7.6.	Line runs to connect Advance Right Centre with 6th Div Arty. Advd Centre (Ramparts YPRES) G Branch of R.A. occupied this Adv. H.2. at 4 pm. Q Office remained open at back H.2. SKC open Report back came into existence & all H.Qr – H.Qr Report Centres for the disposal of wireless traffic. Wireless set installed near right Battn 138th Bde. Visual signalling established between new 138th Bde Hdqrs N.2. and KRUISTRAAT and signallers not carried Adv. H.Q. See Sgd G. to man the later point. Pack horses supplied with 20 pigeons natives of 12 GSO 3 in attendance at Adv. Bn. N.2. GSO 2 in attendance at MAPLE COPSE (N.2; B.36.3a) 139 IB occupied Redt N.2. MAPLE COPSE	
2 a.m. Aug 9/15 KRUISTRAAT	Bombardment of enemys trenches commenced. Communication between Redts N.2, 139 Bde and Redt N.2. broken down. Communication kept up through runners. 23rd Bde R.F.A. Communication established through...	

Army Form C. 2118.

WAR DIARY
or
INTELLIGENCE SUMMARY.
(Erase heading not required.)

Instructions regarding War Diaries and Intelligence Summaries are contained in F.S. Regs., Part II. and the Staff Manual respectively. Title pages will be prepared in manuscript.

Hour, Date, Place	Summary of Events and Information	Remarks and references to Appendices
Aug 9/15 G.H.Q. 2nd	Arrival. Staff requires telephone speech between h.q. and MAPLE COPSE than has been tried and found impracticable. Wireless station found to be out of order and not used. Naval stations ZILLEBEKE LAKE and REVISTRAAT not workable after daylight owing to enemy snipers. Battle W/T arrangement often broken – wire frangible. Pack mules lost. Only Artillery comms. broken – wire frangible. Pack mules lost. Get in another unit?	
Aug 10/15 "	G.S.O.3 returned to H.Q. Brigade H.Q. still up. Laying of new cable ZILLEBEKE LAKE to MAPLE COPSE commenced	
10:30 am Aug 11/15 13 pm "	Brigade Artillery advanced H.Q. closed. Battle H.Q. at " (commenced) closed	
Aug 12/15 "	Normal.	

Army Form C. 2118.

WAR DIARY
or
INTELLIGENCE SUMMARY.
(Erase heading not required.)

Instructions regarding War Diaries and Intelligence Summaries are contained in F.S. Regs., Part II. and the Staff Manual respectively. Title pages will be prepared in manuscript.

Hour, Date, Place	Summary of Events and Information	Remarks and references to Appendices
Aug 13. 15 G.U.C 16.	Installing 30 lines testphones and protector strip at Marrameded. Change of (Corpo-) we ought to have all trunk lines from through ERE - (5th Corps repertments) complete. but made font FINTER clearing of wire which originally ran through old report centre at KRUISTRAAT. New cable completed between North West Corner of ZILLEBEKE LAKE and NAPIER COPSE. Requisition numbers to town 3 in North of R.2.	Hal
Aug 14 "	New line laid to 6th Siege Battery (Farmyard to YPRES) Report Centre. 6th Div. Report centre closed from 4th F. Ba. Report Centre, and occupied by 14/15 1B.	
Aug 15 "	Lieut. J.S. PARSONS Rose, Sig. Reported sick and examined by Divisional Hospital. Lieut FINTER relieves him.	

Army Form C. 2118.

WAR DIARY
or
INTELLIGENCE SUMMARY.
(Erase heading not required.)

Instructions regarding War Diaries and Intelligence Summaries are contained in F.S. Regs., Part II. and the Staff Manual respectively. Title pages will be prepared in manuscript.

Hour, Date, Place	Summary of Events and Information	Remarks and references to Appendices
Aug 13/15 G2C 7.6.	Rode through ZILLEBEKE LAKE to 18th Aus Bn HQ trenches and afterwards to looking at down the Austrian trench.	
Aug 14/15	Normal	
Aug 15/15 "	"	
Aug 16/15 "	"	
Aug 17/15	13/A.I.B. Bde. out to Rest & Communication of	
Aug 18/15 —	SKR.I. III Bn with Bn HQ Hdqrs established at Chapman Well. No. 14 received.	

(3 29 6) W 3332—1107 100,000 10/13 H W V Forms/C. 2118/10

Army Form C. 2118.

WAR DIARY
or
INTELLIGENCE SUMMARY.
(Erase heading not required.)

Instructions regarding War Diaries and Intelligence Summaries are contained in F.S. Regs., Part II. and the Staff Manual respectively. Title pages will be prepared in manuscript.

Hour, Date, Place	Summary of Events and Information	Remarks and references to Appendices
Aug 1/15 G.2. C.7.6	Took over role line from E Coys from H.Q. 4th K.S.L.I. & E.R.C.	
Aug 2/15	Normal	
Aug 3/15	13th Brigade took up the line at Wood Co to H.S.E. Communication with Bois Ne In Khale	

(9 29 6) W 8332—1107 100,000 10/13 H W V Forms/C. 2118/10

Army Form C. 2118.

WAR DIARY
or
INTELLIGENCE SUMMARY.
(Erase heading not required.)

Instructions regarding War Diaries and Intelligence Summaries are contained in F.S. Regs., Part II. and the Staff Manual respectively. Title pages will be prepared in manuscript.

Hour, Date, Place	Summary of Events and Information	Remarks and references to Appendices
Aug 24 GHQ 76	Quiet. One man from Report Centre to 137th Bde Hd slightly shaken by shell but was warned that there was more [illegible] coming. 36th Commencing [illegible]	
Aug 25/15	Making further dug out trenches to 137 & 138 Bdes from Report Centre.	
Aug 26	Classes commenced to instruction of Officers & Drivers at HdQrs S.A.C. Lieut ARNOLD Instructor Lieut HARDING { Making further dug out trenches for horses cables 137 & 138 Bdes to Report Centre.	

Army Form C. 2118.

WAR DIARY
or
INTELLIGENCE SUMMARY.
(Erase heading not required.)

Instructions regarding War Diaries and Intelligence Summaries are contained in F.S. Regs., Part II. and the Staff Manual respectively. Title pages will be prepared in manuscript.

Hour, Date, Place	Summary of Events and Information	Remarks and references to Appendices
Aug 17/15. G.u.C 76.	Working parties of MMR trenches for hours cables to 137th Bde.	
Aug 18/15	MMR horses trench to working parties trenches from 137th Bde to Rupert Cantine	
Aug 21/15 "	Working parties filling in trenches to horses cables from Rupert Cantin to Bayards front. J.S. PARSONS left for ENGLAND to hand over of instruction	

Army Form C. 2118.

WAR DIARY
or
INTELLIGENCE SUMMARY.
(Erase heading not required.)

Instructions regarding War Diaries and Intelligence Summaries are contained in F.S. Regs., Part II. and the Staff Manual respectively. Title pages will be prepared in manuscript.

Hour, Date, Place	Summary of Events and Information	Remarks and references to Appendices
Aug 30/15 GHQ 76	Working party filling in trench for horse exits	
Aug 31/15 G2116 T.C.	Following horse lines completed and holding (1) YDFR to 139 Brigade. Battalion peut Trench (2) 137 Bde to 2nd RFA (3) YDFR Ammunition to 139 Bde. Regret has moved back to original position nr Hulye	

46th Division

46th Divl. Signal Coy RE

Vol III

Sept. 15

Army Form C. 2118.

WAR DIARY
or
INTELLIGENCE SUMMARY.

(Erase heading not required.)

Instructions regarding War Diaries and Intelligence Summaries are contained in F.S. Regs., Part II. and the Staff Manual respectively. Title pages will be prepared in manuscript.

Hour, Date, Place	Summary of Events and Information	Remarks and references to Appendices
Sept 1/15 G.H.Q 7.6.	Brands train load for Belgian Artillery to DICKEBUSCH Rest & Convoy up with Convoy Line from 139 Brigade. Relieved train load of horses 13th A Battle N.O. 6 Carriers up with horses cable to Battn at 9.0	
Sept 2/15	CAPT. DE FORTON 2. (Lieut A. E. G. LEWIS)	
Sept 3/15 "	Line load from 138th Batt to Rest Billets was Ammn Stores. D.A.C connects up at new position 1. 2. 3. 74 Amm Cols also connects up 2nd R.A.R.H.A	

Army Form C. 2118.

WAR DIARY
or
INTELLIGENCE SUMMARY.
(Erase heading not required.)

Instructions regarding War Diaries and Intelligence Summaries are contained in F.S. Regs., Part II. and the Staff Manual respectively. Title pages will be prepared in manuscript.

Hour, Date, Place	Summary of Events and Information	Remarks and references to Appendices
Sept 1st G.H.Q.7b	2 lines laid to Rest Camp By Brigade. Pair in [?] on DM Donnabes line	
Sept 5/15 G.H.Q.76	C.S.M. Parker left for ENGLAND via ROUEN to take up position at mill late. Pair R.D. ESCOMBE attacked from 26 AM + sent to 137th Brigade. Patrol if wires out 1 wandering wires broken by transport between ERC and YCR.	
Sept 6/15 "	Normal	

Army Form C. 2118.

WAR DIARY
or
INTELLIGENCE SUMMARY.
(Erase heading not required.)

Instructions regarding War Diaries and Intelligence Summaries are contained in F.S. Regs., Part II. and the Staff Manual respectively. Title pages will be prepared in manuscript.

Hour, Date, Place	Summary of Events and Information	Remarks and references to Appendices
	Normal	

WAR DIARY
or
INTELLIGENCE SUMMARY.

(Erase heading not required.)

Army Form C. 2118.

Hour, Date, Place	Summary of Events and Information	Remarks and references to Appendices
[illegible] G2 & 7.6	Normal	
[illegible]	"	
[illegible]	"	

WAR DIARY
or
INTELLIGENCE SUMMARY.

(Erase heading not required.)

Army Form C. 2118.

Instructions regarding War Diaries and Intelligence Summaries are contained in F. S. Regs., Part II. and the Staff Manual respectively. Title pages will be prepared in manuscript.

Hour, Date, Place	Summary of Events and Information	Remarks and references to Appendices
Sept 13 GHQ 7.6	Running new permanent line to new front to Gpo	
Sept 14/15	As above	
Sept 15/16.	As above Running cable west of front Report Centori Lieut R ESCOMBE taken over charge of 138th Bde Depots	

Army Form C. 2118.

WAR DIARY
or
INTELLIGENCE SUMMARY.
(Erase heading not required.)

Instructions regarding War Diaries and Intelligence Summaries are contained in F. S. Regs., Part II. and the Staff Manual respectively. Title pages will be prepared in manuscript.

Hour, Date, Place	Summary of Events and Information	Remarks and references to Appendices
Sept 13 G.H.Q. 76.	Preparing wires & roots for removal to new Div'nl Hd. Qrs.	
Sept 14 G.H.Q. 76.	Preparing wires & roots for removal to new Div'nl Hd. Qrs. Lieut FINTER goes on leave	
Sept 15. G.H.Q. 34. 10 am	Removing Div'nl H.Q. to new position. All lines working well after change.	

WAR DIARY
or
INTELLIGENCE SUMMARY.
(Erase heading not required.)

Army Form C. 2118.

Instructions regarding War Diaries and Intelligence Summaries are contained in F. S. Regs., Part II. and the Staff Manual respectively. Title pages will be prepared in manuscript.

Hour, Date, Place	Summary of Events and Information	Remarks and references to Appendices
Sept 19. G 26 3.4	Remained here to hand over to 113. Brigade. Line at west end of Report Centre	
Sept 20. "	Nothing to new report. Had C-C. Remained new here to hand over to 2.	
Sept 21. "	Remained here to H.Q.M.S. near the Cleaning up stuff to new Div. H.Q.	

WAR DIARY
or
INTELLIGENCE SUMMARY.
(Erase heading not required.)

Army Form C. 2118.

Instructions regarding War Diaries and Intelligence Summaries are contained in F. S. Regs., Part II. and the Staff Manual respectively. Title pages will be prepared in manuscript.

Hour, Date, Place	Summary of Events and Information	Remarks and references to Appendices
Sept 22/15 G26C3.4	Completing change of instruments to new office W7A2. Running line from CRA to Field Coy	
Sept 23/15 G26C.3.4	Conference of Signal Officers 10 a.m. Making arrangements to probable move to Battn HQ2. Running line to new position of CRA. CRA moves to new position 3.30 p.m. Line laid from CRA Front. heavy loss by shell fire. Workmen.	
Sept 24/15 G26C3.4	Preparing to remove to Battle HdQrs. Wireless installed working at Report Centre. R4 when TWs office at HY25R at 7.30 p.m. "G.1" Branch stand "j" 10 p.m. 3 men sent to man Visual 138th Bde. ERC (Corps Rep. Centre) Message 5.30 p.m.	Ok

WAR DIARY or INTELLIGENCE SUMMARY.

Army Form C. 2118.

Hour, Date, Place	Summary of Events and Information	Remarks and references to Appendices
Sept 25/15 G 26 c 3.4	"G" Branch 46th Divn remain up at Report centre. R.A. remain at R.C. Report centre closed at 4.30 p.m. and "G" Branch return to Divn. H.Qrs. R.A. return to their H.Qrs 4.30 p.m. Divn assembled 4/6 p.m. "V" Corps Report centre remains open reinstating Sup. Keeping YDFR (R.C.) open on a Transmitting Office. 137th 138th 139th Bdes return from Battle H.Qrs to Brigade H.Qrs. Communication from YDFR to all lines excellent having breakdown during 25th. 3hrs by faulty line being bet. to 138th Battle H.Qrs. and 4th How Bde broken by own men. In no case was communication interrupted either by deciphermen telegraph. Note. Owing to Corps not moving back R.A. had only own line forward from H.Qrs. to Bdes: during night. Nordes Staken material at Stony Farm 137th Rule Verladeremolen. Sup hudyo machine.	

WCR

WAR DIARY
or
INTELLIGENCE SUMMARY.
(Erase heading not required.)

Army Form C. 2118.

Hour, Date, Place	Summary of Events and Information	Remarks and references to Appendices
Sept 26/15 G 26 c 3.4.	E.R.C. closed at 10. am drawing in to reconnaissance communication. All material & extra tools withdrawn from YPER. And installed at Div. Hqrs. C.R.A. Sig. Office completed and an 8 line government instrument 4.10. am. utilized. CRA's communication onto 7 mil OPP's and Div line UIR. Computer considered of Sig. Buckley/Pears and Sergt Haynes.	
Sept 27/15 G 26 c 3.A.	C.R.E. cable line to 7 inch RA needed in 3 cable lines from Div Hqrs to R.A. needed in. Maj. S.A. Lewis proceeded to England on leave. No faults in Communication to report. MIR	
Sept 28/15 G 26 c 3.4.	Sgt Hurd and party completing air line to CRE route home to Stamford, Lincs. Everything above normal and all own pool. MJR	

WAR DIARY
or
INTELLIGENCE SUMMARY.
(Erase heading not required.)

Army Form C. 2118.

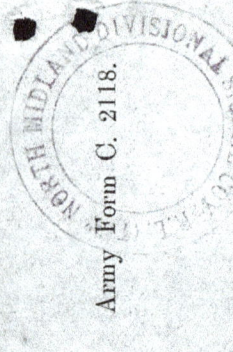

Instructions regarding War Diaries and Intelligence Summaries are contained in F. S. Regs., Part II. and the Staff Manual respectively. Title pages will be prepared in manuscript.

Hour, Date, Place	Summary of Events and Information	Remarks and references to Appendices
Sept 29/15. G.26.c.3.4.	Operation Order No 16 received. Handed over plan of Lewis to O/c Sig 3rd F/Ybsins. Commenced to dismantle YDFR Wind Maj S.A. Lewis return. Lt Pratt returns from 137H/3rd to YDFR R.A. Operation Order No 16 de cancel	
Sept 30/15 G.26.c.3.4.	R.A. Operation Order No 17 received. OC Signals to England recommissioned. Capt Cameron 9th Srim Lakey men. hins Pratt or 4 men attached at YDFR. Intimates that our relays at YDFR. from O.C. No 17 received. In Relief No 2+4 Sectn Stoken column at route at 6.25pm 2/10/15 G 34 D 8.3 Maj S.A. Lewis returned. E R C went on errand with YD5-YDFR. Place legate one G 33 4th and four of early tin of causatin	

131/7519

46th Div: Signal Co.

Oct 1915

vol IV

Army Form C. 2118

WAR DIARY
of
INTELLIGENCE SUMMARY HQ RA 1st Army CRG
(Erase heading not required.)

Instructions regarding War Diaries and Intelligence Summaries are contained in F.S. Regs., Part II. and the Staff Manual respectively. Title Pages will be prepared in manuscript.

Place	Date	Hour	Summary of Events and Information	Remarks and references to Appendices
G26C.3.4	Oct 1/15		Dismantling Office and preparing for removal of Divl Hd Qrs to BETHUNE	GW
"	Oct 2/15		As above	GW
BETHUNE	Oct 3/15		Divl Hd Qrs removed at 12 noon Communication established with XI Corps and 1st Army.	GW
"	Oct 4/15		normal	GW
"	Oct 5/15		normal	GW

Army Form C. 2118.

WAR DIARY
INTELLIGENCE SUMMARY.
(Erase heading not required.)

4th Army CRA

Hour, Date, Place	Summary of Events and Information	Remarks and references to Appendices
Oct 6/15 GOSNEY	Divisional Hd Qrs. remained at midday. Communication established with 3rd Corps. Telephones run to Inf Brigade at Sh FOUQUIERES and HESDIGNEUL two lines (telegraph telephone) runs to CRA. Also lines to RA Brigades.	Sh
Oct 7/15 "	Normal	Sh
Oct 8/15 "	Normal	Sh
Oct 9/15 "	Preparing to move. Advanced Hd Qrs Qrs to SAILLY LA BOURSE taking over area from French Divn.	Sh

Army Form C. 2118.

WAR DIARY
or
INTELLIGENCE SUMMARY.
(Erase heading not required.)

Instructions regarding War Diaries and Intelligence Summaries are contained in F.S. Regs., Part II. and the Staff Manual respectively. Title pages will be prepared in manuscript.

Hour, Date, Place	Summary of Events and Information	Remarks and references to Appendices
Oct 1/15 GOSNEY	[illegible handwritten entry regarding officers, report, march through trenches to Brigade HQ]	
Oct 2/15	As above. Signal Co. orders to be issued. Meeting of all signal officers in Divn.	
Oct 3/15 SAILLY LA BOURSE	Opened new Centre at 10 noon. All wires working well. [illegible] collide at [illegible] in VERMELLES [illegible] Augustus.	

Army Form C. 2118.

WAR DIARY
—or—
INTELLIGENCE SUMMARY.
(Erase heading not required.)

Instructions regarding War Diaries and Intelligence Summaries are contained in F.S. Regs., Part II. and the Staff Manual respectively. Title pages will be prepared in manuscript.

46th Div. Signal Coy R.E.

Hour, Date, Place	Summary of Events and Information	Remarks and references to Appendices
13/10/15 SAILLY LABOURZE	[illegible handwritten entry regarding 137th & 138th Infantry Brigades at HOHENZOLLERN]	Lee [illegible]
14/10/15 SAILLY LABOURZE	[illegible handwritten entry]	
11am 15/10/15 SAILLY LABOURZE	137th Inf Bde march from [illegible] to [illegible] 3rd Bde occupied SAILLY LABOURZE 138th Bde left for FOUQUIERES PRIEUR ST [illegible]	
3pm	[illegible]	
7.15pm GOSNEY	[illegible]	

Army Form C. 2118.

WAR DIARY
or
INTELLIGENCE SUMMARY.
(Erase heading not required.)

Instructions regarding War Diaries and Intelligence Summaries are contained in F.S. Regs., Part II. and the Staff Manual respectively. Title pages will be prepared in manuscript.

Hour, Date, Place	Summary of Events and Information	Remarks and references to Appendices
4/30 am 16./10/15 GOSNEY	139th Brigade arrived FOUQUIERES. Whole Brigade telephone communication with Group H.Q. established	
17/10/15 GOSNAY	2/Lieut. MacGuire joined as Supernt. Officer to 46th South Sig.	
	Lieut. H.C.C. Lewis on leave.	
	Situation normal.	

Army Form C. 2118.

WAR DIARY
or
INTELLIGENCE SUMMARY.
(Erase heading not required.)

Instructions regarding War Diaries and Intelligence Summaries are contained in F.S. Regs., Part II. and the Staff Manual respectively. Title pages will be prepared in manuscript.

Hour, Date, Place	Summary of Events and Information	Remarks and references to Appendices
18th Oct. Gosnay.	NORMAL	
19th Oct. Gosnay.	139th Bde move from Anzin, at 2.30. 13th Batn. commenced by plane to take over billets on arrival. 137th Bde move from Chateau de Paly to ALLOUAGNE at 11am (28 lorries sent detached army) Ammunition column return Ry DIR. Telephone lines run to all Bde CMY	
20th Oct. Gosnay. Chateau.	Lay day. 13th Upland line from Anzin to 139th B.M. 137th at ALLOUAGNE and Ammunition columns at K.1/2 a Bn CMY here in billet. Orderly Room removed from Chateau to get Mess. Inspection of horses with Batn Major R.A. & Major E.A. Lewis on torn at 7am. Officers Antinal Animal	

Army Form C. 2118.

WAR DIARY
or
INTELLIGENCE SUMMARY.
(Erase heading not required.)

46th Div G.H.Q

Instructions regarding War Diaries and Intelligence Summaries are contained in F.S. Regs., Part II. and the Staff Manual respectively. Title pages will be prepared in manuscript.

Hour, Date, Place	Summary of Events and Information	Remarks and references to Appendices
21/10/15 GOSNAY.	Relieving Aeroplanes seen from August 5 139th, 131st Bdes. 1/2nd Fd Coy. Colliery Scrum. Reveille in old Dr. lines from 5th August 139th & 137th Bdes. Gunner Stralian wounded.	G.M 4.4.R
22/10/15 GOSNAY	NORMAL	4.4.R
23/10/15 GOSNAY	Div. O.O. No 23 rec.	4.4.R
24/10/15 GOSNAY.	R.A. Operation order No 23 received and acted. HQrs at HAM-EN-ARTOIS. Bties at ST HILAIRE and BOURBEC. Lieut H.S.C Lewis returned from leave.	

Army Form C. 2118

WAR DIARY
or
INTELLIGENCE SUMMARY
(Erase heading not required.)

Instructions regarding War Diaries and Intelligence Summaries are contained in F. S. Regs., Part II. and the Staff Manual respectively. Title Pages will be prepared in manuscript.

Place	Date	Hour	Summary of Events and Information	Remarks and references to Appendices
GOSNAY	25th	9 am	Divn Arty Operation Order No 23 cancelled	
			137th 2nd Bde moved HdQrs from Chateau at ALLOUAGNE to FOUQUERIL	
		2 pm	and communication established from Bde HdQrs. XDivn HdQrs at 2 pm	SH
				UR
GOSNAY	26		138th Inf Bde moved from Headquarters to Verkin (Vaugan)	
			139th " " " " " Labourreur to Bethune	
			Div Arty " HdQrs from Mil at Gosnay to chateau	
			in Bethune. Communication established all round without delay.	
			Div Arty Bde service in at Labourreur	UR
			Signal Coy moved to new HdQrs	
FOUQUIERES	27	10 am	Divn HdQrs move from Les Chammont to Prieuré St Pry	UR
			and 15th Divn HdQrs move to Chateau des Pres	
			HdQrs + Sig Office at Gosnay handed over to 16th Divn	

SECRET.

ORDERS RE COMMUNICATIONS.

1. **Telegraphs and Telephones.**

    From XIth Corps to Divisional Headquarters Advanced 1 Telephone and 1 Telegraph. Communication with Divisional Head Quarters will be obtained through XIth Corps.

    Communication will be available between :-

    Telephone
    Div'l Head Qrs. Advanced
    and
    (1. Guards Division.
    (2. 12th Division.
    (3. 12th Division Advanced.
    (4. 2nd Division.
    (5. 137th, 138th and 139th Bdes.

    Lines between Divisional Head Quarters Advanced and Brigades will be allotted as shewn in diagram (Appendix 1) and it must be noted that these lines form alternative routes for each Brigade. Linemen will be stationed at Divisional Head Quarters Advanced FOUNTAIN KEEP (G.2 c.77) and at each Brigade Head Quarters, and their duties are to keep the Brigade lines through at all times.

    The 139th Infantry Brigade will come in circuit on each of the Brigade Lines.

    From Brigade Head Quarters to Battalions one line will be provided, with linemen stationed at very frequent intervals along their lengths. These men will devote the whole of their attention to keeping these lines working, and each man will be responsible for a given portion of each line.

    Battalion trench lines and inter Battalion lines will be maintained under the direction of Battalion Signal Officers.

    D.5 cable specially wound on portable drums is provided for Battalions and this is to be used in the attack, when every endeavour is to be made to maintain communication with Battalion and Brigade Head Quarters, by carrying forward telephones and wire.

    Lateral communication to all similar formations on the left of 138th Brigade and the right of 137th will be provided and maintained.

2. **Wireless.**

    The 46th Divisional Signal Companies wireless Station will be at the RAILWAY DISC (G.3 c.5.2) (The DISC formerly used by the Railway is still standing at this point). All messages handed in at this station must be in cypher or coded The station will be under the direct command of O.C. Signals, 137th Brigade, who will ration the operators and be responsible for the removal of the station when the Brigade Head Quarters advances. Messages will be transmitted from this station to the Wireless Dugout at L.18 a.33, and sent thence by wire to Divisional Headquarters Advanced.

    N.B. Wireless is only to be made use of in case of breakdown of ordinary communication.

3. **Visual.**

    Visual communication has been established at the following

    points

points :-
(a) FOSSE No. 9 ANNEQUIN.
(b) RAILWAY WELL (G.3 b.25)

These stations will pick up any messages sent from the front and the station at FOSSE No. 9 will be in direct telephonic communication with Divisional Head Quarters Advanced.

During the attack Visual Stations will be established whether telephones be successful or not. The South West corner of the DUMP will be specially looked for and afterwards the N.W. corner. Telescopes will be trained on these points, and it is expected that the Battalion Signallers of 137th Brigade will establish Visual Stations at these points.

The Battalion Signallers of the 138th Brigade will establish a Visual Station (1) at G.4 b.33, and afterwards at any possible point between A.28 d.15 and A.28 d.49, and these lines will be watched from the Stations behind.

Each Brigade Signalling Officer will have 4 men at his disposal from the Battalion Signallers with a complete visual apparatus. He will keep them until they are needed and he will then send them to a definite position to establish a visual station.

The proposed Stations will also be looked out for by Observers in our present system of trenches, and these Observers will be placed at positions close to present telephone dugouts. They will be supplied with periscopes. These arrangements will be made by Battalion Signallers in co-operation with Brigade Signal Officers, who will see that all concerned are acquainted with the arrangements.

Visual messages will be signalled straight through at a rate not exceeding six words per minute. They will then be repeated "DD".

It must be remembered that short messages are more likely to get through than long ones and messages must be made as short as possible - one or two words if possible.

4. Runners.

Four runners will be kept at Brigade Head Quarters and two close to each telephone dugouts in the trenches. These will be used only if the lines break down.

5. Pigeons.

A pigeon loft will be established at the 137th Brigade Head Quarters. These birds will be sent on at the discretion of O.C. 137th Brigade Signals. There will be a direct wire to Divisional Headquarters Advanced for pigeon messages.

6. Despatch Riders.

A station consisting of three motor cyclists will be established at VERMELLES in a position to be pointed out by O.C. Signals 138th Brigade. These will be used by the two Brigades in action.

Existing Artillery Communications will be taken over at Brigade Signal Offices.

The following arrangements must be specially noted and most carefully adhered to.

Periodic weather reports will be sent to Corps Head Quarters from Section Gas Officers over the telephone systems of Companies

and

and Battalions. "Clear the line" facilities must be given for those messages, from 8 a.m. to 8.15 a.m., 10 a.m. to 10.15 a.m., 12 noon to 12.15 p.m., 1 p.m. to 1.30 p.m. on 13th inst. The urgency of this must be impressed on all concerned. All work must be stopped to allow these messages to pass.

Issued to :-
    XIth Corps Signals (1)
    Signal Coy. Officers & Signalmasters (8)
    Battalion Signal Officers (12)
    War Diary (1)

11/10/15.   E.A. LEWIS, Major,

                                O.C. 46th Div'l Signal Coy. R.E.

[Handwritten annotation:]
5 am to 5.15 am
7   7.15
12   12.15
1   1.30

APPENDIX 1.

DIAGRAM OF COMMUNICATIONS
46th DIVISION

Sept 30/15
W/T Burrys Sgls

- F2YD5-3 1st Div
- E17Y7-3 139 Bde
- 136 Bde E2qc4-5
- L.C.O. K4 Bo-5
- E16A6-5 C.R.A.
- G. Roberts
- E21A8-8 C.R.E.
- E21A4-6 137 Bde
- E21D5-9
- Orderly Room
- CQMS
- Q. Branch
- O.C. Sigs
- E25B3-7 Sds Div
- J11B4-5 ART. ADES
- 1st Army

Army Form C. 2118

WAR DIARY
or
INTELLIGENCE SUMMARY
(Erase heading not required.)

WK Army CRE

Place	Date	Hour	Summary of Events and Information	Remarks and references to Appendices
FOUQUIERES	28th	8 a.m.	Laying new telephone line from Chateau Prise St Pry (Hqrs) to 138th Bn to 138th Bn. Linked in C.R.E. on telephone line to 137th Ben. Otherwise situation normal. Major E.A. Lewis returned 3.30 a.m. 2/Lieut C.A. Magure proceeded to heat (Telegraph 29th Bn)	Sgd Sgd
"	29		Lieut U.G. Roberts proceeds on leave from 3 a.m.	Sgd
"	30		Constructing Newproject lines	Sgd
"	31		— Do — Communication Normal	Sgd

4th Sept. Sigs.

Nov. 1915

Vol V

12/7663

Army Form C. 2118

WAR DIARY
or
INTELLIGENCE SUMMARY
(Erase heading not required.)

Instructions regarding War Diaries and Intelligence Summaries are contained in F. S. Regs., Part II. and the Staff Manual respectively. Title Pages will be prepared in manuscript.

Place	Date	Hour	Summary of Events and Information	Remarks and references to Appendices
FOUQUIERES	1915 May 1	8 am	Improving present lines and billets. Communication trench made.	
"	2	"	Visiting Indian Corps H.Q. at MERVILLE and arranging to take over lines from MEERUT and LAHORE Divns.	
"	3	"	Running lines and installing telephones, preparation to takeover No Aprs. O.O. 24 Received.	
"	4	"	As above. Takeover order No 1 received. No " " No 2 " 25 "	
LESTREM	5	10.0 am	Divnl H.Qrs closed at 10 am and opened at LESTREM. Reconnaissance roads. O.O. No 26 Recd.	

Army Form C. 2118

WAR DIARY
or
INTELLIGENCE SUMMARY
(Erase heading not required.)

46th Div Signal Co R.E.

Place	Date	Hour	Summary of Events and Information	Remarks and references to Appendices
LESTREM	1915 Nov 6	8 am	Running lines for CRA and to connect Divisional and Brigades	Int.
"	7	"	Lieut G.R. Roberts returned from leave. Running lines and fitting up new HeadQrs.	Int.
"	8	"	All working parties running lines for new movements	Int.
"	9	"	As above. Detachment sent to O.C. 137th Brigade for Battn lines	Int.
"	10	"		Int.
"	11	"	O.O. No 27 received	

Army Form C. 2118

WAR DIARY
or
INTELLIGENCE SUMMARY
(Erase heading not required.)

Instructions regarding War Diaries and Intelligence Summaries are contained in F. S. Regs., Part II. and the Staff Manual respectively. Title Pages will be prepared in manuscript.

Place	Date 1915	Hour	Summary of Events and Information	Remarks and references to Appendices
LESTREM	May 12	6am	Improving Infantry Organisation and preparation for removal of artillery batteries	Enh
"	13	"	As above	Enh
"	14	"	Normal	Enh
"	15	"	Conveying troops to have leave and making various alterations	Enh
"	16	"	Improving communication lines and making use of other districts here	Enh
"	17	"	As above	Enh

Army Form C. 2118

WAR DIARY
or
INTELLIGENCE SUMMARY
(Erase heading not required.)

Instructions regarding War Diaries and Intelligence Summaries are contained in F. S. Regs., Part II. and the Staff Manual respectively. Title Pages will be prepared in manuscript.

Place	Date	Hour	Summary of Events and Information	Remarks and references to Appendices
LESTREM	Mar 18	8 pm	Intense Artillery Commencement	Gen Sh
"	19	"	on alarm	Sh
"	20	"	Enemy starting hole in communication trench. what seemed to be abandoned not filled in.	Sh
"	21	"	as above	Gen Sh
"	22	"	testing hole which our posts not to forward communication trench & recovering same.	Sh
"	23	"	as above	Sh
"	24	"	138 Bde relieve at 2 pm. in front trenches an arpm at X 17 C. 7.1 above have been	Sh

1875 Wt. W593/826 1,000,000 4/15 J.B.C. & A. A.D.S.S./Forms/C. 2118.

WAR DIARY
or
INTELLIGENCE SUMMARY

Army Form C. 21

Place	Date	Hour	Summary of Events and Information	Remarks and references to Appendices
LE STREM	[illegible]	[illegible]	Running end lines to new formation of 138th Bde Sigs	
"	26	"	Relaying traffic Kia Daiva brigade signal company motor cyclist traffic etc	
"	27	"	Reforming lines of Infantry communication etc	Etc
"	28	"	As above	Etc
"	29	"	Reforming lines of artillery communication etc	Etc
"	30	"	As above	Etc

46th Dn. Signal Coys

Dec 1915
———
Vol VI

Army Form C. 2118

WAR DIARY
or
INTELLIGENCE SUMMARY
(Erase heading not required.)

H.Q. Divnl. Signal Co. R.E.

Place	Date	Hour	Summary of Events and Information	Remarks and references to Appendices
LESTREM	1/3/15	—	Improving lines. Renewing cables rendezvous-taking wire	G.S.
"	2/3/15		Building "comic" aerial lines to recover cable	E.h. E.h.
"	3/3/15		Having one communication to 19th Divn Rifle (Lt. BELL) Arranged with Lt. BELL to keep 137th Bde on lines through 19th Div Signal Office	E.h.
"	4/3/15		Loading up & preparing for move	E.h.

Army Form C. 2118

WAR DIARY
or
INTELLIGENCE SUMMARY
(Erase heading not required.)

Instructions regarding War Diaries and Intelligence Summaries are contained in F. S. Regs., Part II. and the Staff Manual respectively. Title Pages will be prepared in manuscript.

Place	Date	Hour	Summary of Events and Information	Remarks and references to Appendices
ST-VENANT	5/10/15	—	D.in H.Qrs. moved from LESTREM to ST VENANT	
"	6/10/15	—	Joining up communication with 136 & 139 Inf Bde	
"	7/10/15	—	No operations	
"	8/10/15	—	Inspecting equipment. machine loading test. Searching area about to 19th Div Reserve & Corps Reserve.	

WAR DIARY or INTELLIGENCE SUMMARY

Army Form C. 2118

Place	Date	Hour	Summary of Events and Information	Remarks and references to Appendices
ST VENANT	9/2/15	—	Checking stores and equipment. Indenting for same	
"	10/2/15	—	As above. Same	
"	11/2/15	—	As above. Same	
"	12/2/15	—	Inspection of vehicles. Packing tents. Same	

Army Form C. 2118

WAR DIARY
or
INTELLIGENCE SUMMARY

(Erase heading not required.)

Instructions regarding War Diaries and Intelligence Summaries are contained in F. S. Regs., Part II. and the Staff Manual respectively. Title Pages will be prepared in manuscript.

Place	Date	Hour	Summary of Events and Information	Remarks and references to Appendices
ST VÉNANT P4c 9.9.	13/10/15			
"	14/10/15		SITUATION NORMAL	
"	15/10/15			
"	16/10/15			

WAR DIARY
or
INTELLIGENCE SUMMARY

Army Form C. 2118

(Erase heading not required.)

Instructions regarding War Diaries and Intelligence Summaries are contained in F.S. Regs., Part II. and the Staff Manual respectively. Title Pages will be prepared in manuscript.

Place	Date	Hour	Summary of Events and Information	Remarks and references to Appendices
ST. VENANT	17/5/15		Situation normal. Inspection of kite equipment etc.	J.L.
ST VENANT P4c 9.9	18/5/15		Divnl O.O. No 31 received and acted on. Situation normal. Lines stopped. Major Lewis proceeded on leave to England. 2.30 a.m. Lieut Davis 38th Divn Sig. Stores nr lines etc.	W.R.
LAMBRES N10d 7.7	19/14/15	11 a.m.	Division moved from Hingh at ST VENANT to LAMBRES. Sig Office open at LAMBRES at 12 noon. Communication with 1st Army. XV & XI Corps established at 1.30 p.m. No wire taken over running 38th Divn. Take over Office at ST VENANT 11 a.m. Sig Cnt. marched off 9 a.m. All horses and men billeted in houses and barns. Cable line laid from MOLINGHEM to 2nd Bde RFA at P&C 5.8 Sig Office to CRE and Sig Coy Hdrs. " " " from Divn Hd Qrs to {137th R.A. at O 3d 8.6. – ISBERGUES 138th " " 1220 4.8. THIENNES 139th " " 1 3C.10. BOSECHEM Telephone around ST VENANT BOSECHEM (by phone)	W.R. W.R.
LAMBRES N10d 7.7	20/5/15		Permanent line MOLINCHEM to THIENNES vis ST VENANT handed back to Sig. 1st ARMY	W.R.

1875 Wt. W593/826 1,000,000 4/15 J.B.C. & A. A.D.S.S./Forms/C. 2118.

WAR DIARY
or
INTELLIGENCE SUMMARY

Army Form C. 2118

(Erase heading not required.)

Place	Date	Hour	Summary of Events and Information	Remarks and references to Appendices
LAMBRES N10d 7.7	21/12/15	—	Poling wire from C.R.A. to R.F.A. Bdes in P.14, P.8, P.1 Div. Arty O.O. No 32 received and acted. Copy 10. All lines good — Situation normal. Loaned old D5 wire from 38th Div Sig. Coy. Awaiting to return surplus R.E. offrs received.	W.B.R
LAMBRES N10d 7.7	22/12/15	—	Divn. Am. Col. moves from J.21.c.5.1 to neighbourhood WITTERNESSE. Line laid from Hd Qrs C.R.A. N10d 8.8 to Hd Qrs D.A.C. Intended for all calls & Remount to complete establishment. Armoured D/R service as per D.R.O. 22/12/15. Lines erect but liable to troubles due to wet weather. 1st Army Sig Coy called re cable wire laid out. Allotted 12 miles D1. Situation otherwise normal.	W.B.R
		7.30pm	Operation Order No 33 Div. Arty re and acted.	W.B.R
LAMBRES	23/12/15	—	Changing carried exchange at 2nd Bde R.F.A. to 1st Bde R.F.A. at St Venant. 2nd Bde R.F.A. move from ST VENANT to ST QUENTIN. Line laid from 2nd Bde to ST QUENTIN to exchange at DAC at WITTERNESSE.	
		1.55pm	Divn O.O. No 31 received and acted.	

Army Form C. 2118

WAR DIARY
or
INTELLIGENCE SUMMARY
(Erase heading not required.)

Place	Date	Hour	Summary of Events and Information	Remarks and references to Appendices
LAMBRES	24/10/15	—	Normal	Enh
"	25/10/15	—	Signal Sec. No 2. H.Q. 139th entrain. Lorries and drivers left behind with 139th Inf. Bde. O.O. No. 32 received	Enh
"	26/10/15	—	Situation Normal. Wagon reequipment overhauled.	
"	27/10/15	—	Route marches recommence	Enh
"	28/10/15	—		
"	29/10/15	—		
"	30/10/15	—		
"	31/10/15	—		

46 Div Signal Co.
Jan 1916
Vol. VII

Army Form C. 2118

WAR DIARY
or
INTELLIGENCE SUMMARY
(Erase heading not required.)

Hd Qrs Div Signal Corps

Instructions regarding War Diaries and Intelligence Summaries are contained in F.S. Regs., Part II. and the Staff Manual respectively. Title Pages will be prepared in manuscript.

Place	Date	Hour	Summary of Events and Information	Remarks and references to Appendices
LAMBRES	1/1/16	–	Normal	
"	2/1/16	–	Route march on foot 8 mile	Ent
"	3/1/16	–	Inspecting No 4 Section	Ent
"		7 pm	O.O. No 33 received	Ent
"	4/1/16	–	Visiting No 4 Section & 1st Army Signals	Ent
"	5/1/16	–	Repairing Company for entrainment	Ent
BERGUETTE	6/1/16	11 am	Entraining Hd Qr. No. 1 Sect. Repair Co for MARSEILLES	
IN TRAIN	7/1/16			
"	8/1/16	11 pm	Detraining at MARSEILLES. Marching men to SANTI CAMP and driving wagons to BERILY PARC	

Army Form C. 2118

WAR DIARY
or
INTELLIGENCE SUMMARY
(Erase heading not required.)

Instructions regarding War Diaries and Intelligence Summaries are contained in F. S. Regs., Part II. and the Staff Manual respectively. Title Pages will be prepared in manuscript.

Place	Date	Hour	Summary of Events and Information	Remarks and references to Appendices
MARSEILLES	9/1/16	—	Changing tents at SANTI	
"	10-1-16	—	Inspecting wagons at BERILY. Infantry drill for men	
"	11-1-16 to 20-1-16	—	Normal. Men at SANTI CAMP. Wagons at BERILY PARC. Horses at VALENTINE CAMP	
"	21-1-16	—	Embarking on Cunard H.M.T. ANDANIA. Embarking completed at 2.35pm. Horses not embarked	
"	22-1-16	—	Disembarking. Men returned to SANTI CAMP. Wagons " " BERILY	
"	23-1-16 to 24-1-16	—	Normal. Inspecting wagons, horses	

Army Form C. 2118

WAR DIARY
or
INTELLIGENCE SUMMARY
(Erase heading not required.)

Instructions regarding War Diaries and Intelligence Summaries are contained in F. S. Regs., Part II. and the Staff Manual respectively. Title Pages will be prepared in manuscript.

Place	Date	Hour	Summary of Events and Information	Remarks and references to Appendices
MARSEILLES	25/1/16	11 am	Entraining at GARE D'ARENC. Horses, wagons & men entrained	Ends
IN TRAIN	25/1/16			
"	27/1/16	10 pm	Detraining at PONT REMY	Ends
PONT REMY	28/1/16 to 31/1/16		Inspecting wagons, harness. Running lines to 139th Inf Bde & Batteries Brigade. Awaiting arrival of expected drafts of 137th & 139th Batteries.	Ends

Sent

40th Div Signal Co Operation order No.34

5th Jan 16.

1. Hdqrs 40 and No 1 Section will entrain on 6th inst at BERGUETTE Station.

2. Train will be ready to move off from LAMBRES at 8.20 am

3. Rations for journey will be supplied as per separate instructions issued with this order.

4. All vehicles will be taken but no horses or mules. Personnel harness and remounts will be attached to No a.5.3 Coy Divl. Train

5. Nos 3 & 4 Sections will entrain under orders of Brigades to which they are attached

6. Lieut LEWIS will report at BERGUETTE Station to R.T.O. at 10 am and hand over entraining state to R.T.O. and Staff Officer

7. Lieut ROBERTS will command the march to the station

8. Parties as detailed in separate instructions issued with this order will load vehicles on train

These vehicles will have to be taken by the Exchange & down to the French Railway authorities.

9. On arrival times & numbers of pairs of mules to water, feed and food will be decided on later after entraining party.

10. Nothing is on any account to be placed on the Guards van.

11. Men reporting sick before or during journey will be reported to the M.O. in charge of train, who will have the best kind at his disposal.

12. As many vehicles as possible will be loaded on to the first train. The water lorry will however be taken on the second train. Any vehicles not loaded on the first train will be handed over to O.C. 2nd [echelon] who will have them loaded by him onto the second train.

13. No N.C.O. or man must leave the train at any time without permission.

14. The Officers and parties detailed for entraining duties will also form the similar detraining parties

10. All drivers, grooms and others in details in reports not moved with this file will remain behind. They will be under the command of Lieut. MAGUIRE who will be responsible for all details of personnel, equipment, horses & stores not taken. An inventory of all stores to be left behind will be prepared by the C.S.M., this list will be handed to Lieut. MAGUIRE who will forward one copy to 1st Army Signals giving the position of same.

11. After the departure of the Company communications will be maintained by the Staff left behind at C.R.A. 3 No. to cyclists will remain behind and be attached to Divnl. Hd. Qrs. for .... It has been arranged that all officers up to cyclist and horsemen will be transported by C.R.A.

3

remain there under command of Divnl Hdqrs.

Motor Cyclists ordinarily with the RFA will remain with RFA and embark with them together with operators, linemen and technical equipment left with R.F.A.

(2) In connection with the embarkation of personnel on 21st inst either 2 G5 waggons or 1 motor lorry will be drawn from Camp Adjt SANTI CAMP for the purpose of collecting any stores not loaded on transport i.e. Kits re required on board the ship during the voyage. This will be arranged for & conducted under the command of Lieut ROBERTS.

(d) The time of marching from SANTI Camp on 21st inst will be 6 am.

(e) Embarkation States and all necessary certificates (see F.S.R.) will be prepared and handed over by Lieut LEWIS.

(3) RATIONS — Rations for the day of embarkation will be carried.

(Sgd) E A Lewis Major
4b th Div Sig Co Jan 19/16.

(2)

The guard on duty at BORELY Camp at the time of departure will accompany the transport to the quay where they will be met by Lieut LEWIS with an adequate loading party. Lieut LEWIS will be in command of embarkation and disembarkation of vehicles & personnel on the vessel.

(b) Lieut MAGUIRE will assist as far as possible with the embarkation of vehicles or personnel on the 20th & 21st inst. after which he will proceed to VALENTINE CAMP where he will remain in command of personnel & horses remaining behind.

(c) The Officers (less Lieut MAGUIRE) N.C.Os (less as below) and men at SANTI CAMP will embark at 9 am on 21st at same place as (a) & on the same vessel.

*1 Motor Cyclist (Corpl DEELEY) will remain with 139 Bde HQ at Parc BORELY.

3 motor cyclists to be detailed by Br (the 5 or) will report at Divnl Hqrs BORELY Parc at 6 am on 21st and will remain

Order for Embarkation
46th Div Sig Co RE(T)
By Major EA Lewis RE

1. The embarkation of this Company will take place as follows

(a) The vehicles will leave BORELY PARC at 6.30am on Jan 26th. Teams will be provided with drivers by OC 2/1st NM Field Co RE with whom arrangements for this have already been made. The vehicles will be arranged on the quay ready for craning at 9am. The point of embarkation is Berth 13 Hangar 8/+ the name of the vessel is ANDANIA. Vehicles will include all cable wagons, GS waggons, cooks carts, Water cart, maltese Cart, motor Lorry, Sunbeam car, motor cycles and ordinary cycles. All vehicles will be packed in accordance with regulations before Embarkation and all loose implements and stores must be made fast. Detachment Commanders will be held personally responsible for this. The

Army Form C. 2118

WAR DIARY
or
INTELLIGENCE SUMMARY
(Erase heading not required.)

46th Divl Signal Coy

Place	Date	Hour	Summary of Events and Information	Remarks and references to Appendices
PONT REMY	1/2/16	—	Improving communications to 138th Bde. 139th Bde and Artillery	9th
"	2/2/16	—	As above	9th
"	3/2/16 to 7/2/16	—	Normal	9th
"	8/2/16	4-15 pm	O.O. 42 received re 21/1st Field Co. moving to new position	9th
"	9/2/16	2-0 pm	O.O. 43 " " 139th Bde moving to new position	9th
"		5-30 pm	O.O. 44 " " 5th Leicester Regt 1 1/2 Bn 7D. Amb moving	
"			In connection with O.O. 42 & 43 arrangements made with 55th Div. to use their line via DOMART for communication to 46th Div. via XVII Corps	

1875 Wt. W593/826 1,000,000 4/15 J.B.C. & A. A.D.S.S./Forms/C.2118.

Army Form C. 2118

WAR DIARY
INTELLIGENCE SUMMARY

Place	Date	Hour	Summary of Events and Information	Remarks and references to Appendices
PONT REMY	10/2/16	—	M. Du CHATEAU joins Company as Interpreter vice M. MORACCHINI. Lieut H.E.C. LEWIS rejoins Company from Wireless Course at 3rd Army H.Q.	
"	11/2/16	—	O.O. 45 received.	
"	12/2/16	—	O.O. 45 modified by D.H.2. memo.	
"	13/2/16	—	Normal	
"	14/2/16	—	Normal	
"	15/2/16	—	O.O. 46 received	
"	16/2/16	—	Normal	
"	17/2/16	—	Memo received stating that D.H.Qrs. Clerks at PONT REMY at 10 am and operators at W. Hdqrs. Clerks at PONT REMY at 10 am and operators at RIBEAUCOURT at noon on Monday next week.	
"	19/2/16	—	Leave commenced for men	

Army Form C. 2118

WAR DIARY
or
INTELLIGENCE SUMMARY
(Erase heading not required.)

146/K Div ADMS RE

Place	Date	Hour	Summary of Events and Information	Remarks and references to Appendices
PONT REMY	20/7/16	—	Normal	Enc
"	21/7/16	—	School for operators lecture & opens at D.A.C. Surgical Officer closes at 10 am & opens at RIBEAUCOURT at noon. All ranks and Brigadiers Enc under XVII Corps.	
RIBEAUCOURT		12 noon	137th Inf Bde go to LONGVILLERS 136 Inf Bde to FIENVILLERS 139 Inf Bde to HOUDENCOURT Enc	
"	22/7/16	—	Advance office shifted from forward floor to 1st floor on removal of Harper Staff	Enc
"	23/7/16	—	O.C. visited 36th Bde Dressing Station at ACHEUX. 146th Div taking over right Inf Bde. Enc O.O. 47 received. Postponing O.O. 47. O.O. 48 received.	
"	24/7/16	10/15 pm	O.O. 49 received. 138th Inf Bde removes from FIENVILLERS to MONTRELET. Scheme for operation at D.A.C. closes. Enc	

WAR DIARY
INTELLIGENCE SUMMARY

Army Form C. 2118

46th Div Sig Co RE

Place	Date	Hour	Summary of Events and Information	Remarks and references to Appendices
RIBEAUCOURT	26/7/16	8am 3pm	Cable detachment sent to ACHEUX to run artillery lines. This detachment arrived up at BEAUVAL. Communication connected with little routine. Weather at times (snow & sleet) that motor despatch service has to be suspended.	
	27/7/16	9am 3pm	Detachment still held up at BEAVUAL. They proceed. Motor despatch service resumed. Normal. Commencing training class at the Div 137/16 Inf Bde. Absent Permanent Leave	
	28/7/16	3pm 9pm	Orders received to be prepared to move early tomorrow so receive. Lieut MAGUIRE relieves Lt/Cpl 137/Bde O.i/c (?)	
DOULLENS	29/7/16		Div. moved to DOULLENS. Communication established at HeadQtrs Inf Bdes and Arty HQs in accordance with WD. O.D. SD. Eng.	

46

Signal Coy R.E.
Vol IX

Army Form C. 2118

WAR DIARY
or
INTELLIGENCE SUMMARY
(Erase heading not required.)

46th Divn Signal Coy RE (T.F.)

Place	Date	Hour	Summary of Events and Information	Remarks and references to Appendices
DOULLENS	1/3/16		Movements of Infantry Bde Battalions covers areas as far march to O.O 51 of 29/2/16 viz (1) 137th Batts to BOISBERGUES	Departure of 46th A.S.C. [HARDINGVAL?] (2) 138th " " DOULLENS units now near RIBEAUCOURT AREA to DOULLENS (1½) 139th " " GEZAINCOURT
"			D.H.Q. remain at DOULLENS probably for H.V 5 days longer 46th R.A. units remain in billetty area at LE MEILLARD - Communication established UUR	
DOULLENS	2/3/16		138th H.Q. moved to DOULLENS - Communication established. Aeroplane Situation normal. Communication established with DAC and RA HQ. 17th Corps collect exchange etc from Signal Office FIENVILLERS to LE MEILLARD Handed over air line to Corps. Cpl Robinson, Cp Holmes & CMS James returned from English leave	
DOULLENS	3/3/16	5 pm	O/c conference with Q.O.C. NORMAL	UUR
"	4/3/16		NORMAL	UUR
"	5/3/16	9.15 am	O.O 52 Copy 5 received and noted for movement of D.H.Q on 6th/7th & also were R.A. LE CUROY. Local lines laid in. Also lines to 137th/138th/139th Bdes and R.A. Line from R.A. 15 Bdes and DAC redrawn. R.A. O.O. No 43 Copy 12 received and noted. " " " " 24th/152th/17th [Island?] " " " 44 " 17 " " " " "	UUR

1875 Wt. W503/826 1,000,000 4/15 J.B.C. & A. A.D.S.S./Forms/C.2118.

WAR DIARY
INTELLIGENCE SUMMARY
(Erase heading not required.)

Army Form C. 2118

A.6th Div Sig Coy R E (T.F.)

Place	Date	Hour	Summary of Events and Information	Remarks and references to Appendices
DOULLENS to	6/3/16	—	46th Divn R.A. move from LE MEILLARD to MANCHEUX. All R.A. Rides move to new billeting area of RENIN - MAIZIERES - GUYEN-TERNOIS - MONCHEAUX - SIBVILLE. R.A. Hd.qrs. opened at 9 a.m. Communication established with D.H.Q. at	
LE COUROY	"		LE COUROY at 10.30 a.m. 138th Bn to MAGNICOURT 139th " to GEZAINCOURT Communication 2 s. Listheret with all Bries. to "G.T.Q." No telephone line allotted by Corps, only telegraph via Bergueneuse. Corps remaining at DOULLENS. D.H.Q. closed at DOULLENS at 9 Bonon and opened at LE COUROY at 10.30 a.m. A/154 Battery allotted to Divn and were Heavy Battery attached	TAR
LE COUROY	7/3/16		139th Bn move to IVERGNY - Line laid LE COUROY to IVERGNY.	
"	7/3/16	9.15 am	Divn O.O. 53 received and ackd. re meet of French tomorrow viz 137th B - 24th K Bn 138th " - 17th " 139th " - 152nd " other are normal	TAR

WAR DIARY or INTELLIGENCE SUMMARY

Army Form C. 2118

46th Divn Signal Coy RE (T.F.)

Place	Date	Hour	Summary of Events and Information	Remarks and references to Appendices
LE COURCY	8/3/16	—	RA O.O. 46 received and acted. Copy (II) Otherwise situation normal. 137/B/B received from amendments to O.O.53 received for 11th instant in 4-5. References to Penin	4/4/R
LE COURCY	9/3/16		Hostile R.A. Cld at MONTENEUX at 10am and opened at CAMBLIGNEUL at 12 noon. Two actzal movts. Ordered to proceed to CAMBLAIN L'ABBÉ to take over French units with Lieut Laval Lieut-R'taute. at X8 & B.P. Communication established with R.A. and 2nd Bde R.F.A. marches to CAMBLAIN L'ABBÉ. 137th Bde to ECOIVRES "" French Heavy Bde at 139th to MONT ST ELOY "" "" Connected up to chateau of 17th Fr. Divn. 138th "" VILLA D'ACQ	4/4/R Received French only by 4/4/R
LE COURCY	10/3/16	7.30pm	Amendment to O.O.53 received and acted. RACD. No 147.	1st Bde connects to R.A. Pigeon "30"(30,) "" to 46th CRA Metalline from Corps R.A. to 46th CRA 4/4/R
LE COURCY TO CAMBLAIN L'ABBÉ	11/3/16	9am	D.H.Q. close at LE COURCY and open at Chateau CAMBLAIN L'ABBÉ 9am Communication with 137/8/9 Inf Bde and all other units established. DAC move to SAVY. HAR connected up to RA from MAREUIL 1st Bde R.F.A R/ACQ. 2nd district to Camblegnens. 3rd to Cambl'au L'Abbé. Corps take over at AUBIGNY.	Auth 46 4/4/R
CAMBLAIN L'ABBÉ	12/3/16		Later to 23rd Divn HQ+RA at Chateau de la Haur Rue. Otherwise normal	4/4/R

Army Form C. 2118

WAR DIARY
of
INTELLIGENCE SUMMARY
(Erase heading not required.)

46th Divn Sig Coy RE

Place	Date	Hour	Summary of Events and Information	Remarks and references to Appendices
CAMBLAIN L'ABBÉ	13/3/16		Laid to 51st Divn and 3rd RFA established at MONT ST ELOY } Communication existing. 4th " " ECOIVRES Wagon Lines 1st/1 Bn RE ACR employed on letter Box lines Personnel from A VILLA D'ACQ with Summer Supervened	UPR
"	14/3/16		4th How Bde moved from ECOIVRES to BERTHONVAL FARM. Survey of Signal Officer RA Bde & Battn with 13th Maj.R. Reconny of French lines. Making approach for office thrown across	UPR
"	15/3/16		1 a.m. Power advanced Lis run from DHQ to 182 Tunnelling Coy at MINGOVAL 3rd Bn H.Q. shelter at MONT ST ELOY	UPR
"	16/3/16		Line to DADOS laid Attack Otherwise normal A.T. HQ 137th established at Aux RIETZ	UPR
"	17/3/16		Line from Aux RIETZ (nr. 137 Bn) taken to back trench at ECOIVRES. 2 lines from signage. Coys in Kitchener Bay metallic circuit from Aux RIETZ to "IT" planned.	UPR

Army Form C. 2118.

WAR DIARY
or
INTELLIGENCE SUMMARY
(Erase heading not required.)

A1st Div Sig Cy R.E. (T.F.)

Place	Date	Hour	Summary of Events and Information	Remarks and references to Appendices
CAMBLAIN L'ABBÉ	18/3/16		NORMAL.	WAR
"	19/3/16		To Steiner 1 R.Co. + 3men to 137th Divine in Circles	WAR
"	20/3/16		2nd Lieut M V JONES reported for duty	WAR
"	21/3/16		NORMAL	WAR
"	22/3/16		Lieut Jones attached 139th Bde.	WAR

Army Form C. 2118

WAR DIARY
or
INTELLIGENCE SUMMARY
(Erase heading not required.)

46th Divn Sig Coy RE (T.F)

Instructions regarding War Diaries and Intelligence Summaries are contained in F.S. Regs., Part II. and the Staff Manual respectively. Title Pages will be prepared in manuscript.

Place	Date	Hour	Summary of Events and Information	Remarks and references to Appendices
CAMBLAIN L'ABBE	23/3/16		Laying line through network	WWR
"	24/3/16		Fresh exchange released and run down the metallic installed here. H.E.L. PORTER attached for two weeks instruction from England O/c went to AUX RIETZ.	WWR
"	25/3/16		Inspection of programme to Rpt centre at BERTHONVAL WOOD by Hut-LEWIS. Area & heard. Cleaning up our line to Calonne	WWR
"	26/3/16		Position of Report Centre considered. Otherwise normal	WWR
"	27/3/16		Programme new position of Report Centre F.3 central Otherwise normal	WWR

1875 Wt. W593/826 1,000,000 4/15 J.B.C. & A. A.D.S.S./Forms/C. 2118.

WAR DIARY
INTELLIGENCE SUMMARY
(Erase heading not required.)

Army Form C. 2118

46th Divn Sig Coy R.E. (T.F.)

Place	Date	Hour	Summary of Events and Information	Remarks and references to Appendices
CAMBLAIN L'ABBÉ	28/3/16		New zone exchange delivered from Corps. Munition Returnal	WR
"	29/3/16		Personnel from A/137R. for 1 platoon at E COUTURES Maj. S.A. LEWIS to 139th T138R. Maj. of Maj Lewis proceeds on leave	WR
"	30/3/16		Lieut H.E.L. PORTER returns to XVII Corps. Acting rank permanent.	WR
"	31/3/16		Col Newbigging called and inspected Sig Office. Reported that rumours too small to permit of new one to be built	WR

Major R.E.(T)

Confidential

Memorandum on Signal Communications

With reference to Card O.B. 630 sent you today, entitled "Orders regarding the sending of messages within 1500 yards of the firing line." Please note that all the orders issued on this card are to be <u>strictly</u> adhered to.

In order to carry out the provisions of Order No 4 I have allotted the <u>station</u> calls and codes shewn in the attached diagram and list. The idea is that the <u>station</u> shall have a call which will not change although the units occupying that station may change.

You must take immediate steps to ensure that all units in your Brigade are acquainted with the station calls and the reason and method of their adoption.

The code name of each unit will be the present signal code for that unit. <u>This will never be used as a call in the dangerous zone</u> but simply as the <u>name</u> of the unit.

Please explain this to all officers NCO's

NCO's & men connected with Signal
work and make sure that your
staff and the staffs of all units
are acquainted with the methods

Mch 2/16

E.A Lewis Major
46th Div. Signal Co R.E.

Station Calls
For use in dangerous zone

46th Division Report Centre   G.N.R.

Infantry Brigades of Division
Stations from left to right

Left Brigade	RYA
Centre "	RYB
Right "	RYC &c.

Battalions
Stations from left to right

Battalion Stations for Left Bde   KA
                                                 KB
                                                 KC &c.

"   "   " Centre Bde   LA
                                                 LB
                                                 LC &c.

"   "   " Right "   MA
                                                 MB
                                                 MC &c.

Trench Stations from left to right
For stations of left Battn
                 (KA)   KAA
                              KAB
                              KAC &c

"   "   "   LA   LAA
                              LAB
                              LAC &c

Pioneer Battalion   PA

Station Calls continued

Artillery Brigades

    Brigade on left   OA

       "   in centre   OB

       "   on right   OC

            Howitzers   OD

Batteries

    Stations from left to right

    Battery Stations for left Bde.   OAA

                                        OAB

                                        OAC &c

       "   "   " Centre Bde   OBA

                                        OBB

                                        OBC

       "   "   " Right Bde   OCA

                                        OCB

                                        OCC

    Howitzers   left Batty   ODA

                     right   "   ODB

   The above should be read in conjunction with the diagram attached

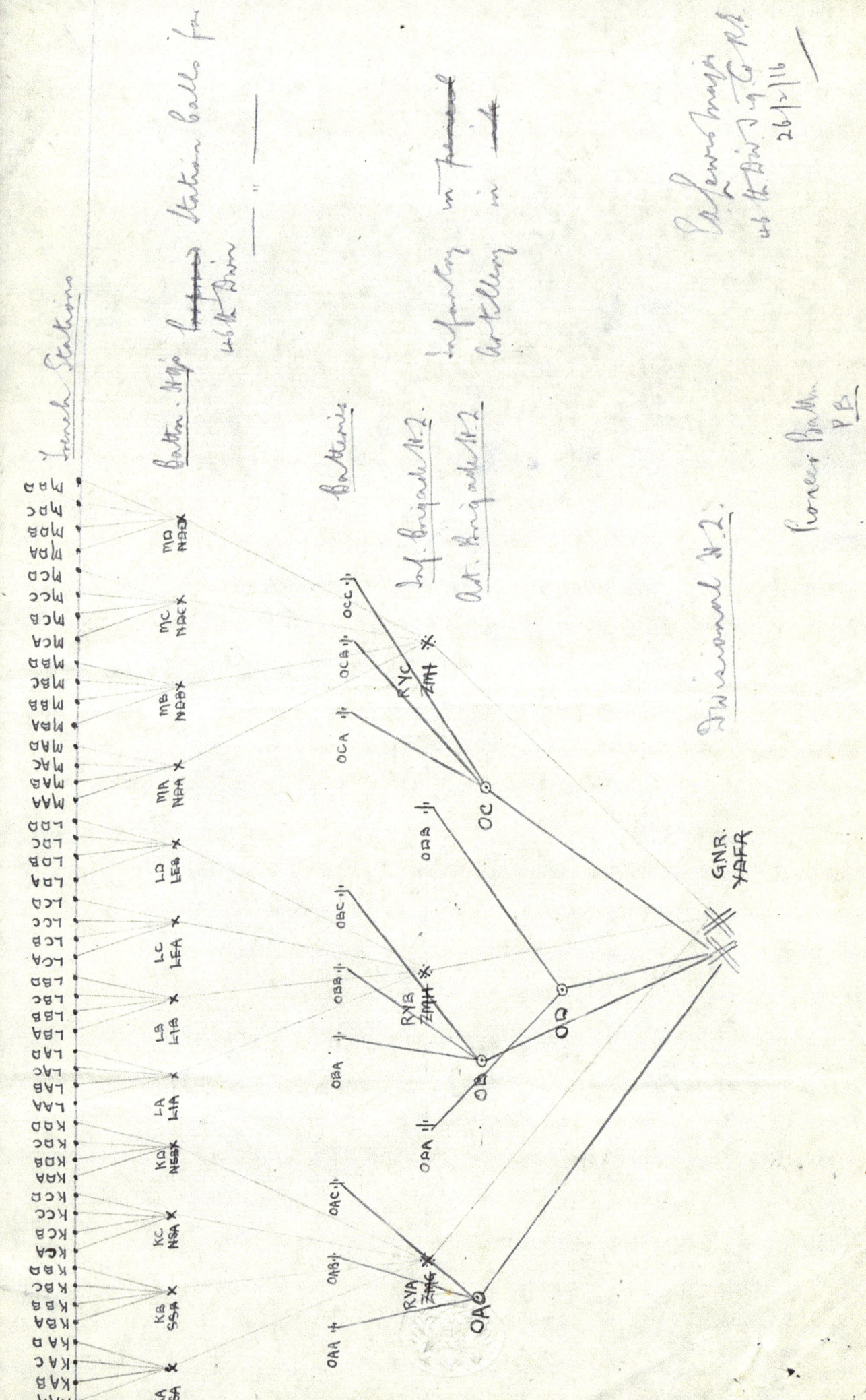

46

46 Div Signal Co RE
Feb 1916
Vol XVIII

46

Signal Coy R.E.

Vol X

Army Form C. 2118

WAR DIARY
INTELLIGENCE SUMMARY
(Erase heading not required.)

46th Divn Sig Coy RE (TF)

Place	Date	Hour	Summary of Events and Information	Remarks and references to Appendices
CAMBLAIN L'ABBE	1/4/16		Lieut Smith arrived with Col Claudet Smith - inspected newly opened Sig Office Survey route for Report Centre commenced. Reports commenced to hand.	Rob. T.S.R.
"	2/4/16		Started Survey Rpt Centre. m.g. 1st TRoute 137th Bde 138th Bde Bn Btns Commenced 6 line out the route	Rob T.S.R.
"	3/4/16		Wiring up Report centre.	Rob T.S.R
"	4/4/16		Cables ran in line function but for Report centre wiring	Rob T.S.R

WAR DIARY
or
INTELLIGENCE SUMMARY

(Erase heading not required.)

Army Form C. 2118

46th Div Sgt CN RE (TF)

Place	Date	Hour	Summary of Events and Information	Remarks and references to Appendices
CAMBLAIN L'ABBE	5/4/16	—	Burying tram for Report Centre. Working party to repair & improve trench cable. Cpl. Thorney relieved by Humphrey.	initials
"	6/4/16	—	Burying wires from trench cable from Report Centre to A.D. 138th or CABARET ROUGE. Working party on Cabaret Rouge trench dropping by night at junction. Capt. Thorney returns to AIX RIETZ.	initials
"	7/4/16	—	Sample trench Schneider Corps. Same order as above. Test was carried out with in 137th Div. Cpl. Smith into England on leave. Lewis leave begins. Capt Thorney (now Sgt Murray) and Capt Murray (now Sydney) and 40 eyebolts dropping standby wire Div. R.P.C. at S.3 extras to ANRIETZ. to R.P.C. to detachment. A.D. 138th Rn. Retirement leaving wire at CABARET ROUGE. Cpl Buchanan. 1 Offr + 40 OR working on CABARETROUGE TRENCH with hut & scrub. working party 60 men supervised by Staff. ELECTRIC LIGHT 3.O.R. returned from Army.	initials
"	8/4/16	—	A. Cy. S.A. LEWIS returned about 3 a.m. Cable attached length 1 to 6 to work to R.P.C. Re-laying in all wires to Sig. office. 3½ miles in Div. returned to Engr. 4 men dropping trench to trench cable to 138th Rn. Working party 60 OR 137th dipping trench to Report Centre.	initials
"	9/4/16	—	Cpl. Scott and party laid trench cables in Bayan de Bois Ravine to 2nd Bde R.F.A. Sgt. Mullinger completely attaching dropping Cpl. Jenner working on leads to Report Centre Sanders an returning from Column. Recoveries electric light installed. Hut Office. A.D.H.Q. I to now dropping trench to Army cable Trav. 138th Bn. Sgt. Buchanan with man to England on musketry course. Filling up wiring for H.Q. Offices.	initials

1875 Wt. W593/826 1,000,000 4/15 J.B.C. & A. A.D.S.S./Forms/C.2118.

Army Form C. 2118

WAR DIARY
or
INTELLIGENCE SUMMARY
(Erase heading not required.)

46th Divn Sig Coy R.E. (J.F.)

Place	Date	Hour	Summary of Events and Information	Remarks and references to Appendices
CAMBLAIN L'ABBE'	10/4/16	—	(1) Air line detachment commenced work on 4 line permanent route from HQrs to arty DHQ. - Sgt Mulrooney. (2) Cpl Jenns with 6 men laying wires to Report centre. 5 Sets Fullerphone received to CRA new listening lines. (3) Col Newberry D.A.D.S. 3d Army visiting to "IT" Arry Lewis at 139th ORs. also Lieut Hopgoss Lieut Lewis at arty R.P.C. 139 Bde. Cpl Innes to 139th Inf. Bn. for duty. (4) 2 Officers & 100 O.R. digging tunnel for tunnel at 139th Bde at CABARET ROUGE	Int.
"	11/4/16	—	Sgt Salt and party laying ground cable in stone trench to 2nd Bde R.F.A. Cpl Jenns employed along. Sgt Mulrooney went to air line alone. Capt Forman proceeds on leave. Lieut Escombe and 100 O.R. continuing digging tunnel for buried cable to CABARET ROUGE. Work delayed owing to rain. Weather bad.	Int.
"	12/4/16	—	Cpl Jenns and party wiring Report Centre. Bryant for Report centre also in reserve of construction. Sgt Mulrooney and party commenced laying air line from Cambelain to Bon Aleur. Working parties of 40 girls, 160 O.R. 139th Bn. employed. Heavy rain. Town of Batteries with Bde. Major RA T O/c.	Int.

Army Form C. 2118

WAR DIARY
or
INTELLIGENCE SUMMARY
(Erase heading not required.)

46th Divn Sig. Coy. R.E.

Place	Date	Hour	Summary of Events and Information	Remarks and references to Appendices
CAMBLAIN L'ABBE.	13/4/16		Cpl. Jenner many Report Centre. Sgt Mulroney etc completed 4 our lines from Chandlers to area South in charge of Sgt Souttsville material for R.A. Hee. Permanent from No 5 to lead in CR+ office at Camblignine. lines. Permanent c/o Sig XVII Corps channumero, unat o/c ceive returns Major Y MR Brown 18th inst. Capt ? our own etc. All leave stopped + all officers + men to return by 18th inst. Capt ? our own informed. Order No 54 received re recepts commencing on 20th. Operation order No 54 received re CABARET ROUGE for 137th Bde canteen. Working parties enjoy French to CABARET ROUGE for 137th Bde canteen. channumero about 9.30 p.m. linnes thro' was transferred	
"	14/4/16		Work as on 13/4/16 Maurine manual Reactor - main	

Army Form C. 2118

WAR DIARY
or
INTELLIGENCE SUMMARY
(Erase heading not required.)

46th Divn Sign Coy RE (T)

Instructions regarding War Diaries and Intelligence Summaries are contained in F.S. Regs., Part II. and the Staff Manual respectively. Title Pages will be prepared in manuscript.

Place	Date	Hour	Summary of Events and Information	Remarks and references to Appendices
CAMBLAIN	15/4/16		Same as 14/4/16 Weather – Rain.	
"	16/4/16		Visit to O/C Sigs 25th Divn re taking over Rest Billets at ROLLECOURT. Sgt Salt + party ready to leave from Coy HQ to Hq'rs R.A. Parties ready to install all cable (Branch exchs) West of D.H.Q. Sgt Mulroney leaving to run earth exchange at D.H.Q. (R.A. south Branch). C.R.A. main exchge installed in Hq'rs Sig Office. Waterworthy shelter – Working Party Staffords. Cpl Jenner employed drawing to Report Centre. 20 D 5's Ammo from River. Company wagons frozen. 25 D 3 } 6 D's	
"	17/3/16		NORMAL	

Army Form C. 2118

WAR DIARY
or
INTELLIGENCE SUMMARY
(Erase heading not required.)

46th Divl Sigl Coy R.E.

Place	Date	Hour	Summary of Events and Information	Remarks and references to Appendices
CAMBLAIN L'ABBE	18/4/16		NORMAL	
"	19/4/16		46th Sigl. Coy men working on the R.E. route to Report centre. Cpl. Jarvis. NORMAL.	Ent
"	20/4/16		Allworkingparties cancelled due to bad weather. Cpl Jarvis, his twenty men completely (geographically) aunt C.R.A. Lieuts day & Holmes advance new party and route for brains from Report Centre to adv. repl. of 139th & 137th Bdes. Engineer Coy wagons employed for moving off trench stores.	Ent
"	21/4/16		All working parties cancelled due to bad weather. Lieut. Toy & Holmes new from 25th Divn. of 12 Rifle Bde in line etc. NORMAL.	Ent
"	22/4/16		Lieut Lewis and twenty to take over from 25th Divn. answer men to R.A. Co. No 49 received.	Ent

Army Form C. 2118

WAR DIARY
or
INTELLIGENCE SUMMARY
(Erase heading not required.)

Instructions regarding War Diaries and Intelligence Summaries are contained in F. S. Regs., Part II. and the Staff Manual respectively. Title Pages will be prepared in manuscript.

Place	Date	Hour	Summary of Events and Information	Remarks and references to Appendices
ROELLE COURT	23/4/16		Divn H.Q.rs. arrived at CAMBLAIN L'ABBE at 12 noon and opened at ROLLECOURT the same hour. Divn RA. moving to town RA. moving at CAMBLIGNEUL. REST BILLETS. Lightly installed etc.	Roh. Weather - Fine -
"	24/4/16		NORMAL.	Roh.
"	25/4/16		NORMAL	ditto
"	26/4/16		Capt Thoday joined Hqrs. Lt Haguire to No 2 Section Hqrs 41st Divn RA. move from CAMBLIGNEUL at 8.30 am and open at new Hdqrs. GRANDCAMP at 10 am. Telephonic communication restored with D.H.Q. + R.A.H.Q. G.O.C. on leave. Then Campbell in command of Divn.	Roh.
"	27/4/16		Visual communication opened with 137 Bde at BAILLEUL AUX CORNAILLES and 139 Bde at SAVY via Transmitting stn. Lieut Escombe MoTor to Hqs Jr. " " 138th J.B. via Lieut Escombe. Weather fine	Roh.

1875 Wt. W593/826 1,000,000 4/15 J.B.C. & A. A.D.S.S./Forms/C. 2118.

Army Form C. 2118

WAR DIARY
or
INTELLIGENCE SUMMARY
(Erase heading not required.)

46th Divn Sig. Co R.E.(T)

Place	Date	Hour	Summary of Events and Information	Remarks and references to Appendices
ROLLECOURT	28/4/16		Inspection of Signal C&T with wagons etc by C.O. Sunbeam Car returned from M.T. Col! Herts R.A.HQ. GRANDCAMP. Instruction in Visual station Buck Sany 139 1/R.4 Bulline 137 Otherwise situation normal	
"	29/4/16	9.15am	WEATHER – FINE. C.O. Inspection of C.<u>y</u> 9.15 a.m. 16 Artillery new found Signals for Instruction. Visit to R.A.HQ. FOOTBALL MEETING at D.H.Q. Classes in Lamp Signalling – Helio	
		8.45pm	Lecture in Visual Station work by Capt. Thorley. Football Match Signals v Ordnance (1-4)	D.A.S. 3rd Army (Gl Newtagin) visited Lignite. Lend ust to Lecture Room bef..res WEATHER – FINE.
"	30/4/16		Church Parade. WEATHER – FINE. NORMAL.	

Army Form C. 2118

WAR DIARY
or
INTELLIGENCE SUMMARY
(Erase heading not required.)

46th Div S.G. Coy R.E. (T)   Vol XI

Place	Date	Hour	Summary of Events and Information	Remarks and references to Appendices
ROLLECOURT	1/5/16		Maj Lewis & Capt Hurley visited 7th Corps Hqrs to take over lines at PAS with view to communications with Genl le Huttre, and to arrange site of new signal office. Visual practice continued Weather fine	RWL RWL
"	2/5/16		46 Div OO No 59 received re 137 Bde moving to 7th Corps area. Lieut Lewis and party proceeded to New Area, to link up lines to take over their first wagons. Visited our area to take over lines from 143 Bde & 8th Div. Visual practice continued. Helio practice considerably interrupted by clouds. Lieut Roberts visited our area with CRA to look over Artillery positions & communications. Weather fine. Thunderstorm 8pm. Fine evening.	BWT RWL
"	3/5/16		137 Bde marched and billeted for night at IVERGNY. Communication through BERNICOURT via 3rd Army office at FRÉVENT. Interpreter proceeded to PAS to arrange new billets. Weather still very fine	RWL RWL
"	4/5/16		137 Bde marched to ST AMAND. Lieut Robert proceeded to PAS with motor lorry, to see artillery lines taken over from 7th Corps. Lorry broke down at FRÉVENT, repaired at ST POL. D.O. No 58 rec'd from 46 Div re move to VII Corps area. 137 Bde proceeded to ST AMAND and relieved 143 Bde 46 Div at Hue de la Haie during night. Lieut Lewis returned 9.30 PM. Weather fine	RWL RWL

Army Form C. 2118

WAR DIARY
or
INTELLIGENCE SUMMARY
(Erase heading not required.)

Place	Date	Hour	Summary of Events and Information	Remarks and references to Appendices
ROELLECOURT	5/5/16		Coy operation orders for move issued at 11 am. 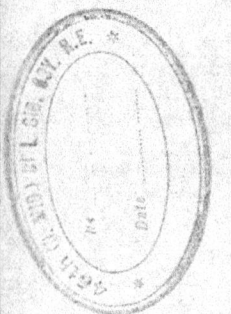 Corp[s] attached. Lieut Lewis went to Wireless course at 3rd Army Hqrs ST POL. Part of Sig Staff moved to PAS. Interpreter proceeded with motor lorry & PAS to complete billeting arrangement for Coy. 137 Bde opened Hqrs at Rue de la Haie at 9.30 am. Weather dull but fine.	JM
"	6/5/16		Company moved to PAS by road. Starting 7 am + arrived 7.45 pm. Communication through to 137 Bde Hqrs was established. Bde Hqrs opened at PAS at 10 am. Major Lewis & Lt Roberts visited 137 Bde Hqrs. 135 Bde moved to IVERGNY. Weather fine.	JM
PAS	7/5/16		Repairing cable with airline in PAS. Major Lewis & Capt Therry visited 137 Bde Hqr. Cleaning up + fixing office. 135 Bde arrived HUMBER CAMP. Communication through 37 Div.	JM
PAS	8/5/16		Weather stormy. 29 Reinforcements arrived from Signal depot ABBEVILLE. (outwork A.9.357) 3/5/16.) Lieut Roberts visited Hqrs of 1st M.M. Bde RFA & looked on [illegible]. Conference of OC's at Divisional Hqrs 4 pm. Capt Freeman visited Hqrs with reference to communication with HUMBER CAMP. Decided to lay airline via GRINCOURT taking in D.A.D.O.S. Major Lewis visited 137 Bde Hqrs. Capt [illegible] went out + decided on Bn Fusial St Hqr.	JM 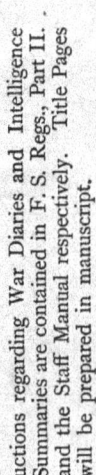

Army Form C. 2118

WAR DIARY
or
INTELLIGENCE SUMMARY
(Erase heading not required.)

Instructions regarding War Diaries and Intelligence Summaries are contained in F. S. Regs., Part II. and the Staff Manual respectively. Title Pages will be prepared in manuscript.

Place	Date	Hour	Summary of Events and Information	Remarks and references to Appendices
PAS	9-5-16		Detachment laying airline PAS to SOUASTRE. Lieut Roberts out with artillery officer deciding re burying wires. 138 Bde proceeded from SAV to LUCHEUX. Laid line into Bde Hqrs office here. Major Farr visited 137 Hqrs re burying. Later visited forward wires to rear Raw.	T.C.
"	10-5-16		Detachment completing airline to SQUASTRE. Lieut ROBERTS surveying route for buried lines for 2nd Brigade RFA. Cable detachment ran buried line to 139th Bde at HUMBERCAMP. Completed 6pm. Fine	Sat
"	11-5-16		Captain L.R. THODAY commenced leave. Burying and laddering of lines in 137 Bde area proceeding	Sat
"	12-5-16		Interviewing DADS re provision of material for burying artillery forward lines for Right sector. Cable will not be available for ten days. Detachment will be carried out in conjunction with Corps Artillery scheme.	Enh
	13-5-16		Normal	Enh

1875 Wt. W593/826 1,000,000 4/15 J.B.C. & A. A.D.S.S./Forms/C. 2118.

WAR DIARY
INTELLIGENCE SUMMARY

Army Form C. 2118

Place	Date	Hour	Summary of Events and Information	Remarks and references to Appendices
PAS	14/5/16		Normal. Church Parade. Testing visual communications	
"	15/5/16		Conference with O.C. Signals 37th & 150th Brig. Corps. Arrangements for re-hours scheme for Corps area. (S.O.E. Brian) Conference	
"	16/5/16		Surveying for new routes to Adv. Div. H.Q. Instructing to Show. Pole. re method of dealing with cable intents and arranging communications. Surveying for lateral route at FONQUEVILLERS inspecting Battn. lines & lofts etc.	
"	17/5/16		Preparing estimate plans &c for scheme of buried cables	
"	18/5/16		As yesterday. Col NEWBIGGING DDAS 3rd Army returned from leave. Capt L.R. THODAY returned from leave. marked offing	

WAR DIARY
or
INTELLIGENCE SUMMARY
(Erase heading not required.)

Army Form C. 2118

Place	Date	Hour	Summary of Events and Information	Remarks and references to Appendices
P.a.S.	19.5.16		Surveying new route to Adv Hq. Advance party commenced work on pylons to HENU. Major Lewis & Capt Thorby visited 138 Bde Hqrs at HUMBERCAMP. 139 Bde Hqrs at Cable trench road FONQUEVILLERS & Hqrs also 4th Bde RFA. Weather fine.	
"	20-5-16		Visited HQrs 56 Div Hqrs. Interpreter Duchatour proceeds on leave to DUNKERQUE. Advance work continued. Arranging route for Latrules. 137 Bde proceeded to LUCHEUX. 139 in action. 138 at HUMBERCAMP? Weather fine.	
"	21-5-16		Arranging diffing parts with Monsalts. Lieut. Hopkins proceeded on leave to England. Commenced diffing at 3rd Bde Hqrs dugouts at 138 Bde Hqrs. Advance worked continued to Henu 6.30 p.m. Leaving line to Dro HUMBER COURT. Weather fine.	
"	22-5-16		Advance work continued through HENU. Major Lewis & Lieut ROBERTS visited Div adv Hqrs & looked over work done by new parties. Major Lewis & Capt Thorby visited 138 Bde Hqrs & 4th Hants Bde RFA. Lieut Escombe proceed to HESDIN for M.S.C. Tot. Weather fine	
"	23.5.16		Major Lewis & Capt Thorby visited 138 Bde Hqrs re burying cable. Capt Thorby Reconnered route for Buried cable FONQUEVILLERS on to BIENVILLERS Weather fine	

Army Form C. 2118

WAR DIARY
or
INTELLIGENCE SUMMARY
(Erase heading not required.)

Instructions regarding War Diaries and Intelligence Summaries are contained in F.S. Regs., Part II. and the Staff Manual respectively. Title Pages will be prepared in manuscript.

Place	Date	Hour	Summary of Events and Information	Remarks and references to Appendices
Pas	24.5.16		Major Lewis & Lieut Roberts went over trunk cable route for St AMAND to FONQUEVILLERS. Telephone proofs made. Capt Shaw visited 137 Bde at LUCHEUX. "B" Coy arrived in wheels this afternoon (57th North'n Fus. Coy) Fine	G
"	25.5.16		Major Lewis & Capt Shaw visited St Bn Div Arty Hqrs re work on cable trenches. Lt Roberts visited Artillery Hqrs & battery positions. Airline route to ST AMAND continued. Capt Shaw visited 137 Bde at LUCHEUX. Rain	G
"	26.5.16		2/Lt McCue arrived on works tour. Lt Lewis attended from wireless school. Major Lewis & Capt Shaw went on a tour from SOUASTRE to FONQUEVILLERS. Lt Roberts tested and tried route for French. Airline work cont'd? Fine	G
"	27.5.16		Major Lewis went over trunk route with E.S.O.? Capt Shaw & Lt McCue visited 138 Bde Hqr FONQUEVILLERS Lt Roberts visited Arty Hqrs. & Bdes. Airline work cont'd? Fine	G
"	28.5.16		Church parade 10.15. Lt Col Hope & Capt Shaw's took part Investing cable for buried Scheme. Bombardment heard on 56th Division 10.30pm Fine	G

WAR DIARY or INTELLIGENCE SUMMARY

Army Form C. 2118

Place	Date	Hour	Summary of Events and Information	Remarks and references to Appendices
PAS	29.5.16		Lieut Roberts buried out new route for buried cables. 150 men 13th Bn working in trenches E of SOUASTRE. 250 men working on Reserve SOUASTRE - FONQUEVILLERS. Carpentering. Lt Roberts visited parties. Wire work continued. 16 men arrived from Sig Depot. Rain.	A
PAS	30.5.16		Working as above. St AMAND SOUASTRE + dispatch Service. Burying route completed. Major Lewis Capt Thornycroft Roberts visited Hd Qtrs. Capt Shaw + Lt Lewis visited parties working behind FONQUEVILLERS 9pm. Fine.	A
	31.5.16		Digging continued at ST AMAND. Car went into Depot Column for repairs. 40 Div O.O. 61 received. Night park continued on trench to FONQUEVILLERS. 6 Juice phones received from E Corps + distributed to Inf Bdes. 4 Cable twisting apparatus started. Fine.	A
	1.6.16		Digging continued at ST AMAND. Lt Roberts visited burying from St AMAND. Capt Thornycroft visited night party near SOUASTRE. 1" 4 Sig to begin digging tomorrow. Fine. Mr Luckeyk.	A

SECRET

W/Div

Operation Order No 58 by
Major L. A. Lewis R.E.
Commanding 46th Div Signal Co R.E.

Map Reference LENS. II. 1/100,000   5th May/1916

1. Divisional Hqrs will be established
at PAS at 10am on May 6th, for troops
in ~~XVIII~~ VII Corps Area
   Divisional Hqrs for troops in XVII Corps
Area will remain at ROELLECOURT.

2. Hqrs & No 1 Section Signal Co LESS
1 N.C.O, Corps Operator, 3 Motor Cyclists,
3 Operators, 3 Cyclist Orderlies.
will move at 7am on May 6th.
Starting point
   Meeting of roads immediately
above 2nd R in ROELLECOURT

3. The party left behind will keep the
Signal Office at ROELLECOURT open for
communication with troops still in
XVII Corps Area

4. ~~Divisional Hqrs Cancelled~~

5. Lieut ESCOMBE will be i/c Column

6. March discipline will be strictly
maintained, attention being paid to
halts at 10 mins to clock hours, & a
suitable halt for water & feed at NOON

Over.

7. Acknowledge.

Issued at   am

Copy No 1 to O.C.
" " 2 " F ESCOMBE
" " 3 " C.S.M.
" " 4 " War Diary
" " 5 " "
" " 6 " File

L. Thodos
Capt
for Major R.E. (T)
Commdg. Nth. Mid. Divl. Signal Co.

WAR DIARY
INTELLIGENCE SUMMARY

Army Form C. 2118

Place	Date	Hour	Summary of Events and Information	Remarks and references to Appendices
PAS	1.6.16		Digging continued at ST AMAND. Major Lewis and Lt Roberts visited trench digging at from SAILLY-AU-BOIS to FONQUEVILLERS. Capt Moday visited digging party near SOUASTRE, n of Signal Co Drivers digging. Capt Moday visited 137 Bde Hdqrs LUCHEUX. Fine	

WAR DIARY or INTELLIGENCE SUMMARY

Army Form C. 2118

Place	Date	Hour	Summary of Events and Information	Remarks and references to Appendices
PAS	2.6.16		Lt Roberts + Lt McCoy visited artillery OPs re buried cable scheme. Cable testing + digging continued. Gunline from Lebihen + Lealvi through O61 46 Div sec^t.	R.
"	3.6.16		Fine. Finals of FOC's Football Cup Compⁿ won by ck 1st Leicesters by 1-0. All digging continued. Slow cable testing. News of North Sea Naval battle received.	J.M.R.
"	4.6.16		Fine. Lt Lewis proceeded on leave. 2nd Lt A° Coy b^{tt} 1/c Coy. Church parade 10:15 am. Cap^{tn} Murray every continuation of different between Cable testing continued. St AMAND + SOUASTRE Lt Roberts test light different parts of PONQUEVILLERS + arranged continuation of both Major Lewis attended formation Scheme attack at LUCHEUX.	G.
"	5.6.16		Fine. Slight showers. hay in Lewis awarded D.S.O. Major Lewis + Lt Roberts visited Posts in action + artillery hgr. Capt Murray attended Scheme attack demonstration near LUCHEUX. Lt Roberts visited artillery digging party during evening. Layout line from 233 Bde RFA - 234 Bde RFA. Showery. no working parties on account of Relief	J.M. G.

WAR DIARY
INTELLIGENCE SUMMARY
(Erase heading not required.)

Army Form C. 2118

Place	Date	Hour	Summary of Events and Information	Remarks and references to Appendices
PAS.	6-6-16		Lt Roberts visited hqrs of artillery forks. Party laying lines in trenches ST AMAND - SOUASTRE and 232 Bde RFA - 233 Bde RFA. Capt Sharp visited SOUASTRE to see progress of cable French. Lieut Roberts met artillery working party at FONQUEVILLERS 7pm. The infantry parties on account of relief.	JM
PAS	7-6-16		Major Lewis went with ADAS VII Corps to decide position for listening apparatus in FONQUEVILLERS. G 269 46 Div received	JM
			The working parties on account of relief. Standing by.	
"	8-6-16		Signal continued on ST AMAND trenches and at night behind FONQUEVILLERS. Capt Sharp & Lt Roberts looked over work done during evening. G 270 46 Div recd. G 408 " recd. bet.	JM
"	9-6-16		Capt Sharp & Lt Roberts typed line from FONQUEVILLERS to BIENVILLERS. Also looked for site for Visual Viewing Stn. Major Lewis looked over work on Atty Hqrs + Gn obs line. Capt Sharp met night party + afterwards visited 137 Bde Hqrs. G. Div G 270/1 rec.	JM

WAR DIARY / INTELLIGENCE SUMMARY

Army Form C. 2118

Place	Date	Hour	Summary of Events and Information	Remarks and references to Appendices
PAS	10-6-16		Digging continued behind FONQUEVILLERS. Capt Thomas visited 137 Bde Hqrs Humbercamp. G270/5 rec'd. Rain	
PAS	11-6-16		Church Parade at Coigneux Hqrs. Conference of Signal Officers 11am - 5pm	
"	12-6-16		Showery. Capt Thomas fixing visual stn at ST AMAND & FONQUEVILLERS & arranged for future Major Lewis Mr Roberts topped int BIENVILLERS trench. digging parties with 137 Staff Capt. Digging continued. About 300 men working. G270/3 rec'd. Showery.	
"	13-6-16		Lieut Roberts carrying on buried cables behind FONQUEVILLERS. Digging continued Capt Sloan visited FONQUEVILLERS to prepare site for visual stn & dugout for same. G297 rec'd. G300 rec'd. Rain	

WAR DIARY
INTELLIGENCE SUMMARY
(Erase heading not required.)

Army Form C. 2118

Place	Date	Hour	Summary of Events and Information	Remarks and references to Appendices
PAS	14/6/		Cable laying & differing continued. Naval started through between FONQUEVILLERS & ST AMAND. Capt Shropshires (13) Bde re trophies parties. Road crossing completed. at D.11 063 recd. Rain.	S.M.
"	15/6/		Cable laying & differing cont'd. Visual practice continued. Dugout for Visual commenced at F'VILLERS. Capt Kennett 63 Div Cyclists visited hqs re alarm dugout. CRA 0055 recd. RAIN	S.M.
"	16/6/		Lt Roberts met Bde Officers re ground lines. Diffing cont'd. also cable work. Pidru carrying bar & Staples procured in DOULLENS. Fr Bdes & Batties. Major Lewis visited SOUASTRE re diffing between Thos & 232 Bde RFA. FINE	S.M.
"	17/6/		Cable laying continued. Visual dugout completed at F'VILLERS. Signalling practice mineral status. 1651/5/ recd. Fine	S.M.

WAR DIARY / INTELLIGENCE SUMMARY

Army Form C. 2118

Place	Date	Hour	Summary of Events and Information	Remarks and references to Appendices
PAS	18-6		Cable laying continued. Wireless test at FONQUEVILLERS twin cable brought to Brigade Hqrs of 139. Commenced wiring Adv Div Hqrs. G 270 rec'd. Fine. 137 & 139 laying their cables & wiring their Hqrs. G 314/1. G 316A + G 270 rec'd	
"	19-6		Laying of cables continued. Drilling in Trench Trenches. Lamp practice with Rice Balloon. Successful. Fine.	
"	20-6		Cables laid & Kites from R.C. to Brow. Extraordinary number of German aeroplanes over. 46 Div 00 64 rec'd. Fine.	
"	21-6		Wiring Adv Report Centre commenced. Line down to 37th Div. G 270 rec'd. Fine.	

WAR DIARY

INTELLIGENCE SUMMARY

(Erase heading not required.)

Army Form C. 2118

Place	Date	Hour	Summary of Events and Information	Remarks and references to Appendices
PAS.	22-6		Wiring of Adv RC continued. Line run to Kansel St. Visual Stn + dugouts completed. Sitting in trenches continued. G314 Rec? Div 46Div Appendix K rec?	Cm
"	23-6		Adv RC work continued. All lines tested OK Div 0065 Rec? Line laid to 3) artillery G353 Major Lewis visited Visual Stn + Adv Base Hqrs. Q301/148 rec? Sitting in of trenches cont? P341 Thunderstorm. L39 Cm	
"	24-6		Leading wires into Adv Hqrs. 46 Div 0065 rec? Wires laid to 37 Div Bazerque + Bazeque Inn G372 G373 9/373/1 rec? Showery.	Cm
"	25-6		Bombs dropped on PAS + SAUDEMPRE G327 rec? Major Lewis + Lt Lewis visited Adv Hqrs. 46Div OO 66 rec? Wiring continued. G393 Wireless Stns took up fwd positions. G396 " " Fine 0064 " "	Cm

WAR DIARY
INTELLIGENCE SUMMARY
(Erase heading not required.)

Army Form C. 2118

Place	Date	Hour	Summary of Events and Information	Remarks and references to Appendices
	26-6		Adv Hqrs completed. All lines working well. 137 Bde at Chau La Haie. 138 " " WARLIN COURT. 139 " " HUMBER CAMP. Showery.	G 409 G 413 G 410 G 418 } Rec^d Lnh
	27-6		Line laid to Hospice Gaudiempre. Arrangements made for delivery of Pigeons to Bde. Capt Storey & Lt Roberts stayed at new Hqrs during night. Line all good. 137 Bde proceeded to their adv Hqrs 10 p.m. Showery.	@ 414/7 rec^d G 420 rec^d 0068 rec^d Lnh
	28-6		Divisional Hqrs moved to Adv position. Cancelled. Signal Office Official opened at 2 P.M. do 137 Bde moved back to Chau La Haie. Very wet t-storms	Lnh
	29-6		Communications from adv Hqrs at 7 p.m. 00 69 820^d Rabbit wire laid by Bde section in their Battalion circuits. Major Lewis visited Adv Hqrs in afternoon. 00 71 rec^d. Fine & cloudy.	Lnh

WAR DIARY
INTELLIGENCE SUMMARY

Army Form C. 2118.

Place	Date	Hour	Summary of Events and Information	Remarks and references to Appendices
P.9.5.	30-6		Divisional Hqrs moved up to Roba Hqrs at 2 P.M. Signal Off. opened at 2 P.M. All wires good	
ST AMAND			230 Bde R.F.A. to 137 Inf Bde wire broken	

Army Form C.2118

WAR DIARY
or
INTELLIGENCE SUMMARY
(Erase heading not required.)

Instructions regarding War Diaries and Intelligence Summaries are contained in F.S. Regs., Part II and the Staff Manual respectively. Title Pages will be prepared in manuscript.

Signal Coy pt 13

Place	Date	Hour	Summary of Events and Information	Remarks and references to Appendices
BAS.	30-6		Divisional Hqrs moved up to Adv Hqrs at 2 P.M. Signal Office opened at 2 P.M. All lines tested.	
ST AMAND			23s Bde RFA to 137 Inf Bde line broken	
ST AMAND	1-7-16		Bombardment commenced about 6.15 am. All lines front at 5.50 am. 137 Telephone broken down 6.30 am, working again 7.20 am. 6.30 am Jos with for Visual. 7.29 lines all tested. 8.30 am. Aeroplane dropped message saying shutter working at FONQUEVILLERS sent OK. Von miah & hand sinistre hanging our trenches, impossible to read visual signals. Lines working well during day. Correct at 5.30 p.m. Men this laid to SOUASTRE from spare pair at Jemninal Pole, for Staff Capt 137 Bde. Lieut Roberts visited 230 Bde RFA Hqrs & found at lines working with Visual Stn reported flashes from direction of litter Z. Intense bombardment continued till afternoon about 4 pm. Left Bde for 4 lines across to German trenches. 2 were broken at once and the Star I StB was on after a short time. 137 Bde through to all Battalions at 5.30 p.m.	

2449 Wt. W14957/M90 750,000 1/16 J.B.C. & A. Forms/C.2118/12.

Army Form C. 2118.

WAR DIARY
INTELLIGENCE SUMMARY
(Erase heading not required.)

Instructions regarding War Diaries and Intelligence Summaries are contained in F. S. Regs., Part II. and the Staff Manual respectively. Title Pages will be prepared in manuscript.

Place	Date	Hour	Summary of Events and Information	Remarks and references to Appendices
ST AMAND	1-7-16		46 Div. O. 72 rec^d. 138 Bde to relieve 137 Bde. Tried lamps to RCA Balloon. The signals in the front attracted considerable shelling & had to be abandoned. By midnight all lines correct.	JW
ST AMAND	2-7-16		Telephone "down" to 138 Bde 9.30 a.m. through at 10.5 a.m. Divisional Adv Hqrs closed at 4 pm and moved to PAS. OC Sig & wires Capt Thorby, Bavincourt. 137 Bde at ST AMAND 138 " in Trenches 139 " moved from trenches to GRINCOURT-WARLIN COURT. RFA remaining at ST AMAND. Lt Roberts and 1 cable detachment left with them.	JW
PAS	3-7-16		137 Bde moved to BAILLEULMONT 138 " " " BIENVILLERS 139 " " " SAULTY Capt Thorby & Lt Lewis taking over lines at 37 Div Hqrs BAVINCOURT. Lt Roberts conducted 58 Div Sig Officer over buried cable route, list huts &c. 168 Bde relieves 138 Bde Hqrs at SHRINE FONQUEVILLERS. Connects 168 Bde to 4 Army Probrs of 46 Div Cct^s.	JW

2449 Wt. W14957/M90 750,000 1/16 J.B.C. & A. Forms/C2118/12.

Army Form C. 2118.

WAR DIARY
INTELLIGENCE SUMMARY

(Erase heading not required.)

Instructions regarding War Diaries and Intelligence Summaries are contained in F. S. Regs., Part II. and the Staff Manual respectively. Title Pages will be prepared in manuscript.

Place	Date	Hour	Summary of Events and Information	Remarks and references to Appendices
PKS	4.7.16		Div. Hqrs. moved to BAVINCOURT. Lt. Lewis & party left 5.15 a.m. to take over office. Signal Co. wagons marched at 10 a.m.	
BAVINCOURT		10 am	Office opened & all lines through to Bdes & Arty. All lines at ST AMAND handed over with plans to 56 Div SIGS. 3 linesmen left here to Bgde. Heavy rain 2-6 pm	Sgt
BAVINCOURT	5-7-16		Lt. Lewis went through SAULTY ROUTE. 45th Div relieved 56th Div Artillery. CRA office now in BAVINCOURT (Mairie) Wiring up to new exchange in Signal Office. Enemy put shells into BAVINCOURT. Capt Stevenson visited Hqrs. & handed in his report on the operations of July 1st. Lt Lefevre left Bafume.	Sgt
BAVINCOURT	6-7-16		Major Lewis + Lt. Lewis visited pigeon loft at BARLY. Party testing DAC lines into CRA office. Wireless station listed with DAC Bdes. 10 am and 10 pm. Major Yeo Stuart Worthy relinquished command of the Division. Fini.	Sgt

WAR DIARY / INTELLIGENCE SUMMARY

Army Form C. 2118.

Place	Date	Hour	Summary of Events and Information	Remarks and references to Appendices
BAVINCOURT	7-7-16		Capt Thorp visited BG Bee HQrs SAULTY. Exchange boards completed in Signal Office.	
"	8		Very wet. Heavy storms. Streets flooded. Instruments affected by wet. Major Lewis visited 13s Bee HQrs & 135 Bde HQrs. Checking stores on hand. Capt Thorn visited HQrs. Fine.	
"	9		Major Lewis visited 13) Bee HQrs. Lt Maguire visited HQrs. Churchparade. Larbrik exchange hut to WARLINCOURT. Lewis hut to SLACKFORD for transport lines. Fine	
"	10		Lewis hut from BAILLEULMONT to BASSEUX. RA laying lines from BAVINCOURT to BASSEUX. Fine.	

WAR DIARY or INTELLIGENCE SUMMARY

Army Form C. 2118.

Place	Date	Hour	Summary of Events and Information	Remarks and references to Appendices
BAVINCOURT	11-7-16		139 Bde go into action BASSEUX 139 " " " lost SAULTY. Division staff Side shifted Northwards 139 Bde Hqrs at BERLEZCOURT 9 P.M. Rain through.	
"				
BAVINCOURT	12-7-16		Capt Shenley met O.C. S.C. 17 Div re hutmul to R.A.S. also visited No 5 R.B. Park re stpealing.	
			Rain	
"	13-7-16		Major Lewis visited Battalion Hqrs (3) Bde.	
			Rain	
"	14-7-16		135 Poole took over line in front of Bienvillers. Genl Thwaites inspected Bonshaw Detachment not laying wire into their hqrs. Col Newbigging visited Same office.	
			Rain	

WAR DIARY

INTELLIGENCE SUMMARY

(Erase heading not required.)

Army Form C. 2118.

Place	Date	Hour	Summary of Events and Information	Remarks and references to Appendices
BAVINCOURT	15-7-16		137 Hqrs BAILLEULMONT. 138 " POMMIER. 139 " BASSEUX. Sects. line reeled up. Fine	RW
=	16-7-16		Church Parade. Testing electric lamps with signalling keys. Artillery route reeled up at SOUASTRE - HENU - by parties of divisional LOCAVILLE units. Rain	RW
=	17-7-16		Major Lewis visited ADAS III Corps re. reeling up spare lines. Capt Jordan visited 137 & 138 Bn Hqrs also BELLACOURT. Rain	RW
=	18-7-16		Rain	RW

WAR DIARY
INTELLIGENCE SUMMARY

Army Form C. 2118.

Place	Date	Hour	Summary of Events and Information	Remarks and references to Appendices
BAVINCOURT	19.7.16		Major Lewis visited 137 & 139 B/130 battery. Lieut Lewis building new airline route to Div Sig dugout. Capt Storey visited to learn topr Bank.	
			Fine	
	20.7.16		Major Lewis visited Div Sig Dugout. Battalion Hqrs of 137. Party continued airline work. Enemy bombarded our front line 12.15 am to 1.30 am	
			Fine	
	21.7.16		Major Lewis & Lt Rotall visited 232 Bde RFA. & 139 Inf Bn Hqrs. Capt Storey & Lewis arranging for communications from ADS Div Hqrs.	
			Fine	
	21.7.16		Normal	

Army Form C. 2118.

WAR DIARY
or
INTELLIGENCE SUMMARY
(Erase heading not required.)

Instructions regarding War Diaries and Intelligence Summaries are contained in F. S. Regs., Part II. and the Staff Manual respectively. Title Pages will be prepared in manuscript.

Place	Date	Hour	Summary of Events and Information	Remarks and references to Appendices
BAVINCOURT	2,3		Capt Sharon & Lt Lewis fixing up Bn adv Sig Office Church parade. 12 noon. Normal. Major Lewis visits trenches of 138 Bde	
"	24		Capt Sharon visits 138 & 137 areas. in fixing up wires and repairing Dis cam with 83. 30 miles required. Normal	
"	25		Wiring & fixing up Signal Shelter. GOVY - LAHERLIERE airline led into office and also RE path.	
"	26		Major Lewis visits 137 Area. and inspects & Tar huts at ETRUN bd Div. inspected front line comms of 137 Bde. Normal	

Army Form C. 2118.

WAR DIARY
INTELLIGENCE SUMMARY
(Erase heading not required.)

Instructions regarding War Diaries and Intelligence Summaries are contained in F. S. Regs., Part II. and the Staff Manual respectively. Title Pages will be prepared in manuscript.

Place	Date	Hour	Summary of Events and Information	Remarks and references to Appendices
BAVINCOURT	27		Capt Shirley visited 139 area re-visual. Fixed points for stations. Cable testing up in trenches continued.	Sm
	28		Major Lewis visited pigeon loft BARLY. Normal. Laid airline to BARLY	Sm
	29		Reeling up cable in trenches forward are continued. Reeled up BARLY cable and LAMERLIERE cable	Sm
	30		Fine. Church parade 10 am Normal. Fine	Sm

2449. Wt. W14957/M90 750,000 1/16 J.B.C. & A. Forms/C.2118/12.

Army Form C. 2118.

WAR DIARY
INTELLIGENCE SUMMARY
(Erase heading not required.)

Instructions regarding War Diaries and Intelligence Summaries are contained in F. S. Regs., Part II. and the Staff Manual respectively. Title Pages will be prepared in manuscript.

Place	Date	Hour	Summary of Events and Information	Remarks and references to Appendices
BAINCOURT	31		Capt Thorp fixing up Divnal in 13f Area. also visits Bullo rTowthyn RA in their area. Normal Fine	

Head Qrs
46th Div

Attached is War Diary
of this Company for month
of August 1916

E.A Lewis Major

20.9.16 46th Div Sig Co R.E.

Army Form C. 2118.

WAR DIARY
or
INTELLIGENCE SUMMARY

(Erase heading not required.)

Instructions regarding War Diaries and Intelligence Summaries are contained in F. S. Regs., Part II. and the Staff Manual respectively. Title Pages will be prepared in manuscript.

Place	Date	Hour	Summary of Events and Information	Remarks and references to Appendices
BAINCOURT	Aug 1		Div Sports in afternoon. Normal.	Enc
"	2		Fine. Paid visits to S.O.E.'s of LA COUCHIE. Arranging visual stations in 138 area. Normal	Enc
"	3		Fine. Wireless at BASSEUX moved to BELLACOURT. Normal	Enc
"	4		Fine. ADMS visits hops. Major Lewis & Capt Thorby went to PAS to collect forms & labels, also drew cash for pay. Normal	Enc

Army Form C. 2118.

WAR DIARY
or
INTELLIGENCE SUMMARY

(Erase heading not required.)

Instructions regarding War Diaries and Intelligence Summaries are contained in F. S. Regs., Part II. and the Staff Manual respectively. Title Pages will be prepared in manuscript.

Place	Date	Hour	Summary of Events and Information	Remarks and references to Appendices
BAYENCOURT	5/6/16		138 Bde occupied advanced position for raid during night. '137 Bde Sports Bailleulmont. Wireless Sec ans working at BERLES AU BOIS. Fine	
"	6/6/16		Two church parade. Company bathing all day. Normal. Fine	
"	7/8/16		Major for's visits 135/138 trps. Sixing kill for Gas Alarm in Town bring Office Lachet. Normal. Fine.	

WAR DIARY

Place	Date	Hour	Summary of Events and Information	Remarks
BAVINCOURT	8.9.16		Hugh Jemi Visits 137 & 138 2 Pole offices and 233 & 235 A. Pole "	
		10 pm	Pm alet.	
	9		Reconnaissance of Novembers Regiment. Company found with three horses. Major Lench visits improved Backrange at BRETANCOURT and O.P. to be connected to it. Lieut H. HOOPER joins Coy as Recpti. Officer	
	10.	9.30 am	Gas alert earlier. Normal Lieut H. HOOPER joins left Group R.A. to arrive Artillery Officer	
	11		Normal	

WAR DIARY
or
INTELLIGENCE SUMMARY

Army Form C. 2118.

Place	Date	Hour	Summary of Events and Information	Remarks and references to Appendices
BAVINCOURT	12.8.16		Instruction of all arms of Company. Maj. Lewis visits working parties on Railway line likely to be damaged by the felling. Gas Alert.	
"	13.8.16	11.20pm	Gas alert ended.	
"		9am	Preparation for Divisional Signal School. Students arriving (N.A.). Lieut ARMESLEY forms Class for Signalling Course.	See School programme Appx I
"	14.8.16	6pm	Lieut H.E.F. LEWIS joins 137 Bde. vice Lt MAGUIRE on that Bde. comg. undergo Signalling Course. "Elementary Electricity Interpretation" no Sig. applies to Field Telephony	
"	15.8.16		Divisional Order 85 received. Major FRENCH R.E. leaves for XVII Corps. lecture on Office Organisation. Light Signalling Platoon for Report.	
"	16.8.16	7.30	MAJOR E.A. LEWIS lectures on Telephones to Signal School. Musical Signalling between Classes out by day and night Sig	

Army Form C. 2118.

WAR DIARY
or
INTELLIGENCE SUMMARY

(Erase heading not required.)

Instructions regarding War Diaries and Intelligence Summaries are contained in F. S. Regs., Part II. and the Staff Manual respectively. Title Pages will be prepared in manuscript.

Place	Date	Hour	Summary of Events and Information	Remarks and references to Appendices
BAVINCOURT	17.8.16		Captain THODAY lectures on "Helio". O.C. visits Left Front O.P. Exchange. 137 & 139 Divisions Offices.	
"	18.8.16		Major Innis visits O.P. Exchange O.P.Yo. Making of home standings commences. Capt. THODAY lectures School on its telescope, scale lamping.	
"	19.8.16		Normal. Capt THODAY lectures on "reckoning". Making of home standards proceeding. Weather very wet.	
"	20.8.16	2 pm	Church Parade O.O. No. 91 received	
"	21.8.16		O.C. Company visits Batt. H.Qrs. & Front Line Trench 139 Bde.	
		8/30 p	O.O. 92 received. G.S.4+/2 recd.	

WAR DIARY
INTELLIGENCE SUMMARY

Place	Date	Hour	Summary of Events and Information	Remarks and references to Appendices
BAVINCOURT	22/8/16		Normal	
		4/40p	O.O. 93 received	
"	23/8/16	1 am	Gas alert	
			O.C. Company visits Rubin Pt. 2, 137 2 Bde. Norman. Dispatch riding scheme by Divisional Dispatch Riders	
"	24/8/16	9 am	Normal. O.C. Coy visits 137 Bde. Divisional front except in D Section where it is returned	
"	25/8/16	9/30 am	Gas alert. m.g. fired on 139 aH 80 a.m.	
		3 pm	O.C. Company visits 139 Bde. Pt. 2. Wireless Station. O.C. v/Cpl JERVIS attempts demonstration to Corps Commander	
		9/30	Night signalling with lamps to tent students	
"	26/8/16		Major E.A. LEWIS lectures to school on the Fullerphone	
			Normal	

WAR DIARY
INTELLIGENCE SUMMARY

Army Form C. 2118.

Place	Date	Hour	Summary of Events and Information	Remarks and references to Appendices
BAVINCOURT	27/8/16	4pm	Church Parade. Schedule for second course Signal School assemble	
"	28/8/16	6am	Second course Signal School commences. O.C. Coy visits Signal Officer of Brigades 3 HPA, Motor Batt. Capt. THODAY Lectures on the Message Form (Div Artillery)	
"	29/8/16	am 10/25 6/10pm	Gas alert. O.C. Coy visited Battery Sig. Officers Gas alert off.	
"	30/8/16	9am	Major LEWIS Lectures on Telephones Lt. Coy visits 138 Bde & & Report for Signal Officers	
"	31/8/16		Normal	

DIVISIONAL SIGNAL SCHOOL.
PROGRAMME OF WORK.

MONDAY.

6 a.m.-7 a.m.	Flag drill.
9 a.m.-10 a.m.	Telephones. Internal construction. Care of &c. Elementary Electricity.
10a.m.-12-30p.m.	Reading & Sending. Flag. Helio. Disc.
2p.m.-4-30p.m.	Cables. Types of. Laying. Labelling. Jointing. Crossings.
8-30 p.m.	Lecture. "The message form".

TUESDAY.

6a.m.-7a.m.	Flag Drill.
9a.m.-10a.m.	Setting up & Packing up Stns.
10a.m.-11a.m.	Discussion on Cable laying
11a.m.-12-30p.m.	Map Reading. The Compass.
2p.m.-4p.m.	Station work. Discipline.
8-30 p.m.	Lecture. "Organisation of Signal Offices". (Sgt. MILLER.)

WEDNESDAY.

6a.m.-7a.m.	Flag Drill.	NOTE.
9a.m.-10a.m.	5 minute Lectures.	Written NOTES should
10a.m.-12-30p.m.	Transmitter Work.	be taken on all
3-30 p.m.	Long distance scheme.	Lectures.

THURSDAY.

6a.m.-7a.m.	Flag Drill.
9a.m.-10a.m.	Disc & shutter. Reading & sending.
10a.m.-12-30p.m.	Despatch Riding.
2p.m.-4-30p.m.	Establishing chain of Visual Stns.
8-30 p.m.	Lecture. "Station Discipline".

FRIDAY.

6a.m.-7a.m.	Flag Drill.
9a.m.-12-30p.m.	Station work. Visual & Phone.
3-30p.m.-4-30p.m.	Discussion on Work Done. 5 Minuet Lectures.
8-30 p.m.	Lecture. Laying of Field Cables. Induction. Overhearing.

SATURDAY.

6a.m.-7a.m.	Flag Drill.
9a.m.-10a.m.	Telephony in Gas Attacks.
10a.m.-12-15p.m.	5 minute lectures.
8-30 p.m.	Lecture. "Miscellaneous Signals & Their use".

SUNDAY.   Church Parade.

Liable to alteration. According to circumstances, weather &c.

13/8/1916.

46th. Divnl. Signal Coy. R.E.. Capt.

DIVISIONAL SIGNAL SCHOOL.
Programme. 2nd. week.

MONDAY.	6 a.m. - 7 a.m.	Flag drill.
	9 a.m. - 11 a.m.	Helio or flag reading.
	12 noon.	Visual scheme (WARLUZEL).
	8-45 p.m.	Lecture.
TUESDAY.	6 a.m. - 7 a.m.	Flag drill.
	9 a.m. - noon.	D.R. Scheme.
	2-30 p.m. - 4-30 p.m.	5 minute lectures.
	8-45 p.m.	Lamp reading practice.
WEDNESDAY.	6 a.m. - 7 a.m.	Flag drill.
	9 a.m. - Noon.	Sending test. Flag Helio & lamp.
	2-30 p.m. - 4-30 p.m.	do (if possible.)
	8-30 p.m.	Lamp reading practice.
THURSDAY.	6 a.m. - 7 a.m.	Flag drill.
	9 a.m. - Noon.	Cable laying in trenches.
	2-30 p.m. - 4-30 p.m.	Flag reading test.
	8-30 p.m.	Lamp reading test.
FRIDAY.	6 a.m. - 7 a.m.	Flag drill.
	9 a.m. - 11 a.m.	5 minute lectures (examination.)
	11-30 - 12-30 p.m.	Disc reading test.
	8-30 p.m.	Lamp reading test.
SATURDAY.	6 a.m. - 7 a.m.	Flag drill.
	9 a.m. - Noon.	Cable laying test.
	2-30 - 4-30 p.m.	Picking up stations test.
	8-30 p.m.	Lamp reading.
SUNDAY.		Return to UNITS.

Army Form C. 2118.

WAR DIARY
or
INTELLIGENCE SUMMARY
(Erase heading not required.)

Instructions regarding War Diaries and Intelligence Summaries are contained in F.S. Regs., Part II. and the Staff Manual respectively. Title Pages will be prepared in manuscript.

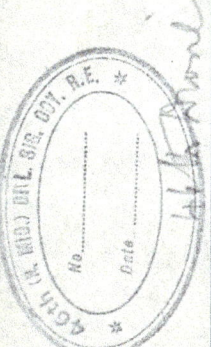

Place	Date	Hour	Summary of Events and Information	Remarks and references to Appendices
BAUNCOURT	1/9/16		Signal Officer A 233 Batty. 139 Bde. Battn H.q. 137 Bde visited. Also O.P. Richecourt 139 & 137.	Sch
	2/9/16	2.15 pm	O.C. visits trenches on 137 Bde front and inspects arrangements for communication during tonight's raid. O.O. 95 received.	Sch
	3/9/16	9.30 am 2.30 pm	O.C. visits Brigade Signal Officers 137 & 139. O.C. attends C.O's conference at Divnl. H.qrs.	Sch Sch
	4/9/16		Normal	Sch
	5/9/16	7 am	O.O. 96 received.	Sch

WAR DIARY or INTELLIGENCE SUMMARY

Army Form C. 2118.

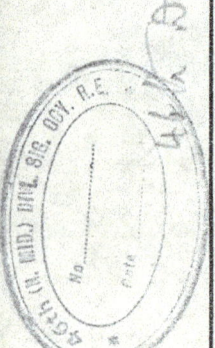

Place	Date	Hour	Summary of Events and Information	Remarks and references to Appendices
BAVINCOURT	6/9/16		Normal	
"	7/9/16		Open wire experiments	
"	8/9/16	11.30 am	Major Lafevre lectures to Divisional Signal School on "Buckhausing and the Fullaphone"	
BAVINCOURT	9/9/16		Hutts and cable trenches examined. Officers students of Signal School visit O.P. Exchange.	
		10 noon	Divisional School Closes	
			2nd/Lt WOOD reports for duty as Area Officer (Supervision of lines)	

Army Form C. 2118.

WAR DIARY
or
INTELLIGENCE SUMMARY
(Erase heading not required.)

Place	Date	Hour	Summary of Events and Information	Remarks and references to Appendices
BAVINCOURT	10/9/16		Lt Lewis returns to Hqrs. Lt Haynie returned to No 2 Sect 137 Bde. Capt Sharpe visited 137 & 135 Bde Offices also 135 adv hqrs.	Sch
	11/9/16		138 Bde sports LaBazeque Fm. No 4 Sect from 1st forge with 2 sect winless. Cleaning up on harness to for S.O.C. inspection. Archbp order parade No 1 Caber Section. Drilling harness.	Sch
	12/9/16		Cleaning up harness etc for S.O.C. inspection. Marching order parade 9 am.	Sch
	13/9/16		G.O.C. inspected Hqrs & No 1 Section 9 am.	Sch

Army Form C. 2118.

WAR DIARY
or
INTELLIGENCE SUMMARY
(Erase heading not required.)

Instructions regarding War Diaries and Intelligence Summaries are contained in F. S. Regs., Part II. and the Staff Manual respectively. Title Pages will be prepared in manuscript.

Place	Date	Hour	Summary of Events and Information	Remarks and references to Appendices
BAVINCOURT	14-9-16		Major Lewis visited Bde Hqrs. Lt Jones visited hqrs. Latham to 12th Div reserve.	Sgd
	15-9-16		Capt Shoddy went over Bde Bstelies and held Court of Inquiry on Motor cycle burnt. also visited 137 Bde Hqrs.	Sgd
	16-9-16		Major Lewis attended Conference at 39 Div Hqrs with reference to Return to be used for identification of Batta Hqrs in communicating with aircraft.	Sgd
	17-9-16	9.30 am	Church parade. Major Lewis went over to 138 Hqrs re movements.	Sgd

Army Form C. 2118.

WAR DIARY
or
INTELLIGENCE SUMMARY

(Erase heading not required.)

Place	Date	Hour	Summary of Events and Information	Remarks and references to Appendices
BAVINCOURT.	18/9/16		Lt Lewis relieved Capt Dorman at 139 Bde Sig. Capt Dorman came into Hqrs.	Initials
	19/9/16		Rain. Col Newbigging visited Hqrs and 139 Bde offices.	Initials
	20/9/16		Rain. Normal.	Initials
			Rain. Orders received for 46 Div ARTY to take over the whole Corps front.	
	21/9/16		Lt Roberts proceeded to SAILLY and HEBUTERNE to take over artillery lines. 139 Bde raised enemy lines and took 4 prisoners. Telephones used with success over parapet.	Initials

Army Form C. 2118.

WAR DIARY
or
INTELLIGENCE SUMMARY

(Erase heading not required.)

Instructions regarding War Diaries and Intelligence Summaries are contained in F. S. Regs., Part II. and the Staff Manual respectively. Title Pages will be prepared in manuscript.

Place	Date	Hour	Summary of Events and Information	Remarks and references to Appendices
BAVINCOURT	22/9/16		Lieut Roberts again went to SAILLY AU BOIS. Re taking over of new position. Interviewed Capt Sharpe, + Capt Gorman about strength Div Sries.	Ent
	23		Lieut Roberts went on leave to England. Lieut Hooper relieves him as R.A.	Ent
	24		Church Parade.	Ent
	25		10 line route out of action midday through parts knocked down by hopes, trough again 3 pm.	Ent

2449 Wt. W14957/M90 750,000 1/16 J.B.C. & A. Forms/C.2118/12.

Army Form C. 2118.

WAR DIARY
or
INTELLIGENCE SUMMARY

(Erase heading not required.)

Instructions regarding War Diaries and Intelligence Summaries are contained in F. S. Regs., Part II. and the Staff Manual respectively. Title Pages will be prepared in manuscript.

Place	Date	Hour	Summary of Events and Information	Remarks and references to Appendices
BRUAY (OR?)	26/9/16		Capt Shaw attended Div Gas School with 2 NCOs to be in structure in use of Smoke Hire Respirators. Lieut Inspire + 1 NCO of No 2 Section also attended. Major Lewis visited 138 Bde lunched with D.S.I.S 3rd Army.	Seb
	27/9/16		Lieut Jones attended Gas School (as above). Major Lewis visited 137 Bde Trenches Coy R. Battn N.Spros.	Seb
	28/9/16		Lewis attended Gas School. (as above).	Seb
	29/9/16		Lieut Jones attended Gas School (as above). Major Lewis + Capt Farrow walked through Divisional lines.	Seb

Army Form C. 2118.

WAR DIARY
or
INTELLIGENCE SUMMARY
(Erase heading not required.)

Instructions regarding War Diaries and Intelligence Summaries are contained in F. S. Regs., Part II. and the Staff Manual respectively. Title Pages will be prepared in manuscript.

Place	Date	Hour	Summary of Events and Information	Remarks and references to Appendices
BAVINCOURT	25/9/16		Capt Thorn & Capt Foreman rode to SIMENCOURT MONCHIET and GOUY to both over 14 IX Div lines, this event of their being required	Ent.

SECRET.   Copy No. 3

46th DIVISIONAL ORDER No. 95.

2nd September '18.

1. The 137th Inf. Brigade will carry out a raid to-night on the enemy's trenches between W.23.d.81.74 and W.23.b.86.00, with the object of :-

    (a) Securing identification of enemy units.
    (b) Killing Germans.

2. The artillery programme has been drawn up by C.R.A. and includes :-

    (a) Wire cutting from 5 p.m. to dark.

    (b) A bombardment from 7 p.m. to 9.15 p.m.

    (c) Sufficient fire to prevent gaps being mended 9.45 p.m. to 10.35 p.m.

    (d) A renewed bombardment 10.35 to 10.55 p.m.

    (e) Barrage 10.55 p.m. to 11.25 p.m.

3. The interval 9.15 p.m. to 9.45 p.m. will be used for patrols to find and mark the gaps in the enemy's wire.

4. The raid will be delivered at 10.55 p.m.

G Thorpe
Lieut.Colonel.,

Issued at 2.15 p.m.   General Staff, 46th Division.

Copy No. 1 to C.R.A.
       2 to C.R.E.
       3 to O.C. Signals.
       4 to 137th Inf. Bde.
       5 to 138th do.
       6 to 139th do.
       7 to A.A. & Q.M.G.
       8 to A.D.M.S.
       9 to 12th Division.
      10 to 17th   do.
      11 to File.
  12 & 13 to War Diary.

O/C Signal
26th Div.

Last night's operations were a complete success. The lines held good from 8 o'clock, when the artillery bombardment started, up till the time "Gas Fire" sounded at 11.18 pm. At 10 o'clock the Phones & III and two drums of D, went over the parapet with a section of the raiding party. At 10.20 the first signals were received from the German wire viz "O.K." This was immediately followed by a message "A & B parties in position in front of gap". At 10.30 the phone went forward to enemy parapet and OK signals were exchanged. From this point OK signals were exchanged every few minutes until 10/40 when another message was received saying. "Have not yet seen runner from C party. OK signals again exchanged until 11/3 when following message was received from German parapet "Assault has started. A party has gone through wire but no definite news yet". At 11/6 another message was received saying

saying "Bombs are being thrown at
front line trench, but no news yet."

At 4/12 "our men in Boche trenches.
officer has sent for further news."

4/16 "'C' party have gone through other
gap and are in enemy front line
trench."

4/20 Bugle sounds the "fall in" and
both parties return with four
prisoners.

I cannot sufficiently praise the
work of all the signallers engaged in
the operations, especially that of the
three who went over with the telephone
apparatus. The line held good all the
time and messages were exchanged with
facility.

All concerned express themselves as
delighted with the signalling arrangements.

H.E.Chauvin Lt
R.E.

3 9/16   No 2 Section

"C" Form (Duplicate).
MESSAGES AND SIGNALS.

Army Form C. 2123.
(In books of 50's in duplicate.)

Handed in at .... Office 9.8 a.m. Received 9.22 a.m.

TO 46 D io Signals

Sender's Number	Day of Month	In reply to Number		A A A

137 Brigade Signal Section did excellent work last night in no mans land aaa accept my best thanks on behalf of the Brigade aaa as far as I old RE signaller I wish to add my personal thanks to the RE's

FROM
PLACE & TIME   H. B. WILLIAMS
                B G.

MESSAGES AND SIGNALS.

Army Form C. 2121.

Prefix......Code......m.	Words	Charge	This message is on a/c of:	Recd. at.........m
Office of Origin and Service Instructions.				Date..........
	Sent		..........Service.	From..........
	At..........m.			
	To			By..........
	By..........		(Signature of "Franking Officer.")	

TO { General H. B. Williams
        137 J Bd.

Sender's Number.	Day of Month.	In reply to Number.	A A A
231	3		

Many thanks for your wire

From   O.C Signals
Place
Time   10.30 am   46th Div.

REPORT on raid of 137th Infantry Brigade, night of 2nd/3rd Septr.

1. The preparation for this raid may be said to have commenced on 27th August when Divisional instructions dealing with the raid were issued, although the raid had previously been considered by the G.O.C., 137th Infantry Brigade.

2. The objects of the raid were :-
   (a) to secure identification
   (b) to kill Germans
   (c) to accustom the troops to moving under close artillery support.

3. The arrangements made worked smoothly, but better arrangements are probably required for getting parties away from front trenches on return.

4. Orders of O.C. 6th South Staffords, and of O.C. Raiding Party are attached marked Appendix II and III respectively, also reports by Officers conducting the various parties, marked Appendix IV.

5. The rough artillery programme is attached, marked Appendix V.

6. A short description of the raid is attached, Appendix I.

7. Attention is drawn to report of O.C. 'C' Raiding Party showing German Gas helmets were lying about, not on the man, and the absence of sentries.

th Sept. 1916.

Lieut-Colonel,
General Staff, 46th Division.

APPENDIX I.

SHORT DESCRIPTION OF RAID.

During the day of the 2nd September, 6" howitzers dealt with the machine gun emplacements on the front of attack and to the south whence the advance could be enfiladed.

At 5 p.m. wire cutting by trench mortars and artillery commenced. This was satisfactorily carried out and two gaps were cut on the front of attack, as well as two further north.

From 7 p.m. to 9.15 p.m. a steady bombardment was carried out of the enemy's trenches about the front of attack. At 8.50 p.m. patrols started out to investigate the wire, and at 9.15 p.m. when the artillery fire lifted, these patrols went in and soon found the gaps. These gaps were marked by tapes after some wire still impeding the gaps had been cut by hand. At 10.35 p.m. a further bombardment was commenced, under cover of which the assaulting parties advanced and lay up just short of the enemy's wire. At 10.55 p.m. the artillery lifted and the raiding parties assaulted. No difficulty was found in walking through the enemy's wire to the tapes which had been fixed to show the gaps. The trenches were entered without difficulty and no sentries were seen. Difficulty was experienced in getting the enemy out of his dugouts, in some cases the men having to go down into the dugouts to fetch them out. About 15 men were killed and 4 men taken prisoners.

OPERATION ORDERS by
Major F.J. Trump,
Commanding 1/6th Bn. South Staffordshire Regiment.

APPENDIX II

Dated 1st September 1916.
Map Reference:- TRENCH MAP. RANSART. 1/10,000.

1. **Raiding Party.**
   On the night of the 2/9/16, the 1/6th Bn. South Staffordshire Regt. will carry out a raid on the enemy's trenches between points W.23.d.81.74 and W.23.b.86.00.

2. **Object.**
   (a) To secure identification of enemy troops holding MONCHY-RANSART Line, by securing prisoners.
   (b) Killing Germans.

3. **Composition of Parties.**
   The party will consist of eight officers and 100 other ranks under the Command of Captain H.V. Mander, and divided as under:-

   "A" Party. 2 officers and 20 other ranks and 3 R.E's.
   "B" Party. 2 officers and 25 other ranks and 3 R.E's.
   "C" Party. 2 officers and 24 other ranks and 2 R.E's.
   "D" party. 1 officer and 22 other ranks.
   Reserve Party. 2 N.C.O's and 10 men.

4. **Objectives.**

   "A" Party. To enter by "R" Gap in enemy's wire and seize and block enemy's front line - sap and C.T. at W.23.d.90.73.
   "B" " Will be sub-divided into clearing party of 15 men and parapet party 10 men. The whole will enter by central gap in wire and the clearing party will endeavour to seize and clear enemy trench by working outwards towards blocking parties "A" and "C". The parapet party remaining outside the trench to support the clearing party to take charge of prisoners and assist wounded.
   "C" Party To enter by left gap proceed to block and hold front line trench and C.T. and suspected sap at W.23.b.86.00.
   "D" " To act as covering party - to remain outside the enemy wire well on outer flanks of "R" and "L" gaps - to fire on enemy either side - and to cover withdrawal of "A", "B", and "C" parties. This party will consist of two Lewis guns with teams and 10 other ranks.
   NOTE:- In the event of the patrols reporting that there are not three practicable gaps in the enemy wire to enable this scheme to be carried out and that only two gaps are cut, O.C., RAID must decide to attack front line in vicinity of gaps, blocking outwards and clearing inwards. Similarly in case of only one gap being found to attack front trench in front of gap and clear outwards.

5. **Assembly, Preliminary.** The Raiding Party will assemble as under:-
   "A" party. Trench 107. Right portion. Point of exit Lewis Gun post.
   "B" party. Trench 107. Left portion. Point of exit Bay 3.
   "C" party. Trench 108. Bays 6, 7, 8 and 9. Point of exit - Bay 7.
   "D" party. Right flank as "A". Left flank as "C". This party will commence to move out 15 minutes in advance of "A", "B" and "C" parties.

   Final Assembly. In "No man's Land" about 40 yards away from the various gaps.

2.

6. Battalion Headquarters.
Trench Battalion Headquarters will be established at TOP end of Nuts Lane, near trench 107.

7. Communication.
Communication will be maintained by telephone and runners. O.C. RAID will arrange to maintain communication with O.C. Battalion by telephone run out into "No mans Land" - one spare instruments and wire will be taken out. Battalion trench headquarters will be connected by telephone to Battalion and Brigade Headquarters. The Brigade Signalling Officer will arrange signalling communication required by O.C. 6th South Staffs Regiment and will be at Battalion Advanced Headquarters at the disposal of the Battalion Commander during operations.

8. Artillery.
The centre Group 46th Divisional Artillery and the 2" Trench Mortar Battery will co-operate in accordance with Artillery programme which will be forwarded later.

9. Equipment.
All ranks will remove identification marks, papers, etc. and will be inspected by their respective party officers before leaving for the trenches.
Rifle Men. Rifle, bayonet, (darkened) 50 rounds S.A.A. and 4 bombs in pockets.
Bombers. No rifle. 12 bombs on bomb carrying waist coat.

Gas Helmets (one per man) Will be taken and carried in the inner coat pocket.
Faces to be darkened. White luminous paint or white cloth to be sewn on underside of collar. Flash lamps will be carried. Mats for crossing enemy barbed wire will be provided by R.E. also 15 ladders (stretcher pattern). "P" bombs will be carried by each party for clearing dugouts. Each man must be provided with some means of cutting wire.

10. Sequence of Operations.
(1) 6" howitzers will fire on selected spots during the day.
(2) at 6 p.m. (or earlier) till 9-15 p.m. general bombardment and wire cutting will take place.
(3) at 9 p.m. three patrols, under the three second officers of "A" "B" and "C" will move out for the purpose of locating the three best gaps in enemy wire and taping the routes to same. The patrols will be accompanied by the R.E. detail who will take out the BANGALORE torpedoes. These patrols should return not later than 9.45 p.m. At 9.15 p.m. to 9.45 p.m. the artillery will not fire on the objective but will keep up the bombardment elsewhere.
(4) 9.45 to 10.35 p.m. artillery will maintain sufficient fire to prevent enemy coming out and discovering and mending gaps in wire.
(5) At 10.35 p.m. to 10.55 p.m. heavy bombardment by artillery.
(6) At 10.55 p.m. the raiding party will attack as arranged.
(7) At 11.20 p.m. unless object is previously attained the raiding party will proceed to withdraw.
(8) At 10.55 p.m. the artillery will lift off the objective but will continue elsewhere, and will not resume firing on objective until O.C. Battalion advises artillery that they may do so.
(9) Machine guns of the 138th Brigade will bring fire to bear on enemy's front trench and saps between W.29.b.15.30 and W.23.c.91.27 between 9 p.m. and 9.45 p.m. and between 10.p.m and 10.55 p.m. and from 10.55 p.m. until "cease fire".
(10) 137th M.G. Co and the 137th T.M. Battery will co-operate under orders from O.C. 1/6th Bn. South Staffs Regt. They will not bring fire to bear on enemy's lines "S" of W.23.b.90.00.
(11) The "cease fire" will be ordered by O.C. Battalion through the F.O.O. who will inform Brigade. The Heavy and Divisional F.O.O's will be with O.C. Battalion.
NOTE:- The artillery will lay the necessary wires and test same. Spare instruments and alternative routes will be arranged for.

11. Countersign.
O.C. RAID will arrange countersign on the day of the operation.

12. **Withdrawal.**
The signal for withdrawal will only be given by O.C. RAID. This will be done by bugle.
NOTE:- O.C. RAID will detail exact method of withdrawal in his orders.

13. The second senior officers "A" "B" "C" will not enter the enemy's trenches, but will remain in gaps and ascertain that their parties have entered the enemy's trenches when they will report to O.C. RAID for instructions at Central Gap.
In the event of the O.C. RAID becoming a casualty the senior of these officers will take command.
These three officers will further accompany the patrol who are to do the taping.

14. **Medical Arrangements.**
(1) The Medical Officer will establish an advanced Regimental Aid post, in the dugout in trench 108.
(2) "A" "B" and "C" parties will be accompanied by two stretcher bearers to each party, using bladder stretchers - four stretcher bearers with stretchers will accompany O.C. Raid and will be under his direction.
Spare bearers will be available at advanced trench R.A.P.
5 stretchers with bearers from the 3rd N.M.F.A. will be at right Company Headquarters.
The R.A.M.C. bearers stationed in the RAVINE will be in readiness if called upon.

15. **R.E.**
The O.C. 1/2 Field Company R.E. will arrange to find the necessary BANGALORE torpedoes and the necessary personnel to operate same. The R.E. will accompany the patrols, and on return to own trenches they will fall in at the head of "A" "B" and "C" parties.
The O.C. 1/2 Field Company R.E. will be at advanced Battalion Hqrs. during operations to advise the Battalion Commander on technical matters.

16. **Silence.**
The importance of absolute silence throughout the operations must be maintained. This must be impressed upon all ranks.

(signed) H. Hanford, Captain.
Adjutant, 1/6th South Staffs Regiment.

APPENDIX III.

OPERATION ORDERS BY CAPTAIN H.V.MANDER,
Commanding 1/6th Batt: South Staffordshire Regt.Raiding Party,
dated 2-9-16.

1. REFERENCE.:- Trench Map RANSART, 1/10,000 and Operations Orders No. 7 by Major TRUMP.

2. OBJECT.
   (1) To secure identification by securing prisoners.
   (2) To kill Germans.

3. COMPOSITION OF PARTIES.
   "A" Party. 2/Lt. T.WALKER in command. 2/Lt.A.JOHNSTON 2nd in command.
   (i) Corpl Russell, J, 3 men and 3 R.Es.
   (ii) Sergt.Pennington, W.A, 6 men.
   (iii) Corpl.Rowley and 5 men.
   (iv) L/Cpl Hale and 3 men.

   "B" Party. 2/Lt.McMillan in command, 2/Lt.Brady 2nd in command.
   (i) Sergt Pritchard, 6 men and 3 R.E.
   (ii) Corpl Hughes and 6 men.
   (iii) Sergt Allen and 10 men.

   "C" Party. 2/Lt.Frew in command. 2/Lt. McGowan 2nd in command.
   (i) Corpl.Payton, 5 men and 3 R.Es.
   (ii) Sergt.Greatorex and 4 men.
   (iii) L/Cpl Morrison and 5 men.
   (iv) Sergt. Harpin and 4 men.

   "D" Party. 2/Lt.Adams in command.
   (i) 1 Lewis gun and team and 5 O.R under L/Cpl Sullivan.
   (ii) 1 Lewis gun and team and 5 O.R under command of Sergt.Whittall.

RESERVE PARTY. Sergt.Aston and 10 B.R assemble at junction of NUTS LANE with front line.

4. THESE PARTIES WILL ASSEMBLE AS PER BATT: OPERATION ORDERS.

5. COMMUNICATIONS.
Each Officer will detail two men to act as runners.
In the event of O.C, Raid, becoming a casualty, 2/Lt.McGowan will take command.

6. EQUIPMENT.
All ranks will remove identification marks, papers, etc, and will be inspected by party officers before leaving for the trenches. Gas helmets (one per man) to be carried in inner coat pocket.

RIFLEMEN.
Rifles, bayonets (darkened) and 50 rounds of S.A.A in bandoliers, to be sewn under tunic. Four bombs in pockets, one wire cutter.

BOMBERS.
12 bombs in bomb jackets - bayonet or knob kerry - one hand wire cutter.
Faces and hands to be darkened - white tape to be sewn underneath collar. Flash Lamps to be carried by all officers and senior N.C.Os and to be used for searching dug-outs.
5 trench ladders to be carried by "A", "B" and "C" Parties to be used as stretchers if necessary.
Two maps to be carried by "A", "B" and "C" Parties. 10 "P" Grenades to be carried by "A", "B" and "C" Parties. Bomb keys will be issued to bombers.
Each party will have a cord to maintain connection between leading and rear officers.

7. OPERATIONS.

2.

7. **OPERATIONS.**

At 8.45 p.m. the second in command of "A", "B", and "C" parties with three other ranks and R.E. party with Bangalore torpedoes will leave our front line trench via gaps in our wire and proceed to examine enemy wire to find suitable gaps. They will lay tapes from gaps in enemy's wire to gap whence they came out. These patrols must be in by 9.45 p.m. when they will immediately report to O.C. RAID at junction of NUTS LANE with front line trench. It is also necessary if possible for these patrols to examine the second line of wire. Sufficient tape must be left at entrance to gap in enemy wire to allow same to be carried through gap to in enemy's trench. At 9.50 p.m. the two sections of "D" party will leave our front line trench via the flank gaps and take up their position in "No mans Land", in order to bring flanking fire on enemy's trenches. They should not open fire until the assault takes place. At 10 p.m. "A", "B" and "C" parties will leave our trenches. On coming clear of our wire they must adopt a close formation and proceed <u>slowly</u> along respective tapes to final assembly place. Runners will be sent by O.C. "A" and "C" parties to O.C. RAID when former are in position.

At 10.55 p.m. Bangalore torpedoes will be <u>fired if necessary</u> and ASSAULT take place.

Prisoners will be sent direct to our trenches - report of same being sent to O.C. RAID.

At 11.25 p.m. the whole party will withdraw in the following sequence :-

(a) "A" and "C" followed by "B" party.

Point of re-assembly will be in RAVINE at end of NUTS LANE. In the event of two gaps being available "A" party will enter by R gap. "C" party will enter by L gap.
"B" party will remain in reserve with O.C. RAID at entrance to right gap.
"A" party will bomb to "R".
"C" party will bomb to "L"

In the event of finding only one gap "A" party will enter first and bomb to right and "C" party will enter second and bomb to left.
"B" party will remain with O.C. RAID.

In case of flare lights hindering advance all ranks will keep still but must waste NO time in getting forward.

A duplicate copy of nominal roll will be made by O.C. parties and handed in to Battalion Trench Headquarters.

8. **R.E. Party.**

3 R.E's will be attached to "A", "B" and "C" parties - they will accompany the patrols and carry with them one bangalore torpedo, which will only be placed on enemy wire after officer in command of patrol has determined that it is necessary to complete gap. They will not be used if no gap is found. They will return with patrol to own trenches, and taking another torpedo will go out at head of respective parties. On arriving at final assault position at 10.45 p.m. they will go forward and fire the torpedoes if necessary. On explosion they will take forward the second torpedo to blow the second belt of wire if necessary. After the parties have passed through gaps the R.E's will remain at gap to clear same by cutting any remaining wire. They will also carry the tapes forward into German trenches.

9. **STRETCHER BEARERS.**

2 stretcher bearers will accompany the rear of "A", "B", and "C" parties and 4 stretcher bearers will be with O.C. RAID.

10. COUNTERSIGN.

3.

10. **COUNTERSIGN.**
    A COUNTERSIGN will be arranged before leaving for the trenches.

11. **SIGNAL for STRAGGLERS.**
    Flares or rockets will be let off in rear of our line to direct stragglers. This must not be taken as a signal to withdraw.

12. **WATCHES.**
    All watches will be synchronised. Time being taken from F.O.O. in NUTS LANE. All officers will synchronise their watches at 8 p.m.

13. **SIGNALLERS.**
    Three signallers will be attached to O.C. RAID for communication.

14. **PARADE.**
    Parties will be paraded with all inspections finished and ready to march off at 6 p.m.

    ORDER OF MARCH   "D" Party
                          "A" Party
                          "C" Party
                          "B" Party

                          (signed) H.V. Mander, Captain,
              Commanding 1/6th Bn. South Staffs Regt Raiding Party,

APPENDIX IV.

To :-
   Officer Commanding,
      1/6th South Staffs Regt.

Sir,

I have the honour to report that according to instruction, a raid took place last night on the German trenches, the object being to secure prisoners and kill Germans.

The raid was entirely successful, both the parties which penetrated the enemy line secured two prisoners and inflicted casualties.

The parties were in position in our front line trench by 8.15 pm. about this time, for a quarter of an hour, the enemy were shelling our front line and O.Ts.

Three patrols of 1 officer and 3 O.R and 3 R.Es were dispatched at 8.50 pm to reconnoitre enemy wire, mark any suitable gaps, place torpedoes in position if considered necessary, and lay tapes from gaps in enemy wire, to the gaps in our own wire.

At 9.30 pm 2/Lt Johnstone returned wounded and reported to me that there was a good gap through both belts of wire for the right party, and that there was no need to use these torpedoes.

At 9.47 pm, 2/Lt.McGowan reported to me that there was a suitable gap for the left party, and that they had brought the torpedoes back with them, as the gap had been rendered passable by wire-cutting.

At 9.48 pm, 2/Lt Brady reported to me that there was no suitable gap available for centre party. Accordingly (after consultation with Major Barlow), I decided to adopt my second scheme of operations, namely that the left party should make use of their own gap, similarly, the right party should use the right gap, closely followed by the centre party.

At 9.50 pm, according to instructions, two Lewis gun teams and 10 O.R moved out to protect the flanks.

At 10 pm the three parties left our trenches and proceeded slowly and in good order to the final assault position, lying down just short of the enemy wire. The right and centre parties being in position by 10.18 pm, the left party only a few minutes later.

Owing to the wideness of the gap in the wire, I decided to send 2/Lt McMillan with half his party forward along with 2/Lt Walker and his party with orders to act as a parapet party. 2/Lt Brady with the remainder of the party was to stay with me at the gap in the wire.

At 10.55 pm, both parties advanced simultaneously, and were successful in entering the German lines, meeting with little opposition in crossing the wire and hardly any rifle fire.

Shortly after the assault, a runner and one wounded man reported to me that the right party was in the German trench: some bombing meantime being audible.

At 11.5 pm, 2/Lt McGowan reported to me that the left party were all in the German trench, whereupon I sent him back to take up a position on the outer edge of the right gap in the German wire.

Noticing a party of men on the inner edge of the wire, I sent 2/Lt Brady with 4 O.R to investigate same. On returning, he reported that there were three of our men clearing the gap in our wire to assist the withdrawal.

During this period, I found the telephone of utmost value, in maintaining communication with the Battalion Trench H.Q. This was largely due to the efficiency of the three men employed.

At 11.18 pm, runners arrived simultaneously from both parties, with the report that each party had two prisoners, whereupon I ordered my bugler to sound the BUG signal to withdraw.

The withdrawal was carried out in good order, and the parties had re-entered our front line trench by 11.44 pm. Here, there was a considerable amount of blocking before the men proceeded to the point of re-assembly in the RAVINE.

                                                       I then

I then proceeded to Trench H.Q, reported the safe return of the Assault party and suggested to O.C, Battalion, that the covering party be recalled.   This was done by having the bugle blown again.

On re-assembling in the RAVINE, I found that the following casualties had occurred :-
        1 Officer wounded.
        1 man missing (believed killed).
        5 men wounded.

I have, etc,

(sgd) H.Vivian Mander, Captain,
O.C, 1/6th South Staffs Regt Raiding Party.

Report of Patrol "B" Party (Centre Gap).

To :-
O.C., Raid.

I and 3 O.R with 2 Engineers attached left Bay 3 of T. 107 at 8.50 pm, 2/9/16, for the purpose of finding gaps in the enemy wire and laying tape from our own wire to the gap. After proceeding for 150 yards in front of our own wire, we halted in order to allow time for the artillery to lift off the enemy wire.

After waiting the necessary time, we moved on, and reached the German wire. Working along this for some distance we found a gap. On examination this proved to be of little use. It was extremely narrow, was strewn with loose wire, and was impracticable. It was impossible to proceed further than the first belt of wire on account of the heavy shelling to which the gap was being subjected.

I also consider that it was useless to lay the Bangalore torpedo because of this shelling.

The tape was then attached to the edge of the wire at the gap and the patrol withdrew. We straightened the tape on our return journey and got into Bay 3, Trench 107, at 9.48 pm.

I immediately reported to Capt. Mander, O.C, Raid, that the gap was impracticable.

(sgd) I.G.Bray, 2/Lt., O.C.,
Patrol, "B" Party.

Report of Patrol "C" Party, (Left Gap).

To :-
O.C, Raid.

The patrol of "C" Party, consisting of 1 N.C.O, 2 men and 3 Engineers went out from Trench 10B, Bay 7 at 8.50 pm, 2/9/16, and got into "No Mans Land", before the artillery lifted from enemy's front line. The patrol, was under my charge and the task was to find gap in enemy's wire and lay a tape from our gap to the gap in Boche wire.
(1) We arrived at enemy's wire without encountering any opposition.
(2) After a few minutes looking along the wire, we found a gap which after investigation, I thought suitable. The gap was cut very thoroughly by the artillery, and only a few loose strands of wire had to be cut. This done, we fixed the tape. The gap was fully four yards wide until the last belt of wire, when it turned to the right and narrowed down to a few feet. The last part was littered with broken wire and stakes. The gap was cut right through by our artillery. Having ascertained this, the patrol returned along the tape, straightened it out, and I reported to Capt. Mander, O.C, Raid, at 9.45 pm. There was no need to use torpedo.

(Sgd) S.M.McGowan, 2/Lt.
O.C., "C" Party, Patrol.

Report of "A" Party. Right Gap.

1. The party moved off from our own trenches at 10 p.m. The crossing of "No man's Land" was uneventful. As the tape had been led well into the German wire by our patrol, the party halted and lay down about 10 yards inside the outer edge of the German wire. We arrived there at 10.25 p.m. The party was at once organised for the assault. The detachments lying in the order in which they were to enter the German lines. The party was also well closed up so as to enable them all to rush together. Orders were passed for the men to attend to such details as, the turning up of coat collars and the preparing of bombs.

2. At 10.55 p.m. the party went forward taking the German wire in perfect order and in fairly slow time owing to the excellence of the gap which had been made, coupled with the effectiveness retard of our own artillery fire. The only bits of wire left to the progress could not be more than knee high. The party closed up on the inner edge of the German wire and went forward to the trench.

3. They entered the trench in good order until some men who had been held up by the wire collected in front of the parapet and had to be rushed in. The two parties then moved right and left respectively, bombing as they went. When dugouts were encountered, all efforts were made to get the Germans to come up and surrender. In one case, this was successful, and we thus secured our prisoners. When this was not successful, "P" grenades and bombs were used as an inducement to the Germans to come up. The right party did not reach its objective owing to its being held up by bombing from the mouth of a dugout, and two casualties being inflicted. The casualties and prisoners were hurried to the rear with all possible speed. The capture of the prisoners was immediately reported by runner to O.C. RAID. The work of bombing dug-outs was proceeding successfully when the "withdraw" sounded; otherwise other prisoners would have been taken. Although nothing definite be said, the Germans must have had a good many wounded if not killed. can

4. The withdrawal took place in good order, a party waiting for any fully 5 minutes after the withdrawal sounded to collect straggler and any men who might not have left the German trench. After all had been got together by aid of the tape, crossed "No man's Land", and reached our lines, only encountering a small amount of rifle fire from the German lines.

5. Description of German Trenches. At the point of entry of this party the inner edge of the German wire was about 15 yards from the parapet. The trench was about 7' in depth and boards being well raised to allow a good drainage. The trench bottom was very dry and clean. The trenches at the top were much wider than our own and would have given very little protection from shell fire. The firing plat-forms were much on the same principal as our own. No revetments were found.

6. The dug-outs were found in the bays of the trench under the parapet and were from 15 to 16' in depth. In those that had one entrance only, this was in the centre of the bay; where they had two entrances, there was one at either end of the bay. At this point, the Germans had evidently a small support trench very near to their fire trench and running parallel to it. From this trench they attempted to bomb our men in the fire trench, but in every case the bombs went too far and fell out in front of the parapet. Our men on the parapet bombed back at this support trench.

(sd) Thos Walker, 2/Lieut.

5.

Report of O.C. "B" Party.
Right Gap.

To Captain Mander,
   O.C. Raid.

The assault started at 10.55 p.m. and I and 15 O.R. (the remainder of my party being left in reserve under my 2nd in command), proceeded in rear of "A" party through the Right Gap with ease in the enemy's wire, to the point of entry. On reaching this point, I detailed a party to block it, and also detailed a party to bomb to the left flank. The remainder of my party acted as parapet party.

The left party immediately discovered a dugout into which a "P" grenade was thrown. Shortly after, 2 of the enemy were taken prisoners and sent back to our lines. The left party then moved along the trench but no more of the enemy were encountered, and no more dugouts were discovered. A periscope was discovered and the trench round about was searched, but no more of the enemy were discovered.

The bugle then sounded and my party withdrew in good order, the party in trench being assisted during the withdrawal by the parapet party.

The enemy trench at point of entry was about 6' deep and shewed signs of the bombardment. At other places the trench was about 9' deep and was wide at the top. The parados was revetted with continuous brushwood revettment, which was in good condition and was held in position by pickets and anchor pickets.

The dugouts had two entrances, one entrance had about 8 steps down, and the other had 20. The dugout was right below the parapet. The entrance had several little slits which I would say 2 men could get into. These slits were at regular intervals down to the dugout. The entrance was revetted with brushwood. A table and several chairs were inside, also several beds which had blankets on them. The dugout was illuminated by an oil lamp. The walls of the dugout were boarded.

There were steps down into the trench from the parapet. The trench was of saw teeth type.

(sd) Geo. A. McMillan,
   O.C. "B" Party.

REPORT OF "C" PARTY.

To Captain H. Mander, M.C.

We assaulted at 10.55 p.m. The wire had been excellently cut and consisted of two belts. We got into the enemy's trench without delay, and almost immediately encountered 2 Germans (now prisoners).

The trench was 9' deep, and was considerably battered by artillery. The parados was revetted with continuous hurdle work and also over and above anchor pickets.

The parapet was on the step and stairs principle, and was in good condition. The top row was sandbagged. No other sandbags appeared to be in the trench.

The trench was saw teeth shape not traversed as ours are.

The dugouts were substantial. They were placed below the parapet and one entrance was 8 steps down, the other 20. The interior was about 7' broad, with planked walls. At intervals were openings containing 4 bays or beds, 2 and 2. These dugouts held about 14 men in all. There were lamps to illuminate. Chairs and tables. Notepaper was visible. Gas masks in profusion in the dugout. It would appear that the enemy do not continuously wear their helmets, although both prisoners did. The enemy surrendered without hesitation. On entering the dugout, a bell rang. I did not find out how it was worked. The enemy bombed us from their support line, but our parapet party silenced them. The trench is quite lightly held, and appears to consist of a serious of sentry posts. The sentries were certainly not watching when we arrived. On our return, there was little aimed fire, but lots of very lights. We returned at 11.30 p.m. without casualties.

(sd)   James H. Frew, 2nd Lieut.

* * * * * *

APPENDIX V.

ARTILLERY PROGRAMME.

Reference 137th Infantry Brigade Operation Order 89.

5 to 7 p.m.	Wire cutting by Artillery and Medium Trench Mortars.
Phase "A" 7 to 9.15 p.m.	Wire cutting continues. Bombardment of front line objective, communication trenches, support trenches and machine gun emplacements.
Phase "B" 9.15 to 9.45	Bombardment lifts from front line objective to support trenches and strong points and front line on flanks.
Phase "C" 9.45 to 10.35.	Steady bombardment of front line objective.
Phase "D" 10.35 to 10.55	Heavy bombardment of front line objective.
Phase "E" 10.55 to 11.25	Raid goes on. Bombardment lifts to support and communication trenches and trench junctions.

The Artillery will cover the withdrawal until the order to cease fire is given.

A.J.H. SLOGGETT. Major.
Brigade Major, 137th Infantry Brigade.

2/9/16.

Lieut Lewis
 Please see
& give further report

Palerie Maud
4/9/16

O/c Signals
 4th Div

Further report
attached

W E Lewis
         Lieut
8/9/16   RE
    13 y Inf Bde Sigs

For War Diary

ADS

V.II Corps

May like to see the
attached

CaLewis Major
4/9/16   46th Div Sig Co R.E.

O i/c Signals 46th Div.

Seen thank you. I am pleased to hear
that the 137 Brigade Section did well, and
received the praise of the Brigadier. I am
not however convinced of the advisability
of running lines forward for a raid of
short duration. The value of the messages
which can be sent back seems hardly
commensurate with the risk to instruments
and personnel involved
especially in view of Third Army letter
No G.912 20.8.16 (VII Corps GS 1057 of 23-8-16).

It would be interesting to know what
special steps (if any) were taken to prevent the
two D1 lines being cut by enemy fire and
whether the lines were afterwards rolled up
& instruments brought in.
4-9-16.

D. Rampier Jones
Major RE
ADAS VII Corps

O/C Signals
46th Div.

Since the whole operation
worked to "programme", the messages
received from the forward phone were
simply "Progress Reports". Under different
circumstances the phone offered great
possibilities. O.C. Raid could readily
have controlled the Artillery fire if he
had required more time to search the
enemy trenches. He could have called
for assistance had he found the enemy
waiting in force. Requests for more
bombs would have been quickly complied
with.

No special steps were taken against
line breakages by enemy shell fire. As
a matter of fact the enemy did not
retaliate on No Mans Land but their fire
was concentrated on our support line and
Communication Trenches. The weakest
point of the line was considered to be on
our parapet for it was anticipated that
the enemy would shell our front line
trenches. We were prepared to carry
out repairs at this point. I also gave
instructions that should one leg of the
metallic pair be broken, the two lines
were to be bunched and an earth return
used.

There were no casualties amongst
the

the Signallers, who returned with the raiding party, bringing in both instruments. It was not possible to go through the slow process of reeling up in such an exposed position because enemy rifle fire became very persistent when the raiding party were ready to come in. The D⁣³ lines were pulled in as much as possible from our own parapet and then cut adrift.

W. E. C. Lewis, Lieut
RE
137 Inf. Bde Sigs

6 9/16

SIGNALS
137th INF. BGDE.

Date 20/9/16
No. 67

O.C. Signals
46th Division

Handed by 5th North Staff
Telephone Communication.

A special line of twin twisted D5 was run out into a snipers post in No Mans Land about halfway across. Communication was kept up the whole time but only three code signals were exchanged during this period denoted that the party was out, and that they were in the Enemy's trenches. Communication backward consisted of one direct line to Battalion H.dqrs, and from thence to Brigade. The one spare

Company Line was connected direct there to the Centre Group O.P. Exchange. All Communications were good and the Brigadier and O.C. 5th North Staff expressed their satisfaction with the arrangements.
All material except short lengths of wire, was recovered.
Visual Stations were manned and communication test every ¼ hour but no necessity arose for using same.

C Maguire Lieut. R.E.
O.C. SIGNALS,
137th INFANTRY BRIGADE.

O/c Sigs
   46th Div

   Attached summary and
diagram of communications
during raid by 8th Sherwoods
may be of interest to you.

22 9/16   W.E. Lewis Lieut
                              No 3 Sec

Capt Thoday
   War Diary
       Sah May 29.9.16

Report on Communications arranged for Raid by 8th Sherwoods on night of Sept 21/22

The existing wires were used for all communications and no fresh cable was laid out.

Watches were synchronised by the Brigade Signal Officer at 9 p.m.

Left Battalion HQ's were joined direct to Stokes Mortar Guns and to Two Inch Trench Mortars. These guns were also joined direct to their O.P's.

Left Battalion HQ's was given a direct line to Left O.P. Exchange and through the latter place was able to speak to 38th Siege Battery at BERLES who were participating in the preliminary bombardment. The 18 pr batteries covering the Left Sector were, of course, on direct to Battalion HQ as usual. Other batteries (60 pr) taking part, found ready communication via Left O.P Exchange

A detached Heavy Mortar gun was also put in direct communication, but this

this gun did not come into action.
An alternative route from Left
Battalion to 38th Siege Battery was
also provided through 139 and 137
Brigade HQ.

All communications held and
there was not the slightest delay in
getting through at any time.

At 1-10 am it was reported
that raiding party had returned
having captured five prisoners.

A straight line diagram of the
lines as arranged, is attached.

H. E. Lewis Lieut RE
No 3 Sec

22 9/16

Objective

Derby Sap   Liverpool Sap   Lamotte St   Cavendish Sap   from a Sewer Sap   Bay 83 O.P.

Stokes Guns

No 148 gun 2" T.M.

W.T.

No 149 gun 2" T.M.   5 x 6 gun 2" T.M.

Oat St O.P.   Quarries O.P.   Contineé St O.P.

DXA
DXB

DX

Left O.P. Ex
(lines to 16pr Batteries)

D

Centre O.P. Ex

38th Siege Batty

C

"K" is the point from which the raid starts.

Helenish Hunt
22.9
16
R.E.

WAR DIARY or INTELLIGENCE SUMMARY

Army Form C. 2118.

Place	Date	Hour	Summary of Events and Information	Remarks and references to Appendices
BAVINCOURT	1/10/16		Church Parade. Capt Shelley visited 137 Bde Hqrs. re Signal equipment of battalion.	
	2/10/16		Rain. Capt Whelan & Capt Forman rode over Div artillery lines.	
	3/10/16		Rain. Major LEWIS went over 138 Bde lines.	
	4/10/16		Rain. Lt HOOPER wiring new hqrs. of 230 Bde at SOUASTRE. Capt FORMAN went over ST AMAND - FONQUEVILLERS buried lines with up to Coys.	

Army Form C. 2118.

WAR DIARY
or
INTELLIGENCE SUMMARY
(Erase heading not required.)

46th Div Sig Coy RE

Instructions regarding War Diaries and Intelligence
Summaries are contained in F.S. Regs., Part II.
and the Staff Manual respectively. Title Pages
will be prepared in manuscript.

Place	Date	Hour	Summary of Events and Information	Remarks and references to Appendices
BAVINCOURT	5/10/16		Major Lewis held an orderly room at Hqrs. No 2 Sect. 137 Bde. Major Lewis + Capt Thursby + E & O 3 (Capt Guthrie) looked over projected Divl Battle Hqrs at BEAUMETZ-LES-LOGES. With a view to also wiring up an observation post there.	SW
"	6/10/16		Party laying Div OP — BASSEUX Lines. Speaking found good. Capt Forman + Capt Jurber looked over lines from BEAUMETZ for Adv Div Hqrs. Lines found in bad state of repair. 4 pairs found available	SW
"	7/10/16		Airline party out on 4 hire route Nos 52 + 53 straining up wires etc. Capt Forman and Lt Lewis changed over commands of No 3 Section. Lt HEDDERWICK joined the Coy from England.	SW
"	8/10/16		Church parade. Major Lewis went with Lt Hedderwick to POMMIER Capt Thursby + Lt Lewis walked no route helwix BEAUMETZ to inspect work done. Airline party m. b hire route repairing to.	SW

2449 Wt. W14957/M90 750,000 1/16 J.B.C. & A. Forms/C.2118/12.

Army Form C. 2118.

WAR DIARY
or
INTELLIGENCE SUMMARY

(Erase heading not required.)

HQ K Anti-Sig Coy RE

Place	Date	Hour	Summary of Events and Information	Remarks and references to Appendices
BAVINCOURT	9/10/16		Major Lewin visited Roberts went over lines in POMMIER - BIENVILLERS area. Lt Lewis inspected dugout that found at LA CAVERIE with a view to storing stores. Capt Shulay met ADA1 FCD at MONCHIET re joining him there from BEAUMETZ to GOUY for Adv Hqrs. Working parties working on BEAUMETZ MONCHIET lines, staying poles, straining up wires etc.	
"	10/10/16		Joining through on trail to Adv Hqrs BEAUMETZ. Speaking found good. Capt Shulay facing in new dugout at Div OP.	
"	11/10/16		Airline party erecting poles on BAVINCOURT - GOUY line. Capt Shulay & Lt Lewis went over my proposed route. Lt Maguire visited hqrs. 8 phones destroyed by shellfire at BERLES-AU-BOIS - 230 Bde RFA.	
"	12/10/16		Major Lewin had interview with ADAS 7th Corps re some calls. Capt Shulay went over new airline route to GOUY. Poles now in position. Airline party finishing up erecting poles, staying same. Lt Jones Lt Headerwick visited hqrs re new buried route from POMMIER to Bhtn Hqrs. Orderly Room at 137 Rue Hqrs Warren.	

Army Form C. 2118.

WAR DIARY
or
INTELLIGENCE SUMMARY

(Erase heading not required.)

46th Dn Sig Coy.

Place	Date	Hour	Summary of Events and Information	Remarks and references to Appendices
BAVINCOURT	13/10/16		Major Irwin & Capt Shirley walked over new airline route to Gouy.	ELM
"	14/10/16		Poling and two pairs complete on new airline route.	EM
"	15/10/16		Church parade. Laying poles from Sip Mire to terminal pole on new route. Three pairs completed to Gouy route. Capt Shirley visited BEAUMETZ and wired OP line from airport to observation station.	
"	16/10/16		Work continued on airline route. Quads buried from wood to terminal pole at YDF. Four pairs now through to Gouy butt and joined through to movement. Capt Irwin on h: Brun - Callaren visited him.	ELM

Army Form C. 2118.

WAR DIARY
or
INTELLIGENCE SUMMARY
(Erase heading not required.)

4th Div. Sig Coy R.E.

Instructions regarding War Diaries and Intelligence Summaries are contained in F.S. Regs., Part II. and the Staff Manual respectively. Title Pages will be prepared in manuscript.

Place	Date	Hour	Summary of Events and Information	Remarks and references to Appendices
BAVINCOURT	17/10/16		Leading new route into Signal Office. Spanishing from MONCHIET found from Adjutants 7 Corps visited Office, with reference to lateral burial route from BEAUMETZ to BAILLEULMONT. 230 Bde RFA returned to BAILLEULMONT.	EMr
"	18/10/16		Capt Storey & Capt Forman surveyed route for new French Lt Cessen tested lines through from BEAUMETZ to YDP (BAVINCOURT) Major Lewis visited 138 Bde with reference to communication for tonight laid into enemy lines.	EMr
"	19/10/16		Major Lewis visited 138 Bde from 1737 Hqrs. Lieut Heddewick transferred from No 4 to No 2 sec.	EMr
"	20/10/16		Capt Storey laid lines along ARRAS road for police trapping.	EMr

Army Form C. 2118.

46th Div. Sig Co. R.E.

WAR DIARY
or
INTELLIGENCE SUMMARY

(Erase heading not required.)

Instructions regarding War Diaries and Intelligence Summaries are contained in F. S. Regs., Part II. and the Staff Manual respectively. Title Pages will be prepared in manuscript.

Place	Date	Hour	Summary of Events and Information	Remarks and references to Appendices
BAVINCOURT	21/6/16		Major Lewis & Capt Thorn visited 137 Bde HQr with reference to overhearing on lines at BERLES AU BOIS.	Sgd
"	22/6/16		Church Parade.	
"	23/6/16		Major Lewis held orderly room at 135 Bde HQr. Lt. Horn Callander came to take over whole Divisional lines, as new Officer. Lt Lewis then went over divisional lines so far as daylight.	Sgd
"	24/6/16		Lt Lewis & Horn Callander went over new route to BEAUMETZ. Capt Thorn saw Officials of Corps re establish telephones at BERLES & collected same from Corps HQr.	Sgd

2449 Wt. W14957/M90 750,000 1/16 J.B.C. & A. Forms/C.2118/12.

WAR DIARY
or
INTELLIGENCE SUMMARY

(Erase heading not required.)

Army Form C. 2118.

Instructions regarding War Diaries and Intelligence Summaries are contained in F.S. Regs., Part II. and the Staff Manual respectively. Title Pages will be prepared in manuscript.

Place	Date	Hour	Summary of Events and Information	Remarks and references to Appendices
BAUINCOURT	25/10/16		Lt Lewis & Lt Burn-Callender went over buried route to POMMIER & over 138 line. Lt Jones went on leave. relieved by Lt Hopper. 137 Bde carried out raid on enemy trenches capturing 6 prisoners. Communication satisfactorily maintained with raiding party.	
"	26/10/16		Major Lewis & Lt Burn-Callender went over 137 Bde lines. Lt Roberts went to PAS le positions & OPs in Div. area for records.	
"	27/10/16		O.C. Signals 30th Div came over to taking over lines. Lt Hopper visited Lyn. Lt Maguire & Lt Hopper visited hqrs. be moving into new area.	
"	28/10/16		1 Officer & first reponies & horses & 2 signalcarts of 30th Div came to take over lines and Mess. 3 Bdr Signal Officers visited the 3 Bde hqrs to take over lines.	

Army Form C. 2118.

WAR DIARY
or
INTELLIGENCE SUMMARY
(Erase heading not required.)

4th Division Signal Coy R.E.

Place	Date	Hour	Summary of Events and Information	Remarks and references to Appendices
BAVINCOURT	29/10/16		O.C. Signal 36th Div. visited Signal Office. 2 line exchange & local phone relieved. 21st Bde relieved the 137 Bde.	Enc.
"	30/10/16		Church parade. 36th Div. Signals relieved Signal Office. 70th Bde relieved 135 Bde. " " 138 " 135 proceeded to SUS ST LEGER 138 " " HALLOY	Enc.
"	31/10/16		Hqrs closed at BAVINCOURT 10 a.m. & opened at same time at FROHEN-LE-GRAND. 137 Bde at LUCHEUX. 138 " HALLOY 139 " SUS ST LEGER Div transf. to 3rd Army & 137 Bde.	Enc.
FROHEN- LE-GRAND	1/11/16		Inspection of Capt. ... proceeded to	

To,
O.C. Signals
 46th Division

[Stamp: SIGNALS 137th INF. BGDE. 28/10/16 Date...... No. Secret]

Raid on Hostile Trenches by
6th South Staffords on night
of 25th October 1916
———————
Report on Communications

Communications   Three thro' lines were
Back.   provided from O.C. Raid's
                 Dugout to the Right Battalion
                 Headquarters. One was
                 allotted to the Centre Group
                 46th Div. R.A. and was plugged
                 thro' to the Covering Batteries.
                 The remaining two were used
                 for Communication with the
                 Battalion Commander, and
                 to the 137th Bde Hdqs., and
                 also to the 38th Siege Battery
                 thro' the O.P. Exchange.

Communication   Two metallic pairs with
Forward   telephones were taken out
                 into "No Man's Land.
                 One was used by the Lewis
                 Gun Party covering the Gap
                 in Hostile Wire. The other
                 by the O.C. Raiding Party.

The former telephone went out at 6-30pm and signals were exchanged every 10 minutes till 10-45 pm when the party was withdrawn.

The latter telephone went out with the Raiding Party at 10-10 pm and communication was maintained till 10-25 pm when it failed this instrument getting wet in shell-hole occupied by signallers. Use was however made of the Lewis Gun Telephone for further communication.

The lines consisted of D. pairs with the legs spaced about thirty yards apart to prevent both being broken by the same shell list. Earth pins were taken out by both parties of signallers for use in case of one limb being broken, it being arranged beforehand that in the event of failure, both lines would be bunched and the other instrument terminal earthed.

Both metallic pairs were led out the same instrument in the dugout thus enabling the Raiding party to communicate direct this dugout to the covering Lewis Gun.

General.   Communications held good with the exception of the failure recorded above, and all material except one earthpin was recovered.

The G.O.C. Brigade and O.C. 6th South Staffs expressed their entire satisfaction with the Signalling arrangements provided and the way they worked.

Excellent work was carried out by Serg- Lodge the Battalion Signalling Serg- and the Signallers under him, and the success of the communications are due entirely to their efforts.

_____ Lieut. R.E.
O.C. SIGNALS,
137th INFANTRY BRIGADE.

Orders No 54. by Major E.A. Lewis DSO RE

I The Coy will proceed to a new area on Oc. 31st.

II The Coy will parade at 7.45 am in F.S. marching order ready to move.

III The detachment under the command of Lt Roberts will remain behind with the Div Arty. The detachment commander will be L/Cpl Bosley.

IV The Motor lorry will proceed separately. The following men only will travel on it. 2 Drivers ASC, CQMS, Officers Cook, 2 Officers Servants, starting at 9 am.

V Sergt Miller will travel by car with 1 Sounder and 2 ringing phones. He will take with him 2 operators and open up the office at the Mairie FROHEN LE GRAND by 10 am. Car will leave BAVINCOURT at 7.30 am, returning to BAVINCOURT by 10.30 am.

VI Motor cyclists will proceed individually and report to Sergt Miller on arrival at new Hqrs.

VII Lt Lewis will be i/c Column on the march.

VIII The usual halts, and the rules of the road strictly observed. All mounted men will immediately dismount at the halts, and men riding on wagons will inspect same to see that sheets etc are properly tied down.

IX All men mounted on cycles will proceed separately under L/Cpl Parry. They will carry their own kits, starting at 8 am.

X Nosebags will be carried on the horses and Haynets on the wagons.

XI

XI. B'warms and leather jackets will be worn

XII. Blankets will be carried on Section wagons.

XIII. F.S. caps will be packed in kits as far as possible

XIV. Horse rugs will be rolled in bundles of 6. Those of the cable wagon horses on the cable wagon, and the remainder on the footboard of the G.S. Hqrs on their wagon in the same way

XV. Steel helmets will be worn by all ranks.

XVI. Section Sergts will be responsible that billets are left scrupulously clean in every respect.

11 am 30.10.16

1. CSm
2. CQms
3. Sergt. Hall
4. Sergt. Salt
5. Office
6. Lt Lewis

After Order — L/cpl Parry & cyclists will act as clearing up party

Army Form C. 2118.

WAR DIARY
or
INTELLIGENCE SUMMARY
(Erase heading not required.)

Vol 17

Place	Date	Hour	Summary of Events and Information	Remarks and references to Appendices
FROHEN LE GRAND	1/11/16		Major Lewis & Capt Thorn proceeded to ST RIQUIER to look over huts to ABBEVILLE, and to arrange billets. Also visited Signal depot ABBEVILLE about reinforcements.	
"	2/11/16		Advn Hqrs moved to ST RIQUIER. Capt Shorley proceeded early to start wiring Signal office. One pair through to ABBEVILLE. "G" & "Q" phones installed. Also C.R.E.	
ST RIQUIER 3-30pm				
ST RIQUIER	3/11/16		Capt Shorley & Lt Lewis visited 3 Bde Hqrs. One pair found through to YVRENCH (13 Bde). A wire phone installed. Airline pair found to ARGENVILLERS (12 Bde). Cable laid on to MAISON PONTHIEU (14 Bde). DADOS A&MS phones installed. Sommes superimposed on ABBEVILLE pair. Standing times laid all round. Electric light installed.	
"	4/11/16		Wiring in office. 10 line Exchange installed. Capt Thorn proceeded to Signal depot re cable for training. Capt Forman & Lt Hooper visited Bdes re Section training.	

Army Form C. 2118.

WAR DIARY
or
INTELLIGENCE SUMMARY
(Erase heading not required.)

Instructions regarding War Diaries and Intelligence Summaries are contained in F. S. Regs., Part II. and the Staff Manual respectively. Title Pages will be prepared in manuscript.

Place	Date	Hour	Summary of Events and Information	Remarks and references to Appendices
ST RIQUIER	5/11/16		Church parade. Billets arranged for B Section in ST RIQUIER.	
"	6/11/16		Hqrs & No 1 Section marched at 8:30 a.m under Capt Rhodes & met No 2,3 & 4 Sects on the road, the whole company then marched into Hqrs – Inspection by C.O. on arrival. Afternoon spent in billeting & arranging hostelries.	
"	7/11/16		Section drill. Lecture on laying after jointing & labelling by Lt Lewis.	
"	8/11/16		Coy section drill. Lecture on Visual Signalling by Capt Rhodes. Airline commenced to 135 Bde MAISON PONTHIEU	

2449 Wt. W14957/Mgo 750,000 1/16 J.B.C. & A. Forms/C.2118/12.

WAR DIARY / INTELLIGENCE SUMMARY

Army Form C. 2118.

Place	Date	Hour	Summary of Events and Information	Remarks and references to Appendices
ST RIQUIER	9/1/16		Coy drill. Lecture on "Horse Management" to Mounted Orders & Drivers by Capt Hartley M.V.C. Lt Hooke rejoined Artillery at BAVINCOURT. Lt Jones took over NCO's lecture. Airline work continued to MAISON PONTHIEU and AGENVILLERS.	
"	10/1/16		Signal Scheme commenced 9 am. Div Hqrs & Bdes established Hqrs and ran out cable to imaginary battalions. Visual communication also kept up. Airline work postponed owing to scheme.	
"	11/1/16		Capts Thoday & Lewis went over ARGENVILLERS – CANCHY – DRUCAT roads to find lines for 137 & 138 Bdes, moving to CANCHY & NEUILLY L'HOPITAL but found none. Cable was laid & speaking from through to both places by 6 pm. Airline work continued. Signallers practicing Station work under Capt FORMAN. Football Match during afternoon.	
"	12/1/16		Church parade. Capt Thoday visited 137 Bde Hqrs re the making of necessary aeroplane Safos for Bde & battalions.	

Army Form C. 2118.

WAR DIARY
INTELLIGENCE SUMMARY
(Erase heading not required.)

Instructions regarding War Diaries and Intelligence Summaries are contained in F. S. Regs., Part II. and the Staff Manual respectively. Title Pages will be prepared in manuscript.

Place	Date	Hour	Summary of Events and Information	Remarks and references to Appendices
ST RIQUIER	13/11/16		Company paraded in F.S. marching order for inspection by C.O. Signature station work. Airline party continued work on MAISON PONTHIEU route. Company shooting on Range. 1st & 2nd grouping test carried out. Instruction in musketry	
"	14/11/16	9.30 a.m.	Musketry instruction. Company shooting on the Range. Capt Thoday + Lt Israel attended a lecture at HESDIN on "Organisation & work of Signal Service" by Col Hildebrand DDD and Army	
"	15/11/16		Both sections returned to their respective Billets. Airline to MAISON PONTHIEU continued.	
"	16/11/16		Airline work to NEUILLY L'HOPITAL commenced. Detachment reeling up cable to MAISON PONTHIEU	

Army Form C. 2118.

WAR DIARY
INTELLIGENCE SUMMARY
(Erase heading not required.)

Instructions regarding War Diaries and Intelligence Summaries are contained in F.S. Regs., Part II. and the Staff Manual respectively. Title Pages will be prepared in manuscript.

Place	Date	Hour	Summary of Events and Information	Remarks and references to Appendices
ST RIQUIER.	17/11/16		Major Lewis & Capt Shaw went over ground for Visual Scheme. Signallers practising morse etc. Airline work to NEUILLY L'HOPITAL continued.	
"	18/11/16		Visual Signalling Scheme commenced at 8.30 am. Divl HQrs & Bde Rects & 2 Battalion Signal Sections took part. Divnl to Bde Visual scheme was abandoned at 11.30 am. Airline work continued to NEUILLY L'HOPITAL and on to CANCHY. Bdes Trio situated - 137 CANCHY. 138 NEUILLY L'HOPITAL. 139 MAISON PONTHIEU.	
"	19/11/16		Church parade 9 am. Party leeling up cable now replaced by airline to NEUILLY L'HOPITAL and CANCHY.	
	20/11/16		Drilling with lby wounded men.	

Army Form C. 2118.

WAR DIARY
—or—
INTELLIGENCE SUMMARY
(Erase heading not required.)

Instructions regarding War Diaries and Intelligence Summaries are contained in F.S. Regs., Part II. and the Staff Manual respectively. Title Pages will be prepared in manuscript.

Place	Date	Hour	Summary of Events and Information	Remarks and references to Appendices
ST RIQUIER	21/4/16		 Training drill. Normal.	
"	22/4/16		137 Bde moved to YVRENCH 138 " " " BEAUMETZ 139 " " " BERNAUCOURT MAIZICOURT. Company played football match v 1/1 field Co. R.E. + drew 1-1. (Div football comp.) Major Lewis proceeded on leave to England.	
FROHEN-LE-GRAND	23/4/16		Div' H/qrs moved to FROHEN LE GRAND Lt Lewis proceeded to LUCHEUX to look over Signal Office billets. 137 Bde " WAVANS 138 " " BONNIERES 139 " " NEUVILLETTE	
"	24/4/16		Div Hqrs moved to LUCHEUX Saluting drill mounted. 137 Bde " " LE SOUICH Lt Lewis proceeded to LUCHEUX to take 138 " " HALLOY over Signal Office billets. 139 " " SUS ST LEGER	

Army Form C. 2118.

WAR DIARY
INTELLIGENCE SUMMARY
(Erase heading not required.)

Instructions regarding War Diaries and Intelligence Summaries are contained in F.S. Regs., Part II. and the Staff Manual respectively. Title Pages will be prepared in manuscript.

Place	Date	Hour	Summary of Events and Information	Remarks and references to Appendices
FROHEN LE GRAND	25/11/16		Divl. Hqrs moved to LUCHEUX. 137 Bde " " LE SOUICH 138 " " " HALLOY 139 " " " SUS ST LEGER Heavy rain	
LUCHEUX	26/11/16		One cable detachment laying cable to LE SOUICH and another to SUS ST LEGER. Through on phone to MAILLY (138 Bde). Trunk G.co (7th Corps) Capt Skelton visited 137 & 139 Bde Hqrs.	
"	27/11/16		Heavy rain Detachments to 137 & 139 Bdes heating cables safe.	
"	28/11/16		Football Reply v 1/2 Field Co. Won by 2.0. Capt Furner 4th Inspns visited Hqrs. Lt Hooper ? Relieved Lt Jones (138 Bde). On account of weather attending wireless course	

Army Form C. 2118.

WAR DIARY
-or-
INTELLIGENCE SUMMARY
(Erase heading not required.)

Instructions regarding War Diaries and Intelligence Summaries are contained in F. S. Regs., Part II. and the Staff Manual respectively. Title Pages will be prepared in manuscript.

Place	Date	Hour	Summary of Events and Information	Remarks and references to Appendices
LUCHEUX	29/11/16		Lt Jones proceeded to G.H.Q. Wireless School for weeks course.	
"	30/11/16		Capt Shorey & Capt Inman visited H.Q. of 49th Div. Never as taking over line. Capt Inman also visited COUASTRE Bde Hqrs	
"	1/12/16		Both Signal Officers visited new area. O.C. Signals 49th Div visited LUCHEUX	
"	2/12/16		Signal units visited new area. O.C. Signals 137 visited POMMIER and looked over lines there.	

Army Form C. 2118.

WAR DIARY
or
INTELLIGENCE SUMMARY
(Erase heading not required.)

46th Div Signal Coy R.E.

Place	Date	Hour	Summary of Events and Information	Remarks and references to Appendices
LUCHEUX	1/12/16		Bde Signal Officers visited new area. O.C. Signals & the Div. visited LUCHEUX. New Comic airline truck through to LE SOUICH and SUS ST LEGER.	Vol 18
"	2/12/16		Signalmaster visited new area. O.C. Signals, 137 visited POMMIER and looked over lines there.	
"	3/12/16		Lt Lewis sent to hospital. OC's 137 + 138 Bde visited hqrs. Major LEWIS returns from leave.	
"	4/12/16		Normal. Sgt Major visited new area.	

2449 Wt. W14957/M90 750,000 1/16 J.B.C. & A. Forms/C.2118/12.

WAR DIARY or INTELLIGENCE SUMMARY

Army Form C. 2118.

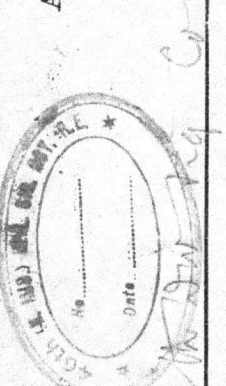

Place	Date	Hour	Summary of Events and Information	Remarks and references to Appendices
LUCHEUX	5/12/16		Major Lewis returned from leave - Lt. Jones returned from Wireless Course. Office instruments taken over to new area.	
"	6/12/16		Major Lewis & Capt Thursby visited new area. Stores & office stuff also Staff for St. Amands exchange went to HENU. 137 Base to POMMIER 131 Base to BIENVILLERS 139 Base to COUASTRE. All lines through at 7am. Office taken over. St Amand Ex. relieved.	
LUCHEUX	7/12/16		Div. HQrs. moved to HENU opening at 10 a.m.	
HENU		10 am	Capt Thursby walked over Div. lines, visited St Amand Exchange - Souastre & Bienvillers.	
"	8/12/16		Major Lewis & Capt Thursby walked over Div. lines. 2/1 Field to put in phone to BIENVILLERS exchange.	

Army Form C. 2118.

WAR DIARY
INTELLIGENCE SUMMARY
(Erase heading not required.)

Instructions regarding War Diaries and Intelligence Summaries are contained in F.S. Regs., Part II. and the Staff Manual respectively. Title Pages will be prepared in manuscript.

Place	Date	Hour	Summary of Events and Information	Remarks and references to Appendices
HENU	9/1/16		A.D. Signals & Corps visited Henu, to position calls & new brined scheme. Capt. Forman (139 Bde) testing line in trenches between SOUASTRE LA HAIE and FONQUEVILLERS. Lieut JONES relieved Lieut HOOPER at BIENVILLERS (139 Bde) Div. School ST AMAND connected to Div Train BELLEVUE connected to R.F.C. 3x.	Sub
"	10/1/16		Church Parade 11am. Parties out repairing lines & staying poles. Lt HOOPER returned to h/qrs. Division on left 30th. on right 21st. Telephones through to (w/T.	Sub
"	11/1/16		Capt Thomas, Lt. Hooper walked over Div. lines. Parly out repairing staying main SOUASTRE Route.	Sub
"	12/1/16		O.D. Signal & Corps visited Henu and discussed trench scheme. 137+139 attended. Posts continued work on Souastre Route.	Sub

Signs.

WAR DIARY

INTELLIGENCE SUMMARY

Army Form C. 2118.

Place	Date	Hour	Summary of Events and Information	Remarks and references to Appendices
HENU	13/7/16		Captain Thorley proceeds on leave. All lines to ST AMAND cut & regulated	
"	14/7/16		Field C in C & Transport lines (Button) connected up to BIENVILLERS & GAUDIAMPRE area. Major Lewis surveyed route & proposed buried lines in POMMIER area	
"	15/7/16		Major Lewis visits ATHIES drawing buried scheme. All lines to SOUASTRE cut & regulated	
"	16/7/16		Lieut W.G. ROBERTS joined HQ from LUCHEUX to take over Div. Arty. Communications	

Army Form C. 2118.

WAR DIARY
or
INTELLIGENCE SUMMARY

(Erase heading not required.)

Instructions regarding War Diaries and Intelligence Summaries are contained in F. S. Regs., Part II. and the Staff Manual respectively. Title Pages will be prepared in manuscript.

Place	Date	Hour	Summary of Events and Information	Remarks and references to Appendices
HÉNU	17/9/16		Church parade. Lt Roberts & Lt Hooper examined Artillery communications from HqArty. O.C. Sigs 31st Div visited to discuss lines scheme	
"	18/9/16		Many wires broken through fall of sansom broken branches on lines already in	
"	19/9/16		Airline run between Hq BREFFAYE farm and RFC hangar for S.S.O. HqRA. Arrangements made for maintenance motorcycle as per corps order	
"	20/9/16		Police Escort sent for APM SOUASTRE. Captain D.P. Tammany (Canadian) on leave was relieved by Lieut J.J. SMITH. RA Brigades visited. Instructions taking over from 49th RA. Lieut G.S. ROBERTS reporting commenced to relieve 49th RA.	

2449 Wt. W14957/M90 750,000 1/16 J.B.C.& A. Forms/C.2118/12.

Army Form C. 2118.

WAR DIARY
INTELLIGENCE SUMMARY
(Erase heading not required.)

46th Div. Sig. Coy. C.R.E.

Place	Date	Hour	Summary of Events and Information	Remarks and references to Appendices
HENU	21/4/16		Front line, support & reserve shelled between STAMANA & GAUDIEMPRE. Demolished BIENVILLERS area commencing work here. Artillery relief completed	JAL
"	22/4/16		Two line wire mats completed between STAMANA GAUDIEMPRE and handed over to 137 and 138 R.E. replace this [ground] wire between two points. Attachment agreed and lines between SOUASTRE and BIENVILLERS imported to [returned] to R.A.F.S.	JAL
"	23/4/16		Training [ ] cables between SOUASTRE and FONQUEVILLERS to bring as many systems of [ ] as with new agree for front night from R.A. [ ] lines broken down in many places. Chiefly this [ ] norms breaking	JAL

WAR DIARY
INTELLIGENCE SUMMARY

Army Form C. 2118.

Places	Date 1916	Hour	Summary of Events and Information	Remarks and references to Appendices
HENU	Dec 24		Captain L.R. THODAY has extension of leave till Jan 6, 1917. Authority War Office. O.C.R.A.S.R. 3rd Army visited 205 T.K. Q. Everything satisfactory. All units standing nothing well. Church Parade. 2 Lieut H. HOOPER leave for wireless course G.H.Q.	46 th Div 3rd Army Corp R.A
"	25		Church Parade. Inspection of equipment.	Sub
"	26		Normal	Sub
"	27		O.C. visited all groups and Brigade Communication section well but lines in trenches very bad. Clearing up proceeding gradually.	Sub

Army Form C. 2118.

WAR DIARY
INTELLIGENCE SUMMARY
(Erase heading not required.)

Instructions regarding War Diaries and Intelligence Summaries are contained in F. S. Regs., Part II. and the Staff Manual respectively. Title Pages will be prepared in manuscript.

46th Divl Sig Co R.E.

Place	Date 1916	Hour	Summary of Events and Information	Remarks and references to Appendices
HENU	Dec 28		O.C. examined buried scheme SOUASTRE to FONQUEVILLERS. Lines but eight of same three lines had then one being constructed (reserve one) tested and working satisfactorily	Enh
"	29		O.C. examined offices and communications of 137 Bde. J. Pha. telephones working more satisfactorily	Enh
"	30	13K	O.C. surveyed proposed route for buried cables 137 Bde H.Q. to Report Centre. Also examined communications of Centre Group R.F.A. Lines temporarily down due to storm	Enh
"	31		Church parades Captain D.P. FORMAN returns from leave	Enh

2449 Wt. W14957/M90 750,000 1/16 J.B.C. & A. Forms/C.2118/12.

Army Form C. 2118.

WAR DIARY
INTELLIGENCE SUMMARY
(Erase heading not required.)

Place	Date	Hour	Summary of Events and Information	Remarks and references to Appendices
HENU	9th		Major Laws visited 134 area & went over lines in GOMMECOURT trench with a view to having the trench cleaned. Lt Roberts visited 137 area. Artillery line in Right Sector 137 R&. improved. Went parts cut out & replaced with new cable.	
"	10th		Normal. Arrangements for tunnel scheme for artillery in connection with 137 R&. now ready. Test bores made, also stakes for route ready. No labour available at present.	
			Capt Inman returned from Wireless Course.	
"	11th		Major Laws & Capt Theday walked over line Henu to Fonada HQ Annual. Arrangements ready for laying line for special Coy R.E.	
"	12th		Normal. New sapper line completed to 135 Bty BIENVILLERS. Special line laid for "N" Coy R.E. in 137 R&. area. New Test board & leading in board installed at 137 R&. in lieu type. Line in BIENVILLERS constantly broken by shellfire.	

Army Form C. 2118.

WAR DIARY
or
INTELLIGENCE SUMMARY

(Erase heading not required.)

Instructions regarding War Diaries and Intelligence Summaries are contained in F.S. Regs., Part II. and the Staff Manual respectively. Title Pages will be prepared in manuscript.

Place	Date	Hour	Summary of Events and Information	Remarks and references to Appendices
HENU	13th		Major Lewis & Capt Thurley worked over festival of lines between STANLAND and POMMIER. and later visited 139 Bde H.qrs. Lt. Roberts went to 138 Bde artillery communications. 138 Scouter line broken by shell fire & repaired.	Enn
"	14th		Church Parade 10 am. Test panels fitted up at 138 Bde Office. Office also revised	Enn
"	15th		Snow	Enn
			Normal	Enn
"	16th		Normal	Enn

WAR DIARY
INTELLIGENCE SUMMARY

Army Form C. 2118.

Place	Date	Hour	Summary of Events and Information	Remarks and references to Appendices
HENU	17th		Normal.	
"	18th		Snow.	
			Capts Hurley & Capt Jordan walked via LOUASTRE - SAILLY trench to try and fish. NB from Jeans to FONCQUEVILLERS	
"	19th		Major Lewis visited all arty groups & Inf Bde HQn to interview OCs & Battalions, be training of Stretcher in aeroplane contact work. Capt Storey inspected St Amand route with a view to building two more posts on it. Stores for same demanded.	
"	20th		Lt Lewin returned from leave.	

WAR DIARY
or
INTELLIGENCE SUMMARY

Army Form C. 2118.

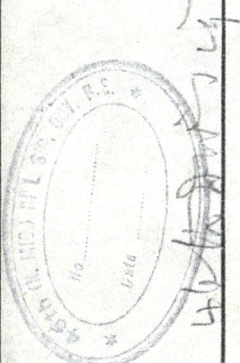

Place	Date	Hour	Summary of Events and Information	Remarks and references to Appendices
HENU	21st		Church Parade 10.15 am. New filed line completed from Support coy Right Batt. 138 Bde to GENDARMERIE trench. Also from 138 Bde to Group R.F.A. line laid from Div 9.P. to Centre Group. New test boards fitted at 137 Bde Hqrs.	
"	22nd		Major Lewis visited 137 area. Capt Murphy & Lt Lewis went over line forward of St Amand testing insulation return. Refunct	
"	23rd		Normal	
"	24th		Normal. OC attended lecture at HESDIN on the methods of communication in the French Army.	

Army Form C. 2118.

WAR DIARY
or
INTELLIGENCE SUMMARY
(Erase heading not required.)

Place	Date	Hour	Summary of Events and Information	Remarks and references to Appendices
HENU	25th		Normal.	
"	26th		Lt Roberts proceeded on leave.	
"	27th		Staying labelling ST AMAND – PONNIER Route. Broken pole on HENU – SOUASTRE Route replaced. Old pole apparently broken by frost.	
"	28th		Major Lewis visited BG Res Hqrs. Church Parade. On route my/ph Group Artillery Hrs. Reconnais. bonds in course of construction.	

Army Form C. 2118.

WAR DIARY
or
INTELLIGENCE SUMMARY
(Erase heading not required.)

Instructions regarding War Diaries and Intelligence Summaries are contained in F.S. Regs., Part II and the Staff Manual respectively. Title Pages will be prepared in manuscript.

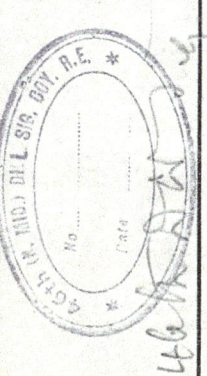

Place	Date	Hour	Summary of Events and Information	Remarks and references to Appendices
HENU	29th		O.C. attends lecture at SOUASTRE on Censorship Regulations. Brigade school of Signalling visited reopened.	
"	30th		O.C. visits FORT DICK and kenneles of 139 Inf. Bde. re relieving up wires in Rue Mar Fracture	
"	31st		O.C. attends Conference on Corps Communications at ADMS Office PAS. Captain L.R. THODAY proceeds to COMPAGNE on machine Gun course	

Army Form C. 2118.

WAR DIARY
or
INTELLIGENCE SUMMARY
(Erase heading not required.)

Vol 20
Signals 13

Place	Date	Hour	Summary of Events and Information	Remarks and references to Appendices
HENU	Feb 1 1919	1	O.C. examines communication of Centre sector. Normal	Apb
"	2		O.C. visits Divisional School. See officers officio from Major WARLINCOURT re Gas alarms S.O's my left Battalion hqrs 137 Bde NAKED ST now occupied	Apb
"	3		O.C. visits 139 Bde School. Interviews hire SHIPLEY re positions of HQ & communications. New front on left of left sector taken over. Communication arranged to accommodate all lectures to side-slip. Everything working well.	Sch
"	4		O.C. visits right Artillery Group re hours scheme and cable for new Gun positions. Normal	Sch

2449 Wt. W14957/M90 750,000 1/16 J.B.C. & A. Forms/C.2118/12.

Army Form C. 2118.

WAR DIARY
or
INTELLIGENCE SUMMARY
(Erase heading not required.)

Instructions regarding War Diaries and Intelligence Summaries are contained in F.S. Regs., Part II. and the Staff Manual respectively. Title Pages will be prepared in manuscript.

Place	Date	Hour	Summary of Events and Information	Remarks and references to Appendices
HENU	5th		O.C. visits 138 Bde area. O.C. wireless examines electric lamps at Bn. H.Q. Difficulties experienced in getting out to him. An additional substation as stand-by adopted	
"	6th		Capt Shodey detained from wireless course. Plan of proposed open lamps lines automatic to A.D.A.S. XVII Corps	
"	7th		O.C. visits 137 Bde area. Freight Group R.A. Capt Inman visited hqrs. Lt Roberts returned from leave O.O. 126 received	
"	8th		O.C. visited A.D. Signals 7th Corps re Communications in that area. 2nd Lt Arden Sgt. Signal Co. R.E. attached for 5 days instruction. O.C. visited 137, 138, 139 Bde areas	

2449 Wt. W14957/M90 750,000 1/16 J.B.C. & A. Forms/C.2118/12.

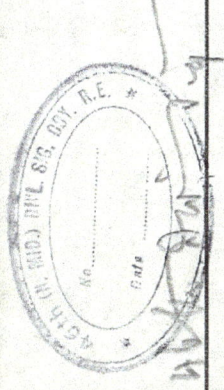

WAR DIARY / INTELLIGENCE SUMMARY

Army Form C. 2118.

Place	Date	Hour	Summary of Events and Information	Remarks and references to Appendices
HÉNU	Feb 9		Normal	Enc
"	10		Normal	Enc
"	11		O.C. and 7th Section officers attend lecture at SOUASTRE by Corps Commander re "the Attack". Working parties staying poles.	Enc
"	12		OC visits 139 Bde Area were forward trenches with A&XXs re-inward depending. All lines relied in in BERLES and NOBBS WALK. O.D. 129 received	Enc
"	13		All lines relied in at BERLES 2nd Lieut ARDEN rejoins 5th Div signal Co.	Enc

WAR DIARY
INTELLIGENCE SUMMARY

Army Form C. 2118.

Place	Date	Hour	Summary of Events and Information	Remarks and references to Appendices
HÉNU	Feb 14		Captain THODAY proceeded to ARRAS (7th Corps.) to take over supervision of tunnel scheme in new area. The 16th Divn occupied by Divn. Demolit line needed in at BERLES	Sh
"	15		Work of ruling up demolit lines continues in Brigade area by section officers	Sh
"	16		As 15th	Sh
"	17		Parties ruling up demolit lines in Divnl Area O.C. & Lt LEWIS visit BAVINCOURT, GOUY & FOSSEUX re communications in new area	Sh
"	18		Relieving 137 Bde Right Battn H.Qr. from KB 59 to KR 40 Laying 3 instrumts from KB 9 to KR 40. Disconnecting Bde line at KB 9 from KB 59 and running up to KR 40. This chiefly completed by 6 hrs. communication gone to all units, including Battn Hrs	Sh

WAR DIARY

INTELLIGENCE SUMMARY

Army Form C. 2118.

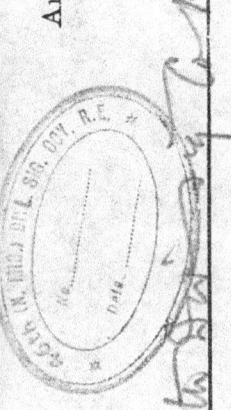

Place	Date	Hour	Summary of Events and Information	Remarks and references to Appendices
HÉNU	Feb 19		O.C. visited trenches 138 R.de area re communications. Parties patrolling, labelling & finishing off new line to K.K.4.9. (See entry of 2nd today)	Sch
GOUY	20	10 am	Joint HQrs moved to GOUY. 137 & 138 R.de sections were made commands of O.C. hip 58th Divn. Parties working in derelict lines in 137 R.de area	Sch
GOUY	21		O.C. visits trenches in new area with Captain THODY reconnaissance tramway scheme at R.E. HQrs. Poles route from K.K.2 to K.K.B.9 restaked. HQ area	Sch
"	22		Lieut HOOPER went to ARRAS to assist in supervision of Corps horse actions for new area. Reclim in derelict lines around BIENVILLERS. O.C. 137 R.de lectures to officers of 5th North Staffs re use of trench life attack.	Sch

Army Form C. 2118.

WAR DIARY
or
INTELLIGENCE SUMMARY
(Erase heading not required.)

Place	Date 1917	Hour	Summary of Events and Information	Remarks and references to Appendices
GOUY	Feb 23		Old man Wireless station installed in RAVINE K.C.6 to work to 137 Bde H.q.	
"	24		O.C. visits ARRAS and ACHICOURT with Capt THODAY and first LEWIS to arrange for cables in that area. O.P. 129 received	
"	25		O.C. visits work at ACHICOURT. Snipers lines in Katana. 137 Bde (Old lines) arrange special communications for lee and it.	See Appx 1.
"	26		New work in front lines of new area inspected by O.C.	
"	27		Normal	
"	28		O.C. inspects new work in ARRAS area. Capt THODAY & O.C. visit ARRAS 74th Corp. re cable scheme. Scheme approved by Corps	

Secret / App.1

Report on Communications
for Raid by 5th North Staffs
25/2/17

Advanced Battalion Hdqrs were opened at a Coy Station (KB57). Three routes were provided from there to the back Hdqs KB40. A line was laid from KB57 out into No Man's Land to control the barrage. This had a tee in and telephone in the Front Trench for the C.O. Raiding Party.

A direct line was obtained thro' an O.P. for the O.P. Exchange providing an alternative route to Batteries, in case the lines to the back Battalion Hdqs were broken.

Communications worked smoothly throughout, and the General instructed me to-day to congratulate my men and the Battalion Signallers on the promptness in which he was able to get thro' from Brigade Hdqs throughout the night.

CMaguire Lieut. R.E.
O.C. SIG. A.S.
137th INFANTRY BRIGADE.

26/2/17

WAR DIARY

Army Form C. 2118.

Instructions regarding War Diaries and Intelligence Summaries are contained in F.S. Regs., Part II. and the Staff Manual respectively. Title Pages will be prepared in manuscript.

INTELLIGENCE SUMMARY
(Erase heading not required.)

Place	Date	Hour	Summary of Events and Information	Remarks and references to Appendices
HENU	Jan 1/1/17		O.C. visited A.D.F.S. at PAS re cable for detached plank and military fronts. Lt. H.E.C. LEWIS resumed duty from Hospital. Working party digging new 6' cable trench to Left Battn 139 Bde. Line in trenches 137 & 136 Bde being relabelled & taped.	Sgd
"	2		O.C. Sig. 137 Bde visited Div. H.Q.; 5 O.R.s proceed on leave. Capt. D.P. FORMAN returned from leave. Working party continuing cable trench 139 Bde. Relabelling & retaping 137 Bde & 136 Bde trenches. Inducting airline. Cpl ? held Scare Reveno. Lafayette Captain L.R. THODAY ?	Sgd
"	3		O.C. visited trenches 136 Bde (Centre Sector). Arrangements made for direct communication between Intelligent O.P.s in GENDARMERIE Forget, CHISWICK Avenue and FONCQUEVILLERS material of them R.A. O.P. etc. Lieut. C.A. MAGUIRE proceeds on leave. Test poles laid in ST MARTIN'S LANE in new cable trench 139 Bde. BAYENCOURT - SAILLY - FONCQUEVILLERS buried route inspected for alternative route to SPRING.	Sgd
"	4		Captain D.P. FORMAN goes on week-end course at G.H.Q. Linesmen working on BAYENCOURT - FONCQUEVILLERS buried trench. Lines renewed in 139 Sector.	Sgd

Army Form C. 2118.

WAR DIARY
INTELLIGENCE SUMMARY
(Erase heading not required.)

Instructions regarding War Diaries and Intelligence Summaries are contained in F.S. Regs., Part II. and the Staff Manual respectively. Title Pages will be prepared in manuscript.

Place	Date	Hour	Summary of Events and Information	Remarks and references to Appendices
HENU	5th		Revised scheme to Left Section 139 Bde completed. 3 parties taken out from SAVOY Inf Bn to VALLEY trench line from Rotary Avenue to K.2.2 - handed over to 138 Bde for O.P. work. Parties refixing up lines in BIENVILLERS area. O.C. M. ROBERTS + 2/Dixie R.F.A. attended lecture on Signal Service at HESDIN	Sch
"	6th		O.C. visited 138 Inf. Bde H.Q. also Centre and Right Groups + Batty. H.Q. (D230) of Centre Group Lieut H.E.C. LEWIS goes on leave	Sch
"	7th		Church Parade Work on new lines/scheme continued - lines tested out. Left Section. Capt Stocks returned from leave	Sch
"	8th		Genl. Allenby visited Bn. Eye+epted metal lifted Captain L.R. THORN receives medal dittoes Compl: within	Sch

2449 Wt. W14957/M90 750,000 1/16 J.B.C. & A. Forms/C.2118/12.

Army Form C. 2118.

WAR DIARY
INTELLIGENCE SUMMARY
(Erase heading not required.)

Instructions regarding War Diaries and Intelligence Summaries are contained in F.S. Regs, Part II. and the Staff Manual respectively. Title Pages will be prepared in manuscript.

4th to 7th April Signal Co R.E.   Vol 2 1

Place	Date 1917	Hour	Summary of Events and Information	Remarks and references to Appendices
HÉNU	April 1	8 am	Dvnl. Hdqrs removes from GOUY. Lieut HOOPER rejoins Coy at HÉNU. O.O. 131 received. O.C. visits new area at GOMMECOURT	Sch
"	2		O.C. visits Rt Rly Ny. Arrangements made to take over lines from 138 Bde. for use of 139 Bde. Captain FORMAN visits Dvnl Hd.q. re communications	Sch
"	3		O.C. visits left Bde Area. Captain THORAY rejoins Company.	Sch
"	4		O.C. visits 138. Bde O.O. 132 received " 133 "	Sch

2449 Wt. W14957/M90 750,000 1/16 J.B.C. & A. Forms/C.2118/12.

Army Form C. 2118.

WAR DIARY
INTELLIGENCE SUMMARY
(Erase heading not required.)

46th Divnl Signal Co R.E.

Instructions regarding War Diaries and Intelligence Summaries are contained in F. S. Regs., Part II. and the Staff Manual respectively. Title Pages will be prepared in manuscript.

Place	Date 1917	Hour	Summary of Events and Information	Remarks and references to Appendices
HENU	Mar 5		O.O. 134 received	Ends
			O.O. 13n cancelled	
"	6		O.O. 135 received	Ends
			ADT.S. 8th Corps visited Hq	
"	7	noon	Division transferred to 5th Corps. D.D. Signals 5th Army visited Hq.	
			O.O. 136 received	
			" 137 "	
			" 138 "	Ends
"	9		O.C. visited 139 Bde advanced re operations	
			O.O. 139 received	Ends
"	10		Captain THODAY lecturing to 136 Bde Battn Signal Officers re Return on general communications and the use of the power buzzer	
			O.O. 140 received	Ends

2449 Wt. W14957/M90 750,000 1/16 J.B.C. & A. Forms/C.2118/12.

Army Form C. 2118.

WAR DIARY
INTELLIGENCE SUMMARY
(Erase heading not required.)

46th Divnl Signal Coy R.E.

Place	Date 1917	Hour	Summary of Events and Information	Remarks and references to Appendices
HENU	Feb 11		Wiring up Advanced Divisional HQrs at Château de la HAYE. Ops 141 1942 received	Ent
"	12	7.30 am	O.C. and Capt THODAY visited new Advanced HQrs — arrangements for communications	
		00 143720	2nd Lieut F.H. STEGGLE joined Company from Div Order 144 received	Ent
"	13	6 am	00 145 received.	
		noon	Offrs to Div. Order 145 received	
		1/45	Amendment to Div Order 145 (G193) received	
		3 pm	Div Order 146 received	
		4/30	Amendment to Div Order 146 received	
		9/45	2nd Amendment to Div Order 146 received Wiring of Advd. Div. HQ. continues	Ent
"	14		Wiring of Advd Div. HQ. completed Normal routine	Ent

Army Form C. 2118.

WAR DIARY
INTELLIGENCE SUMMARY
(Erase heading not required.)

Instructions regarding War Diaries and Intelligence Summaries are contained in F. S. Regs., Part II. and the Staff Manual respectively. Title Pages will be prepared in manuscript.

46th Divnl Signals Co. R.E.

Place	Date 1917	Hour	Summary of Events and Information	Remarks and references to Appendices
HENU	15	1 pm	Advanced No 4 tested & working good. Arrangements made with 5th Squadron R.F.C. for contact aeroplane. Div Order 147 received	Sd.
"	16	1 pm	Warning order NO 2 received	Sd.
		3/30"	" " 2 cancelled	
		5 pm	Div Order 148 received	
"	17	1 pm	Addition and amendment to Div. Order 148 received	
		5/15	Order re Contact aeroplane received	
		5/30	Div. Order 149 received	
		8/10	G 361 amendment to Div Order 149 read. Preparation for removal to advanced Hqrs received	Sd.

Army Form C. 2118.

WAR DIARY
INTELLIGENCE SUMMARY
(Erase heading not required.)

46th Div Signal Co R.E.

Place	Date 1917	Hour	Summary of Events and Information	Remarks and references to Appendices
CHATEAU DE LA HAYE	May 18	10 am	Divisional Advanced HQrs opened. 137 Inf Bde established at FONQUEVILLERS	
		8 pm	Amendment to Div Order No 9 received Div Order 150 received	Sch
"	19		138 Inf Bde advanced to ESSARTS & visited Adv. Rd HQ. Visual working to Brittans.	Sch
"	20		Visual working from Adv HQ to FONQUEVILLERS & from Div. Advd. HQ.	Sch
COUIN	21	10 am	Div HQ removed at 10 am	Sch
		8 pm	Div order 151 received. Great complaints on all telegraph & telephone lines	Sch

Army Form C. 2118.

WAR DIARY
INTELLIGENCE SUMMARY
(Erase heading not required.)

4th Army Sig. G.R.S.

Place	Date 1917	Hour	Summary of Events and Information	Remarks and references to Appendices
COUIN	Feb 22		Communication established to all Rlys 2nd Army.	EMh
"	23	9am	Sin Order 152 received. Preparation made for removal to VILLERS BOCAGE	EMh
"	24		Company marched with Divisional HQrs Column to VILLERS BOCAGE. Telephone communication established with 5th Army HQrs	EMh
"	25		Preparation for move and entraining H.T. Cable section (one) Company from II Corps	EMh
DURY	26		Company marched with Divisional HQrs Column to DURY. Communication established with 4th Army. All lines of H.T. Cable hitherto found to be suffering from damp.	EMh

Army Form C. 2118.

WAR DIARY
INTELLIGENCE SUMMARY.
(Erase heading not required.)

Instructions regarding War Diaries and Intelligence Summaries are contained in F. S. Regs. Part II. and the Staff Manual respectively. Title pages will be prepared in manuscript.

Place	Date	Hour	Summary of Events and Information	Remarks and references to Appendices
BURY	March 27		All names of A.T. Coll'n taken inventoried to 5 men left behind with them. Remaining personnel till tomorrow	Hd/K3 and signal CdS Sd
	28		O.C. went on to NORRENT FONTES to arrange communication for rest area. Company (less motor vehicles) entrained at SALEUX for LILLERS. (mayor of A.T. Coll'n overseen taken to station by other transport)	Sd
NORRENT FONTES	29	6pm	O.C. opened communication with II Corps 186 I Bde. Company marched from LILLERS arrived NORRENT FONTES	Sd

A 5834 Wt. W4973/M687 750,000 8/16 D. D. & L. Ltd. Forms/C.2118/13.

Army Form C. 2118.

WAR DIARY
INTELLIGENCE SUMMARY.
(Erase heading not required.)

46th Divisional Signal Co. R.E.

Place	Date	Hour	Summary of Events and Information	Remarks and references to Appendices
WORRENT FONTES.	1917 Mch 30		Wireless Intersection (Inner) Company. OC visited ADMS re communications	Int.
"	31		OC visited DADS 1st Army re communications from time. Arrangements made for covering scheme	Int.

Army Form C. 2118.

WAR DIARY
or
INTELLIGENCE SUMMARY.
(Erase heading not required.)

Instructions regarding War Diaries and Intelligence Summaries are contained in F.S. Regs., Part II. and the Staff Manual respectively. Title pages will be prepared in manuscript.

41 K? Divisional Signal Coy RE

Place	Date 1917	Hour	Summary of Events and Information	Remarks and references to Appendices
NORRENT FONTES	April 1917			Vol 22
	Mar 1		Smoke helmet respirators drill	S/W
"	2		Training. Checking equipment &c	S/W
"	3		Royal Section personnel brought to strength. Weather too bad to follow training programme. Decided to repeat tomorrow	S/W
"	4		Training. Infantry drill. Visual signalling	S/W
"	5			S/W
"	6		Visual signalling scheme with daylight lamps	S/W
"	7		Brigade Signal Sections returned to their headquarters. Brigade training continued at Brigade Schools	S/W

Army Form C. 2118.

WAR DIARY
or
INTELLIGENCE SUMMARY.
(Erase heading not required.)

A.D.R. Divisional Signal C.R.S

Place	Date 1917	Hour	Summary of Events and Information	Remarks and references to Appendices
NORRENT FONTES	Mch 8		OC reconnaitare ground for Divisional Route march tomorrow. Reynolds schools visited	RR
	9		Divisional route march Brigade schemes march with their Brigade 11 a.m.	RR
	10		Tactical scheme at ESTRÉE BLANCHE Air line parties working on 138 & 139 lines	RR
	11		Air line parties working on 138 & 139 lines. Cable reels up. Maj. E.A. Lewin went on leave. D.O.A. 156 received	RR
	12		all early in area reclothing. D.O. 157 received. Came both 137 Bde at BETHUNE & 63 Bde at LILLERS two 66 Bde	RR
BUSNES	13		Moved to BUSNES. Went to 138, at HQ M1Q115 4 GR115 & CRA failed up. 139 Bde by BR only. DO's 158 & 159 received yesterday	RR

Army Form C. 2118.

WAR DIARY
or
INTELLIGENCE SUMMARY.
(Erase heading not required.)

Instructions regarding War Diaries and Intelligence Summaries are contained in F. S. Regs., Part II. and the Staff Manual respectively. Title pages will be prepared in manuscript.

Place	Date	Hour	Summary of Events and Information	Remarks and references to Appendices
BOSNES	14.		139 Bde moved to NUEUX-LES-MINES. Communication map. 1st Corps	SP2
	15		Advance party on D.A.C. line. O.O. 160 received.	SP2
	16.		138 Bde Section here at VENDIN-LES-BETHUNE. Arrangements made for communications required by O.O. 161. With 1 Army. O.O. 161 received.	SP2
LABOUV-RIERE.	17.		Moved to LABOUVRIERE. Division ended with 1st Corps. O.C. visited 1st Corps Signals. O.O. 162 received.	SP2
	18.		O.C. Lewis visited 24th Division at SAINS-EN-GOHELLE. Also. O.O. 163 received. O.C. Lewis in Jay.	SP2
	19.		O.C. went round 2nd Division area took over signal Bde Section took over from Hd Qrs of 24th Division B2. 24th Division.	
SAINS-EN-GOHELLE	20	10am	Relieved 24th Division. Divers hut to port army hereby manner in which they sig they by the authorities from and positions of Bdes 138 Bde (left) in M.H.Roe of hived water.	

WAR DIARY
or
INTELLIGENCE SUMMARY.

Army Form C. 2118.

Place	Date	Hour	Summary of Events and Information	Remarks and references to Appendices
SAINS-EN-GOHELLE	20		137 Bde (Centre) in LIEVIN. 139 Bde (Right) in ANGRES	SPB
	21.		Heavy treads in forward area.	SPB
	22.		Signal Office at Divisional HQ transferred to cellar of Chateau owing to slight shelling of village, as connection from that point (wireless) to instrument room was a single 25/3 pair cable. Run (?) to Right Centre in CAROONNE cut by 8" shells. Returns during night communication by dues in (?)	SPB
	23.		00.16 received 138 Bde move their HQ (forward line (eng.h?)) Fresh power buzzers used repeatedly (wireless) by centre Bde. Visual by right Bde. Trails into house by some shelling.	SPB
	24.		Have truck with forward Winny. now been laid in German trenches to Right Bde at ANGRES.	SPB
Petit Bussie(?)	25.		Brigades left by 138 Bde in MAROC. Close down 137 Bde with dawn to BULLY GRENAY & Petit Seine	

Army Form C. 2118.

WAR DIARY
or
INTELLIGENCE SUMMARY.
(Erase heading not required.)

Instructions regarding War Diaries and Intelligence Summaries are contained in F. S. Regs., Part II. and the Staff Manual respectively. Title pages will be prepared in manuscript.

Place	Date	Hour	Summary of Events and Information	Remarks and references to Appendices
BAINS EN GOHELLE	25		by 2 Brigades only	SP2
	26		Several wires broken	SP2
	27		New bury (extension of old bury Communicating with M49 b.3) Steel 36.C.S.W.) to M272 commenced. Working party 50 men. Sappers provided by I Corps. OO 169 Received also OO/128 SP2	SP2
	28		Main MAROC buried cut. Line laid from CAFONNE to 138 Bde.	SP2
	29		MAROC Bury again cut. Gas shells in fact the Austria buried. New system has any repairs to lines in MAROC rendered difficult by gas hanging about.	SP2
	30		2/Lt HOOPER wounded in CAFONNE. 137 Bde relieved 139 Bde in ANGRES sector. OO 171 received. Continued trunk work left Bde lines in MAROC.	SP2

… Army Form C. 2118.

WAR DIARY
INTELLIGENCE SUMMARY.
(Erase heading not required.)

Instructions regarding War Diaries and Intelligence Summaries are contained in F.S. Regs., Part II. and the Staff Manual respectively. Title pages will be prepared in manuscript.

Place	Date	Hour	Summary of Events and Information	Remarks and references to Appendices
Samson Potelle	1st August		2/Lt Hooper evacuated wounded. Pair of lines laid from Armand Dirt Exchange to 138 Inf Bde as alternative route, owing to Corps Buries System being shelled and broken.	Sgd
"	2nd		Lines frequently broken by heavy shelling. Communication maintained by Visual and Wireless. Major Lewis returns from leave.	Sgd
"	3rd		2/Lt Mumby and three wireless officers attached for instruction both wounded. Capt. A.A. Saunders joins company from England. O.O. 192 received. Burnet scheme to connect 2 Bde HQrs with forward positions in progress.	Sgd
"	4th			Sgd
"	5th		North Telephone cable broken by shell fire in b' bury? SOUTH of CALONNE. Linesmen sent out and trouble mended in 3 hours. Artillery communications held good.	Sgd
"	6		139 Inf Bde relieves 138 Inf Bde in Northern Sector. All lines found in good order.	Sgd

Army Form C. 2118.

WAR DIARY
or
INTELLIGENCE SUMMARY.
(Erase heading not required.)

46th Div Signal Co R.E.

Place	Date	Hour	Summary of Events and Information	Remarks and references to Appendices
SAINS EN GOHELLE	May 7.		O.C. visits Brigade tracks re-visual signalling and maintenance of lines. Work of burying cables progressing.	Enh
	8		O.C. visits Right Artillery Group re communications. Staff agree to removal of Signal office from Cellar at Div H.Q. to new hut in grounds. Material for this allotted to.	Enh
	9.		Normal	Enh
	10.		O.O. 143 received. Cable trench north of CALONNE upon instructed to shells. Lines repaired. Alterations made per O.O. 143 received.	Enh
	11		O.C. visits Brigade Signalling School. Work of burying cables progressing.	Enh

Army Form C. 2118.

WAR DIARY
or
INTELLIGENCE SUMMARY.
(Erase heading not required.)

Place	Date	Hour	Summary of Events and Information	Remarks and references to Appendices
SAINS EN GOHELLE	12		138th Inf Bde relieves 139 Inf Bde in LIEVIN sector. All lines found over in good order	SH7
	13		R.S. commence touching hut at Div H.Q. for new Signal Office. Cable for new office arrived	SH7
	14		Burying cable from Cellar Div H.Q. to new Signal Office. O.C. visits Brigade Reports	SH7
	15		Burying cables in all sectors. O.O. 176 received O.O. 175 received	SH7
	16		Normal	SH7
	17		OC visits left sector front re abandoned routes cables	SH7

Army Form C. 2118.

WAR DIARY
INTELLIGENCE SUMMARY.
(Erase heading not required.)

Instructions regarding War Diaries and Intelligence Summaries are contained in F.S. Regs., Part II. and the Staff Manual respectively. Title pages will be prepared in manuscript.

H.Q. 7th Div Signal Coy R.E.

Place	Date 1917	Hour	Summary of Events and Information	Remarks and references to Appendices
SAINS EN GOHELLE	May 18		139 Inf Bde relieve 139 Inf Bde in the ST PIERRE sector. All lines handed over in good order. Captain SAUNDERS joins 139 Inf Bde. Signal section to relieve Lt MAGUIRE to 8H-Q for wireless course.	Enc.
	19		Lt MAGUIRE leaves for G.H.Q. Communications Normal. Night working for Divisional Buzzer Exchange scheme connections.	Enc.
	20			
	21		Captain D.P. FORMAN proceeds home to take up appointment of Commanding Signalling Officer CURRAGH.	Enc.
	22		Line laid from ARNOLD O.P. to LEFT GROUP. D.O. 176 received.	Enc.
	23		Fourteen 6 foot buzz lines to LIEVIN also complete. Fourteen 6 foot buzz to Right Battn & Left Bons now through and ready for work.	Enc.

Army Form C. 2118.

WAR DIARY
INTELLIGENCE SUMMARY.
(Erase heading not required.)

Instructions regarding War Diaries and Intelligence Summaries are contained in F. S. Regs., Part II. and the Staff Manual respectively. Title pages will be prepared in manuscript.

Place	Date	Hour	Summary of Events and Information	Remarks and references to Appendices
Souce en Gohelle	24		NASH ALLEY attacked & captured by 137 Bde. Communication through to 2nd Bde. God speaking through to NASH ALLEY	Sd
	25		Normal. Working party in connection with buried routes cancelled by G.S.	Sd
	26		O/C visits proposed new site for advanced divisional Report Centre airline route to BULLY GRENAY broken by bomb dropped from hostile aircraft at 10:30 pm. Communication restored without delay.	Sd
	27		Normal	Sd
	28		Normal	Sd
	29		Rain late from fight from No 5 (139) two Clarry Truncks to Div O.P. in 4th Canadian area	Sd
	30		Normal	Sd

Army Form C. 2118.

WAR DIARY
INTELLIGENCE SUMMARY.
(Erase heading not required.)

Place	Date	Hour	Summary of Events and Information	Remarks and references to Appendices
Simson Steele	31		Lieut C.A. Maguire returns from Wireless Course at G.H.Q.	

Army Form C. 2118.

Vol 24

46th Divisional Signal C.R.E

WAR DIARY
or
INTELLIGENCE SUMMARY.
(Erase heading not required.)

Instructions regarding War Diaries and Intelligence Summaries are contained in F.S. Regs., Part II. and the Staff Manual respectively. Title pages will be prepared in manuscript.

Place	Date	Hour	Summary of Events and Information	Remarks and references to Appendices
SAINS EN GOHELLE	June 1917 1		Map 36 c S.W.1. Normal	
	2		Normal	
	3		Capt A.R. Johnston joins from 5th Army Signals and takes up duties as second in command to Signal Coy. 4th Bn Gordon Hghlrs. Lines laid for communication between Divisional Hd and advanced Inf Bde (138)	
	4		Normal	
	5		Signals 138 Bde. established in BOIS DE RIAUMONT. Lines through	
	6		Normal	
	7		Capt A.A. SAUNDERS. R.E. (attached) Leaves Coy. to take over area under CANADIAN Coy.	
	8		All lines broken during operations between 10 p.m. & midnight. Wireless not found to be good and used.	
	9		Normal	
	10		Normal	

Army Form C. 2118.

WAR DIARY
or
INTELLIGENCE SUMMARY.
(Erase heading not required.)

Instructions regarding War Diaries and Intelligence Summaries are contained in F. S. Regs., Part II. and the Staff Manual respectively. Title pages will be prepared in manuscript.

Place	Date	Hour	Summary of Events and Information	Remarks and references to Appendices
SAINS EN GOHELLE	11th June 1917		Maj. 36.C. Smith. 138 Coy. Pats. relieved 139. Coy. Bets. in Right Sector (Hqrs. M.27 c 8.0) Lines normal	Snt
	12		Raids carried out by 137 and 138 Coy. 137 Coy. Sect. relieved old mine shafts and tunnels from LOOS graves to CAMERON crater to secure cables to bar hqrs.	Enh
	13		Normal	Enh
	14		do	Enh
	15		139 Coy. Sect. relieved 137 Sect. on Left Sector (ST. PIERRE)	Enh
	16		Normal	Enh
	17		do	Enh
	18		do	Enh
	19		do	Enh
	20		Preparations for attack to take place 28th June below. Digging cable trench Barrow from Corps Wired + Cable Head (M.29 b.77) to centre brigade Hqrs. (M.23 b.1.7) and Left Sect. Rt. Right Bde. (M.30 c.35) - Digging party 3rd Australian Tunnelly. Coy R.E.	Enh
	21		Progress made with above work.	Enh
	22		Normal - no digging done in his cable trench as party not available.	Enh
	23		do	Enh

Army Form C. 2118.

WAR DIARY
or
INTELLIGENCE SUMMARY.
(Erase heading not required.)

Army Form C. 2118.

Places	Date	Hour	Summary of Events and Information	Remarks and references to Appendices
SAINS EN GOHELLE	1916 25th June		Digging fours - 3rd Bde. Cavalry from dug trench 15'6" depth from top of BOIS du RIAUMONT at M.23.c.75.65 (Contn Bde. Hqrs) LIEVIN	
	25		Report on Cable Trench progressed - 180 men 8th Leinsters Totalin on working party	
	26		Digging carried on by 1/30 Corps Gelato. Heavy shelled at BUR de RIAUMONT. Little work done. 5 Cables laid in Cable Trench	
	27		1/30 Corps Split Completed trench N.6 in deep from Cable Head Bois de RIAUMONT to Cable Box. Cable Trench on south side of BOIS very shallow. Lines Loop became crossing trench to get Cable over sunken road. Bururd route through LIEVIN completed and from alternate Junct through preparation complete for attack. Cable buried to Bde. from Battn. (Inclay) Battns.	
	28		Preparation complete for attack. Cable buried to Bde. from Battn. (Inclay by) Battns. Turn and armoured cables to Battalion Hqrs in M.23.d. (Centre by) and kiosks in M.30.a. (right tale). Power buzzers at Battalions Hqrs & Bde. Hqrs. with one in each Bde. to go on with attack. Amplifiers at Bde. Hqrs. Trial from BOIS de RIAUMONT to MAISON CABA & ANGRES and from office of 12 MONMOUTHS (J. hater) Audile Bde. Hqrs to ANGRES Station. Verned in charge of Signals	
	29		Communication during attack kept up. Cables laid good.	
	30		Barette Continuing. Communication as above good.	

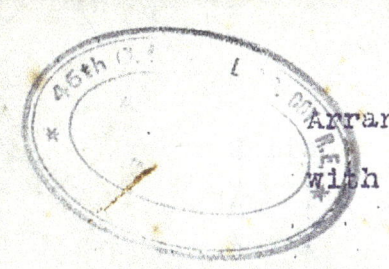

Arrangements for Signal Communications in connection with Operations under 46th Division Orders 191 and 206.

****

Ref: Map Sheet LENS 36 c S.W.1. 1:10,000.

Cables.   Buried lines exist forward to Brigade Headquarters at:-

        M 23 d 50.67   for   137th Inf.Bde.
        M 29 a 7.1   for   138th Inf.Bde.

Also through BOIS DE RIAUMONT between 138th Inf.Bde.Headquarters, O.Ps., in wood and left Battalion 138th Inf.Bde.
    All other cables are secured in trenches and alternative routes are available.

Visual.   Visual Stations will be established near the 137th and 138th Brigade Headquarters. Readers and runners will be stationed at these points. The messages will be transmitted to Divisional Visual Station at M 7 d 3.5 whence they will be transmitted by wire to Divisional Headquarters, and to the respective Brigade Headquarters. In case this visual line should be obscured by shelling of the intermediate area, the messages from 138th Brigade front will be sent by wire to another visual station established at M 29 c 7.6 and transmitted thence to Divisional Visual Station via M 27 c 4.7, where another Station is established.
    In the case of 137th Brigade, the Divisional Visual Station cannot be seen and transmission through M 27 c 4.7 will be the normal route.
    Forward visual posts will be watched for at HILL 65.
    Battalion Signallers will prefix each message with the letter designating their position in the attack as follows:-

138th Brigade.-

Left Company	Left Battalion		D
Centre	:	:	E
Right	:	:	F
Left	Centre	:	G
Centre	:	:	H
Right	:	:	I
Left	Right	:	K
Centre	:	:	L
Right	:	:	M

137th Brigade.-

Left Company	A
Centre	B
Right	C

These letters will be sent four times before commencing the message and (if acknowledgment is not possible) each message will be signalled twice.
    The calls for visual stations which have been established as below are as follows:-

| 137 Brigade. | Visual. | M 23 d 50.65. | Call L |
| 138 | : | M 29 b 80.70. | : V |

P.T.

```
Right Batt: 138th Bde.        M 30 c 75.95.    Call R
Left   :     :     :          M 30 a 10.45.      :  L
Right  :   137th   :          M 23 d 50.67.      :  M
Left   :     :     :          M 23 d 25.72.      :  W
```

Power Buzzers.   Power Buzzers and Amplifiers will be installed as follows :-

138th Brigade.- At Brigade H.Q and at Right Batt: H.Q.
137th Brigade.- At Brigade H.Q and at Left Batt: H.Q.

Power Buzzers will be taken forward by battalion signallers, who will be instructed as to the direction of the earth connections. They will wait at Battalion or Company H.Q until told to move and then, if possible, will go with the officer detailed to control runners and messages.

Wireless.   There will be two wireless sets. One at each Brigade H.Q. They each work to CALONNE, whence messages are transmitted by wire.

Pigeons.   Pigeons will be supplied from Corps Loft and will be released only in case of necessity or at time of relief (after 48 hours). If the birds have to be flown for relief, fresh birds will be supplied from Corps Loft.

Runners.   At each battalion headquarters there will be 8 runners. At each Brigade H.Q 20 and at Brigade Visual Stations 4 each.
There will also be Cyclists at the QUARRIES, M 29 c 4.7 and at Left Brigade H.Q. These will be used in case of all other communications breaking down.

Aeroplanes.   Communication with Contact Aeroplane will be by daylight signalling lamp and signalling panels. It is not possible to receive from aeroplane. Messages will be dropped from contact plane at M 29 a 5.5 for Brigades and R.2 c 8.8 for Division. Orderlies will be provided at the Brigade dropping ground by 137 and 138 Brigades.

Artillery.   Arrangements for artillery communications are being issued separately to all concerned.

E.A. Lewis
Major,
Commanding 46th Division
Signal Company.

26/6/1917.

Issued to 46th Division.
137 Bde Signals.
138 :   :
139 :   :
Sigs, 1st Monmouths.
A.D.A.S.
(Wireless and Power Buzzer only) O.C, Wireless.
O.C, Pigeons, I.Corps, (Pigeons only).
O.C, No. 2 Squadron, R.F.C, (Aeroplanes only).
O.C, Sigs, Div:
War Diary.

Arrangements for Signal Communications in connection with operations under 46th Division Order 182.

Cables. Buried lines exist forward to Left Brigade Report Centre and a point at M.27.b.1.6. Also through BOIS DE RIAUMONT between Advanced Right Brigade Headquarters and O.P's in wood. All other cables are secured in trenches, and alternative routes are available.

Visual. A visual station will be established near the Advanced Brigade Headquarters at M.29.a.65.20. Readers and runners will be stationed at this point. The readers will look out for signals from the attacking battalions. The messages will be transmitted to Divisional Visual Station at M.7.d.3.5 whence they will be transmitted by wire to Divisional Headquarters. In case this visual line should be obscured by shelling of the intermediate area the messages will be sent by wire to another visual station established at M.29.c.7.6 and transmitted thence to Divisional Visual Station via M.27.c.4.7 where another station is established.

Forward visual posts will be watched for at approximately :- M.24.d.5.2 and M.30.d.6.9.

Battalion signallers will prefix each message with the letter designating their position in the attack as follows :-

```
Left Company, Left Battalion    - A.
Centre Company,  "      "       - B.
Right Company,   "      "       - C.
Left Company, Right Battalion   - D.
Right Company,   "      "       - E.
Support Company                 - S.
```

These letters will be sent four times before commencing the message and (if acknowledgement is not possible) each message will be signalled twice.

The calls for visual stations which have been established as below are as follows :-

```
Brigade Headquarters.         M.29.a.65.20    Call Z.
     "    Visual.             M.29.b.80.70     "   V.
Left Battalion Headquarters.  M.23.d.50.65     "   L.
Right    "         "          M.29.d.20.35     "   R.
Reserve  "         "          M.28.b.30.15     "   Y.
Moppers Up.                   M.28.d.75.32     "   M.U.
```

L can get Z through Y. A, B and C can get L and V direct. R can get Z direct. S, D and E can get V direct. Y can get Z direct.

Wireless. There will be two wireless sets. One at Brigade Headquarters, 138th Brigade and one at Right Battalion Headquarters (M.11.b.7.5) of Left Brigade. The calls of these stations are ZD and ZC respectively. They each work to CALONNE M.14.d.8.0 whence messages are transmitted by wire. The working of these stations will be controlled by ZD.

<u>Power Buzzers.</u>

2.

Power Buzzers. Power Buzzers and Amplifiers will be installed as follows :-

<u>138th Brigade</u>. At Brigade Headquarters and at Left Battalion Headquarters.

Power Buzzers will be taken forward by Battalion Signallers, who will be instructed as to the direction of the earth connections. They will wait at Battalion or Company Headquarters until told to move and then, if possible, will go with the officer detailed to control runners and messages.

<u>137th Brigade</u>. The Amplifier is at M.6.a.7.1 and the Power Buzzers at M.6.b.9.4 and M.11.b.8.5. These Power Buzzers will be taken forward if necessary.

Pigeons. Pigeons will be supplied from the Corps Loft and will be released only in case of necessity or at time of relief (after 24 hours). If the birds have to be flown for relief, fresh birds will be supplied from Corps Loft.

Runners. At each Battalion Headquarters there will be 8 runners.
At each Brigade Headquarters 20 and at Right Brigade Visual Station 4. They will wear a red band on the left fore-arm.
There will also be cyclists at the QUARRIES M.29.c.4.7 and at Town Major's Billet, LIEVIN, who will take messages to HOP Ex (M.27.b.1.7). These will be used in case all communications break down.

All runners must carry their messages in the left breast pocket and it is the duty of every officer, N.C.O. or man to search a dead or wounded runner for his message and to get it delivered immediately.

Aeroplanes. Communication with Contact Aeroplane will be by daylight signalling lamp. It is not possible to receive from aeroplane. Messages will be dropped from contact plane at M.29.a.5.5 for Brigade and R.2.c.8.8 for Division.

The most advanced infantry will indicate their positions by lighting flares. These will be called for by means of a Klaxon Horn from the aeroplane.

6th June, 1917.

Major,
General Staff, 46th Division.

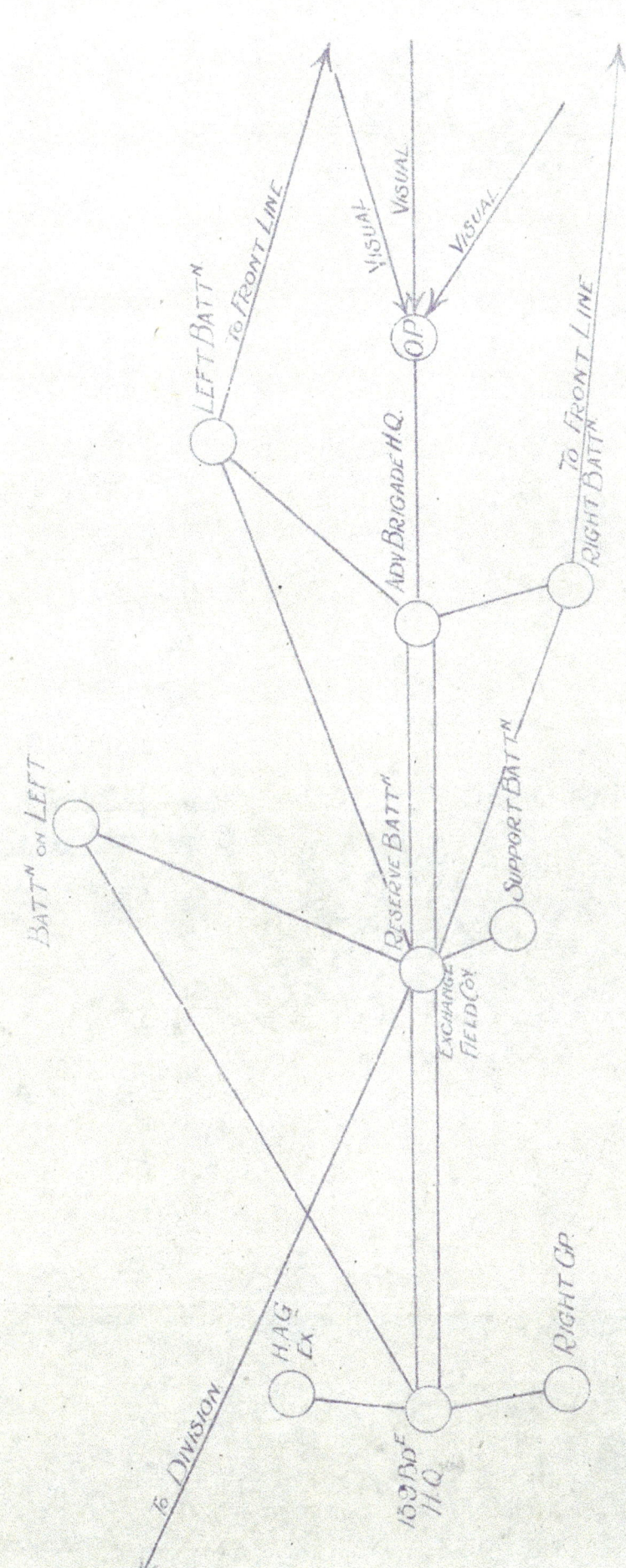

"First Corps Wireless Stations
Directing Stn - ZAA
Sub-Directing Stn - ZH

SECRET

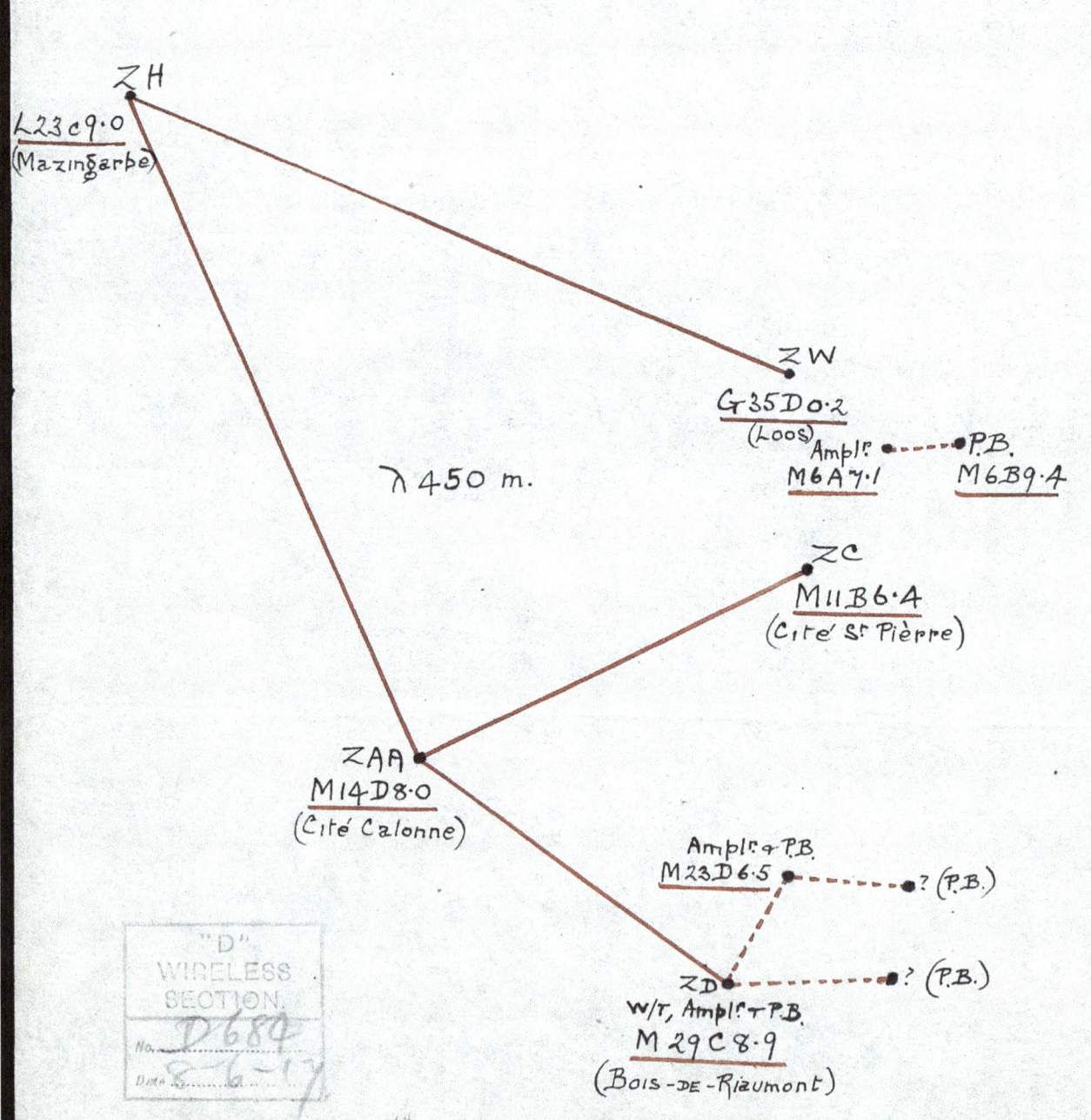

Army Form C. 2118.

WAR DIARY
or
INTELLIGENCE SUMMARY.
(Erase heading not required.)

Instructions regarding War Diaries and Intelligence Summaries are contained in F. S. Regs., Part II. and the Staff Manual respectively. Title pages will be prepared in manuscript.

Vol 25

Place	Date	Hour	Summary of Events and Information	Remarks and references to Appendices
SAINS EN GOHELLE	1 July 1917		Officer of 2nd Canadian Divisional Sig. Co. arrived to arrange "Take Over". Officers at "A.D.H." BULLY GRENAY vacated by 71st Bde. who were attached from 6th Div. & 46th Div. for operations, and relieved by Div. Personnel.	July
	2 July		Arrangements made for circuits in between Div. Hqrs. and Bdes. Change over of circuits made at this hour, and new stations.	July
	3rd		Bde Section officer of 2nd Can. Div. arrived to take over. Section officer took over from No 2 Section at LIEVIN, also lines and 137th & 138th Bde. 6th Can. Bde. took over from No 3 Sect near CITÉ ST PIERRE	5th Can Bde. July
Sheet 36 b. CHATEAU O.10.b.	4th		Div. Hqrs. opened at Chateau (O 10 b - Sheet 36 b) in new area — 137 Bde. at BAILLEUL - 138th Bde. at BAILLEUL AUX CORNAILLES — 139th Bde at ALLOUAGNE Lines arranged with adv First Army from Adv H. Brigade FREVILLERS.	July
	5th		Cleaning up Alques — testing apparatus, transport etc.	July
	6th		do	July
	7th		C.O. Inspection. Drill & Lectures	July
	8th		Church & Bathing parade	July

Army Form C. 2118.

WAR DIARY
or
INTELLIGENCE SUMMARY.
(Erase heading not required.)

Instructions regarding War Diaries and Intelligence Summaries are contained in F. S. Regs., Part II. and the Staff Manual respectively. Title pages will be prepared in manuscript.

Place	Date	Hour	Summary of Events and Information	Remarks and references to Appendices
BOISMONT CHATEAU Map Ref. O.10.6.	9 July		Training as per attached programme.	Ap.
	10		do	do
	11		do. Pigeon Remonstration to 137 Bde (Batt. Signallers) by Corps Pigeon Officer.	Ap.
			do do do 137 Bde (" ")	Ap.
	12		do do 137 Bde (" ")	Ap.
	13		do. Pigeon Demonstration to 138 Bde. (Battalion Signallers) by Corps Pigeon Officer "Poilus Basket" do to 137 Bde (do) A, Distribution, 2nd Sch.	Ap.
	14		do	Ap.
	15		do.	Ap.
	16		do.	Ap.
	17		do	Ap.
	18		do	Ap.
	19		Musketry. Rifle meeting at ROCOURT.	Ap.
	20		do. do	Ap.
	21		139 Bde. Sect.y moved from CAUCHY AUX CORNAILLES to FOUQUIERES	Ap.
	22		138 Bde moved from FOUQUIERES into Line (Hqrs MAZINGARBE) 23rd / 137 Bde moved from rest at MONCHY LE BRETON to FOUQUIERES	Ap.
	24		139 Bde moved into action. (Hqrs PHILOSOPHE.)	Ap.
SAILLY LA BOURSE (CHATEAU).	25.		Divisional Hqrs. moved to SAILLY LA BOURSE — Lines taken over from 6th Div Sigs Co. Command of Div.n-permanent than are lines about 15 brigade - from brigade to battalions and Gateward to Company all lying buried 8 feet 6 inches. Communication very good and safe. Varied from Fay - to FOSSE 3 at MAZINGARBE. Weather not good owing to severe being very light & heavy.	Ap.

Army Form C. 2118.

WAR DIARY
or
INTELLIGENCE SUMMARY.
(Erase heading not required.)

Instructions regarding War Diaries and Intelligence Summaries are contained in F. S. Regs., Part II. and the Staff Manual respectively. Title pages will be prepared in manuscript.

Place	Date	Hour	Summary of Events and Information	Remarks and references to Appendices
SAILLY LA BOURSE	26 July 1917		Normal	Int
	27		do	Int
	28		do	Int
	29		do	Int
	30		do	Int
	31		do	Int

O.C. Signals
46th Division.

Scheme of Training

6-30 am   Reveille
7-0 am - 7-45 am   Physical Drill
9-0 am   Rifle Inspection
9-15 am to 12-30 pm.   Visual Schemes
         or Squad Drill, Gas Drill
         and Firing Exercises
2-0 pm to 4-0 pm   Wagon Cleaning
         Kit Inspection
         Cricket.

Firing on Range two mornings per week.
Lamp Reading 9-0 pm to 11-0 pm two nights per week.
Whole day Visual Schemes three days a week.
Sundays - Church Parade.
Baths - Once a week.

           C. Maguire Lt RE
7/7/17   O.C. Signals
           137th Inf Bde.

To O.C. 46th Div Sig Coy. R.E.

Scheme of Training

7-30am to 8am — Squad Drill and physical training

9 - 12:30 — Flag Drill & reading practice (first two days)

9 - 12-30 — Station work & Schemes (after first two days)

2 - 4 pm — Kit Inspection
Wagon Cleaning
Recreations (football etc).

H Stiggall Lt RE
O.C. Sigs 139 Inf Bde

TRAINING PROGRAMME.

No. 4 Section,
46th. Divisional Signal Company R.E.

Date	Time	Activity
July 7th.	9 a.m. to 12.30 p.m.	Flag Drill amd Message Work, redding, and sending.
	2 p.m. to 4 p.m.	Buzzer Practice.
July 8th.	9-30 a.m.	Church Parade.
July 9th.	9-30 a.m. to 12.30 p.m.	Shutter, Lamp, Flag reading.
	2 p.m. to 4 p.m.	Lecture.
July 10th.	9 a.m. to 12.30 p.m.	Station Work.
	2 p.m. to 4 p.m.	Buzzer and Fullerphone reading.
July 11th.	9 a.m. to 12-30 p.m.	Moving Stations.
	2 p.m. to 4 p.m.	Lecture.
July 12th.	9 a.m. to 12-30 p.m.	Scheme.
	2 p.m. to 4 p.m.	Baths.
July 13th.	9 a.m. to 3 p.m.	Scheme.
July 14th.	9 a.m. to 12-30 p.m.	Heliograph reading.
	2 p.m. to 4 p.m.	Lecture.
July 15th.	9-30 a.m.	Church Parade.
July 16th.	9 a.m. to 12-30 p.m.	Flag Drill and Lamp reading.
	2 p.m. to 4 p.m.	Route March.
July 17th.	9 a.m. to 12-30 p.m.	Scheme.
	9 p.m. to 11 p.m.	Lamp Reading and Sending.
July 18th.	9 a.m. to 3 p.m.	Scheme.
July 19th.	9 a.m. to 12-30 p.m.	Heliograph and Large Flag.
	2 p.m. to 4 p.m.	Buzzer Practice.
July 20th.	9 a.m. to 3 p.m.	Scheme.

The above is subject to alterations to fit in with Brigade Field Days.

2/Lieut. R.E.
O.C. Signals, 138th. Inf. Bde....

7th. July 1917.

Training Programme.

16th Divisional Signal Coy R.E.

Date	Section	6.15 am	9.15 am	11.15 am	2.30 pm
Monday 9 July '17	Drivers & Mounted Sappers	Stables	Squad Drill	Stables	Stables
	Visual	Physical Drill	Communication Hdqrs — 138 Bde 7000 yds	—	—
	Wireless	do	Instruction under Corporal Scott.		
	Old Sappers	do	Squad Drill	Cleaning wagons	Lecture — march discipline
	New Sappers	do	Riding drill	Stables	do
	Junior NCOs	Communicating drill	-	-	-
Tuesday 10 July '17	Drivers & Mounted Sappers	Stables	Full mounted parade and Route march —		Stables
	Visual	Flag drill	do	do	-
	Wireless	Physical Drill	do	do	-
	Old Sappers	do	do	do	Lecture – Line Faults
	New Sappers	do	do	do	do
	Junior NCOs	do	-	-	-
Wednesday 11th July 17	Drivers	Stables	Lecture – Horse Management	Stables	Stables
	Visual	Flag drill, Lamp reading,	Helio Setting & reading	Lecture — Map Reading	
	Wireless	Physical drill	Instruction under Corpl Scott.		-
	Old Sappers	do	Squad drill	-	do
	New Sappers	do	Riding drill	Stables	do
	Junior N.C.Os	Communicating Drill	Squad drill	-	do
Thursday 12th July 17		SAME AS	WEDNESDAY	11th JULY '17	
Friday 13th July 17	Drivers	Stables	Bathing parade or Squad Drill	Stables	Stables
	DR's	-	do	-	Lecture on D.R. duties
	New Sappers	Stables	do	Squad drill	Gas helmet parade
	Old Sappers	Physical drill	do	do	do
	Junior NCOs	do	do	do	Lecture – Line Faults
	Visual	do	do	Moving Stations working	
	Wireless	Overhaul P.O. Apparatus	Power Buzzer Demonstration to 139 Bde (Batt Signallers)		

Training Programme

46th Divisional Signal Coy R.E.

Date	Section	6.15am	9.15am	11.15am	2.30pm
Saturday 14 July '17	Drivers	Stables	Bathing pde or Squad drill (all available)	Stables	Stables
	D.R's	–	do	–	Lecture by Sgt. Kell on DR duties to all DR's not at lecture on 13.7.17.
	New Sappers	Stables	do	Riding drill	Lecture – map-reading –
	Old Sappers	Physical drill	do	Clean Wagons	do
	Junior NCO	do	(C.O's PARADE) do	Practical testing for line faults	do
	Visual	do	do	Communications with 138 Bde 10% of messages	
	Wireless	do	do	Erect & work stations under Lt LEWIS.	
Sunday 15th July 17	Training programme suspended.				
Monday 16 July '17	Drivers	Stables	Bathing parade	Stables	Rifle Stables.
	New Sappers	Riding drill	do	do	Rifle drill & musketry
	Old Sappers	Physical drill and wagons	do	Wagons	do
	Junior N.C.O.	Communicating drill	do	Practical fault-finding	do
	D.R's	do	do	–	do
	Wireless	Physical drill	do	Practice – Setting up trench sets.	
	Visual	do	Open communication with 137 Inf. Bde		
Tuesday 17 July 17	Drivers	Stables	Bathing	Stables	Stables
	New Sappers	Physical drill	do	Riding drill	Clean Harness.
	Old Sappers	do	do	Practical testing – Line faults –	Musketry Exercise
	Wireless	do	do	Setting up Trench sets Communication – Div Hqrs – FREVILLERS	
	Visual	do	Communication – Div Hqrs – 137 Bde.		
Wednesday 18 July 17	SAME AS TUESDAY 17 JULY '17				
Thursday 19 July 17	DIVISIONAL (RIFLE) SHOOTING COMPETITION – ROCOURT –				
Friday 20 July '17	SAME AS THURSDAY 19 JULY '17				

Training Programme

46th Divisional Signal Co RE

Date	Section	6.15 a/m	9.15 am	11.15 am	2.30 pm
Saturday 21st July '17	Drivers	Stables	Bathing	Stables	Stables
	New Sappers	Physical drill	do	Riding drill	Clean harness.
	Old Sappers	do	do	Practical testing (line faults)	~~Riding drill~~ Wagons
	Wireless	do	do	Instruction by Corpl Scott.	
	Visual	do	do	Station discipline & working	
Sunday 22nd July '17	Training Programme Suspended				
Monday 23rd July '17	Drivers	Stables	Bathing	Stables	Stables
	New Sappers	Stables	do	Riding drill	Clean Harness.
	Old Sappers	Wagons	do	Wagons	Lecture Map reading
	Junior NCO	communicating drill	do	Practical fault-finding	do
	DR's	do	do	—	—
	Wireless	Physical drill	do	Instruction under Cpl Scott.	
	Visual	do	do	Station discipline	Flag drill
Tuesday 24 July '17	Drivers	Stables	Bathing	Stables	Stables
	New Sappers	Physical drill	do	Riding drill	Lecture 'Map reading'
	Old Sappers	do	do	Wagons	do
	Wireless	do	do	—	do
	Visual	do	do	Flag drill	do

Capt.,
for Major, 46th Div. Sig. Co., R.E.

Army Form C. 2118.

WAR DIARY
of
INTELLIGENCE SUMMARY
(Erase heading not required.)

Instructions regarding War Diaries and Intelligence Summaries are contained in F. S. Regs., Part II. and the Staff Manual respectively. Title pages will be prepared in manuscript.

49 Bn Signal Co R.E.

Place	Date	Hour	Summary of Events and Information	Remarks and references to Appendices
SAILLY LA BOURSE	Aug 1st 1917		Preparations made for communication in event of enemy moving back in unfriendly manner by 1st CANADIAN DIV on our right. Compher and Powers rigged up two stations in the line 158° & 159°. New wire cable run out & fresh buried pair laid, and no more trouble very satisfactory.	
"	2		Operations of 1st CANADIAN DIV performed to recovery of weather. O.C. visits A.D. Signals to discuss possibilities of visual working in case of withdrawal of enemy.	
"	3		Lieut. C. A. MAGUIRE returns from leave and resumes command of 137 Bde Signals. 137 Bde relieves 138 Bde in line on night 3rd/4th. (O=D=3/2/6/2/17 received)	
"	4		Maps prepared showing all forward visual posts from BORIS and BUNRATY O.Ps at G.23 A 9.1 and G.16 B 3.0 respectively. These forwarded to Bde Adv. Signal Officers from Brigades in line with instructions to send Battery Signal Officers (or through Bn O.Ps) to all forward O.Ps to satisfy themselves what they can see.	

WAR DIARY or INTELLIGENCE SUMMARY

Army Form C. 2118.

Place	Date	Hour	Summary of Events and Information	Remarks and references to Appendices
SAILLY LA BOURSE	4 cont		able to reveal track in case of enemy returning. Consequent on the pending operations by Canadian Division on our right. Captain A. McK. JOHNSTON proceeds on leave O.O. 218 received	
	5		Raid carried out on left Battn. left Brigade front. Right Bttn left up by MG fire. Left reached objective. No identification. Our troops were sent over but it were not successful owing to MG fire & the apparatus was lost. It is proposed to try this again in next raid. Major General FOWLER D.A.S. and Colonel MOORE D.A.A.S. 1st army visited O.C.	
	6		Lance Briggs which was lost in "no mans land" was recovered today Normal O.O. 219 received	

Army Form C. 2118.

WAR DIARY
or
INTELLIGENCE SUMMARY.
(Erase heading not required.)

Instructions regarding War Diaries and Intelligence Summaries are contained in F. S. Regs., Part II. and the Staff Manual respectively. Title pages will be prepared in manuscript.

Place	Date Aug	Hour	Summary of Events and Information	Remarks and references to Appendices
SAILLY LA BOURSE	7		Normal	
	8		Normal	
	9		Proposal made to Brit HQrs that a Div. Signalling School be started to replace the Brigade Signalling Schools.	
	10		Proposed scheme in furtherance of above submitted to Brigade Commanders. Lieut F.H. STEGGALL of No. 139 Bde resumed duty from leave.	
	11		139 Brigade does not approve of formation of Divisional School to replace Brigade School. 137 & 138 Bdes are, however, in favor of the change.	
	12		Normal	

WAR DIARY or INTELLIGENCE SUMMARY

Army Form C. 2118.

Place	Date	Hour	Summary of Events and Information	Remarks and references to Appendices
SAILLY LA BOURSE	1917 Aug 13		Right Batt. left Brigade tonight. Rain commenced about 6pm in favour of Bro. Batten. Power Buzzer taken over two microphone receivers	
	14		Arrangements made for normal reporting observations in connection with consecion operations which commence tomorrow	
	15		Consecion offensive commenced on our left. Overture given by the Divin Artillery work. Communications held well. Captains A. McK JOHNSTON remained duty from 1am.	
	16		For raid fixed to take place tonight 11.45pm arrangements are complete for raiding party (5th Leicesters) to take over one power buzzer to advanced amplifier or alternatively to Corps "IT." This will work back from "IT" to Company HQ's. Right half of Coy Base.	

A.5834. Wt.W4973/M687. 750,000 8/16 D.D.& L. Ltd. Forms/C.118/13.

WAR DIARY
or
INTELLIGENCE SUMMARY.

(Erase heading not required.)

Army Form C. 2118.

for A.D. Signal G. R.E.

Place	Date	Hour	Summary of Events and Information	Remarks and references to Appendices
SAILLY LA BOURSE	17.		138 Bde relieved 139 Bde in left sector during the night. Command of P.O.C. 137 Bde (in the operation) (Tranton) (Lunenburg Trenches) Penner Trigger was taken over — and to manage more safe trade & correctly served by Cpl. IT forcing the enemy's troops and to the rest.	5" Circuits under
	18		Arrangements made to start Divisional Signal School under O.C. Div. Signal Co. at natur. Signal officer & Moments to act as Divisional Signal instructors. Course to commence 22/8/17 and last 6 weeks (years). Capt. Munro (L?) Napier inspected the electric Are circuits & front line sector, with report to probable discontinuance while no tunnels are in progress, maintenance being extremely difficult.	Teacher on left
	19.		Normal.	
	20		do	
	21		(do) Visual Station on Fosse 3 working from Fosse 8 to all Battalions was revived and rebuilt. (Rican lamp used)	
	22		Arrangements made to take over from 2nd Division lines in this forward Right Brigade area — 139 Bde relieved one section from 26th Brigade Divisional Signal School at SAILLY LA BOURSE — W. people from each battalion in Divl. & Arm'y. Howitzers.	
	23		Normal: Major Leiro D.S.O. left for 12 days leave to England.	
	24		Normal;	
	25		Normal;	

WAR DIARY
or
INTELLIGENCE SUMMARY.

Army Form C. 2118.

(Erase heading not required.)

Place	Date	Hour	Summary of Events and Information	Remarks and references to Appendices
SAILLY LA BOURSE	August 1917 26		139th Bde. established headquarters on front line near ANNEQUIN on BETHUNE — LA BASSÉE Road. Having relieved CAMBRIN sector from 99th Bde. 2nd Div. Heavy rain prevented reliefs intended to 11 am. this & Bn. Hqrs. also to provide escorts to right battalion as far as VERMELLES where reliefs were managed to railway line running North-east from A/A Linhouse Café and west of BRICKS Hqrs. 1 from OLD Hq. & Pyt hutt cave on trench ran west and north side of CAMBRIN line to waterworks GARRISON and from north of CAMBRIN line to waterworks. Company lines as in the cellars and [illegible] mined road to Beuvry.	The Div April [illegible]
	27		Normal	
	28		Raid carried out to right 11:30 & 8:30 pm. Lost 1 Officer, 7 prisoners. Enemy barrage not employed. Enemy Lewis Gun fire was used successfully from S. W.	
	29		Raid by right Bn. at 1:30 am. No enemy encountered, though dug outs were penetrated to 1000 ft. Enemy Lewis Gun used successfully from enemy trench signalling to our Hqrs.	
	30		Normal	
	31		Normal	

WAR DIARY
or
INTELLIGENCE SUMMARY.

Army Form C. 2118.

(Erase heading not required.)

H.Q. 46 Div Signal Coy R.E.

Place	Date	Hour	Summary of Events and Information	Remarks and references to Appendices
SAILLY LA BOURSE	September 1		Gas Cylinders discharged by Special Coy R.E. on HULLUCH front. Special signals arranged.	
	2		Normal.	
	3		Arrangements completed for HQ Div Artillery to take over engin of HQ 1 Div Arty. Capt Roberts M.C. of 6th Div. Arty. by 46 Div. Arty. completed Capt Roberts M.C. by Eng'rs. Major Knapp M/c Signals 231 Bns. is acting I/c Signals at DA HQrs 46 DA Chateau du PRES SAILLY LA BOURSE. – 231 Bde. at MAZINGARBE, 230° at PHILOSOPHE; Divvy FA Bdes at ANNEQUIN. Lines taken over as in use.	
	4		Normal.	
	5		Gas alarm during night A/5th. All staff then officials and others were warned by previously prepared messages, sent to Mazingarbe etc but Gas came from concentrated bombardment of various positions (MAZINGARBE, LOOS etc) by no shells. Also from closed gas (cylent) by the enemy in front of down in Rft. Oril deyd. Col M. to down. (Limitation of Eye.) SAP48 LOOS OUEST Stopped with effects noticeable. H.V. Coun during rest stop. Ciphers rec'd down.	
	6		Major Lewis R.S.O. returned from leave to England & resumed command	
	7		Normal.	

Army Form C. 2118.

WAR DIARY
or
INTELLIGENCE SUMMARY.
(Erase heading not required.)

Instructions regarding War Diaries and Intelligence Summaries are contained in F.S. Regs., Part II. and the Staff Manual respectively. Title pages will be prepared in manuscript.

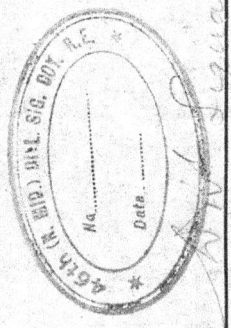

Place	Date	Hour	Summary of Events and Information	Remarks and references to Appendices
SAILLY LA BOURSE	September 8 1917		Raid carried out by 138 Inf. Bde on enemys positions across camp between MAROC & Hulluch against FOSSE 8. Co. CORONS de MAROC. Capt. Ahmuty Willis Stafford descended FOSSE 3 (ANNEQUIN) & reconnoitred H gallery going to telephone line from FOSSE 3 to FOSSE 8 in mine tunnel, the object being to connect air guard at bottom of shaft FOSSE 8 with 139 Bde Hqrs.	
	9		Normal.	
	10		Capt. Roberts MC. arrived from base & England. 2/Lt. Stafford, O.C. sig. 137 Bde. Completed laying line from 139 Bde Hqrs at ANNEQUIN to FOSSE 3, thence down mine shaft & gallery running underground to FOSS 8 (in German lines) while guard of Sumatry Coy is posted. Speaking good. — 5 miles route D.5 cable used.	
	11		139 Bde attempted a raid on enemy trenches which was unsuccessful owing to party being heavily bombarded while coming away — to PO to leave 900 TM bombs. Power buzzer & amplifier was ready — the apparatus fitted at mouth of MINSTER tunnel.	
	12		Normal. 2/Lt. Bickoff left for base & England.	
	13		Normal.	
	14		Normal. 2/Lt. W.H. Allured left for base & England.	
	15		Normal.	
	16		Normal.	

WAR DIARY or INTELLIGENCE SUMMARY.

Army Form C. 2118.

Place	Date	Hour	Summary of Events and Information	Remarks and references to Appendices
SAILLY LA BOURSE	Sept. 1917 17.		50 men of 5th Leicesters and 10 men of 1 Agra. Sgnts. Commenced digging Cable trench in ST ELIE D.I.R. trench necessary to connect existing buried cable to tunnel entrance (STANSFIELD ROAD)	
	18		120 yards of cable trench dug and 1 K Tunnel entrance completed. Bde Signal School G.O.C. Division inspected signal school. Heavy rain. VE buried cable Corps Pack continued suffering reports got down. B K. B.	
	19		10 men of 1 Agra Section continued digging — no infantry available. A Major 47th signal cable ran to H.14 prior to taking over lines of 71st & 18th Bdes. (6th Div)	
	20		OC Sigs. 99th Bde. (2nd Div) visited hqrs. re taking over of CAMBRIN sector by his Bde. Heavy French mortar shoot carried out in CAMBRIN sector with aeroplane observation. Cable damaged.	
	21		99th Bde. (2nd Div) relieved 139 Bde. overnight in CAMBRIN Sector. Lines arranged with 1 Corps division & brigade retaining 139 Bde area.	
	22		139 A.I. Bde returned 71st Bde Lines in H.14 70 (Loos) sector lines to tel. hqrs. on outposts in MAINGATE trench on PONT ST. buried route. M.G. Emm. battalion on PONT ST. buried & 2 Point Angers visited for S.O.S. purpose. 1 Amplifier of 2 Point Angers installed for communication of Signals School. Royal kerr. DSP. gave four bye demonstration to officers attended. G.O.C. Maj-Gen. Jacobs Co. Brig-Gen. Campbell V.C. & Staff officers attended	

Army Form C. 2118.

WAR DIARY
or
INTELLIGENCE SUMMARY.
(Erase heading not required.)

Place	Date	Hour	Summary of Events and Information	Remarks and references to Appendices
SAILLY	October 23, 1917		Normal. O.C. Signals 139 Bde. Reorganising battalion communications in Hill 70 sector.	Enc
LA BOURSE	24		Normal. R/Col. Bowker A.D.S. A.D. Signals VIth Corps inspected D.W. Signal School.	Enc
	25		Normal. 15 men of flying & cable section day to air tests & Courses.	Enc
	26		Party of 15 men completed work on HULLUCH tunnel route.	Enc
	27		O.C. Signals reconnoitred forward area HILL 70 sector with view of proposed lined routes to O.P.'s and Companies.	Enc
	28		Normal.	Enc
	29		Normal.	Enc
	30		Contact Patrol Demonstration and practice carried out by Div. Signal School at Aerodrome of No.2 Squadron R.F.C.	Enc

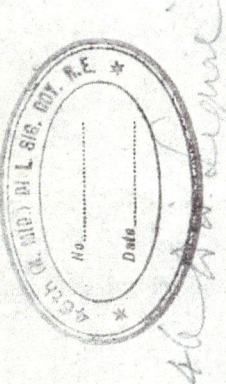

Army Form C. 2118.

Vol 2 H.Q. 46th Div. Sig. Coy. R.E.

WAR DIARY

INTELLIGENCE SUMMARY.

(Erase heading not required.)

Instructions regarding War Diaries and Intelligence Summaries are contained in F.S. Regs., Part II. and the Staff Manual respectively. Title pages will be prepared in manuscript.

H.Q. 46th Div. Sig. Coy. R.E.

Place	Date	Hour	Summary of Events and Information	Remarks and references to Appendices
SAILLY LA BOURSE	Oct 1917 1st		O.C. Signals submitted proposals for using 2½ mile line French alternative front line in LOOS — HULLUCH road. To Old Permanent front line at BOIS RASE.	
	2.		Demonstration given & practice by students of Div Signal School in building portable hut at N.2 Squadron R.E.C.	
			Outside of cable laden etc for above above submitted to 1st Corps, S.G. Braid. O.C. Signals interviewed 6th Res. S.O. referring to reviews Lybonie to front line safety. O.P. on Hill 70.	
			Brig. General John CAMPBELL V.C. inspected Signal School.	
	3.		Normal. Div. Signal School — 1st Course ended 6/10 CO	
	4.		Normal.	
	5.		Normal.	
	6.		General recommended for Command of 1st & Cable Trans. to BOISMITE by Major MILLER O.C. 465 Field Co R.E. & Capt. Bourn S/Sig Co. Major MILLER handed S.Sig Coys to Captn. Brugger amongst November paid by B.C. Signals to Major MILLER DSCY Conv for cable.	
	7.		1st Corps defence & supply cable order termed 15. 6.40 a.m.	
	8.		Cable touch commenced 500 men from Depot Battalion and half course to 4 hour depth. Second Course commenced at Div Signal School =80 Students from Infantry both aux Machine Gun Coys and R.F.A.	

Army Form C. 2118.

WAR DIARY
INTELLIGENCE SUMMARY.
(Erase heading not required.)

Instructions regarding War Diaries and Intelligence Summaries are contained in F.S. Regs., Part II. and the Staff Manual respectively. Title pages will be prepared in manuscript.

46 Div Signal Co R.E.

Place	Date	Hour	Summary of Events and Information	Remarks and references to Appendices
SAILLY LA BOISELE	October 1917 9		LIGOS — BOIS RASE Cable Trench continued. 500 men from Depot Battalion being employed digging.	JH
	10		O.C. interviewed OC/465 Fd Co. R.E. reference digging of Cable Trench that Sept. No digging party today.	JH
	11		500 men from Depot Battalion continued digging LOOS — BOISRALE Cable Trench.	JH
	12		2 Lengths 12 pair twin armoured Cable (each length 440 yds) taken to trench. Lieut BIRD in charge of laying.	JH
	13		2 × 440 yd lengths 12 pairs laid in cable trench. Chateau project deepened by sapper continuing party. Ampliphic Demonstration given to General REGAT & UNITED STATES Army and other officers. — O.C. Signals (Major Lewis A.S.C. Britain) Lab.	JH
	14		150 men from Depot Battalion worked deepening forward portion of cable trench.	JH
	15		O.C. Signals inspected cable trench & picked 30 men worked party from A.D. Signals & Corps Cable Cap 1st completed work. Corps Cable officer working with Lieut BIRD.	JH

Army Form C. 2118.

WAR DIARY
INTELLIGENCE SUMMARY

Place	Date	Hour	Summary of Events and Information	Remarks and references to Appendices
SAILLY LA BOURSE	October	16	30 Cpls Oulick worked in LOOS — Bois RASE Cable Attack	
		17	30 Cpls Oulicks worked in LOOS trenches. Paid 400 yds depth trench laid by others today.	
		18	Four 2 length N Cable laid to Rd German Front line (Bois RASE)	
		19	Nmal.	
		20	Test point in LOOS TRENCH on New board road constructed. Demonstration on Power Buzzer and Amplifier given by O.C. Signals at Sept Rue given to officers of Infantry. Point (LOOS TRENCH) completed	
		21		
		22	Nmal. 2/Lt ALDRICH returned from 6 weeks transfer course at ABBEVILLE	
		23	Demonstration on R.W. Wireless by O.C. Signals to General _____ of the UNITED STATES Army.	
		24	Test point in OLD GERMAN front line extended.	
		25	All Trunks completed on LOOS — BOIS RASE & N new Cable Route	

Army Form C. 2118.

WAR DIARY
or
INTELLIGENCE SUMMARY.
(Erase heading not required.)

Lt. Hon. Reynolds R.E.

Place	Date	Hour	Summary of Events and Information	Remarks and references to Appendices
SAILLY au	26 October 1917		Normal. Lt. McGregor returned from hospital at Base.	
BOURECS	27.		Combined Power Buzzer & Amplifier Instrument installed at 2/4 Right Coy, Right Bn. instead of Power Buzzer.	
	28.		Wireless trench set attached N.W. of LOOS in ENGLISH ALLEY by order of G. Staff, for purpose of intercepting messages and calls from enemy trench and B.Coy. sets.	
	29.		Normal.	
	30.		Cable trench surveyed from cable head in old German front line N.E. of LOOS through right battalion Hqrs of Right Bn. to join buried cable sunk of English front division — and from cable head of NELSON TRENCH branch of right plant division (HILL 70) along rear of right battalion O.P. and right Coys.) to HYTHE ALLEY. (& East up Right battalion O.P. and right Coys.)	
	31.		Amplifier station (HILL 70) and wireless intercepting station at LOOS unable. Aerial blown down by shell fire at pm. Successful daylight raid by battalion of 137 bde, on which 45 prisoners were taken. Communication between raiding party and advanced Bde. Hqr. left op by Lucas lamp from enemy pill-box emplacement. (Bde. Signal Officer report attached).	

Confidential

O.C. Signals
46th Division

Report on Communications
1/6th North Staff Raid 31/10/17
_____

Battalion Battle Hdqrs were established at Right Company A.M.44., and Advanced Brigade Hdqrs at Right Battalion Hdqrs B A 3.

Two routes were provided from A.M.44 to B.A.3, the latter Signal office being taken over and manned by the Brigade Signal Section.

Visual was also provided between A.M.44 B A 3 and the Brigade Visual Station on FOSSE 3. This was not used beyond testing as lines held good.

The raiding party took over two Lucas Lamps which were divided ~~placed~~ between the four Companies raiding.

It was arranged to work these back from two German "Pillboxes" which was successfully done. The receiving station owing to the nature of the ground, was situated at B A 3, the signals being telephoned forward to the

Battalion at AM 44.

The visual worked excellently; the first signals being received 3 minutes after zero, and continued right up to the withdrawal signal, without interruption. A list of the code is attached. The Signal party in each case consisted of one N.C.O. and two men and all regained our trenches without a casualty.
No other special Communications were necessary as the existing ones sufficed

AMaguire Lieut. R.E.
O.C. SIGNALS,
137th INFANTRY BRIGADE.

1/11/17.

Army Form C. 2118.

WAR DIARY
or
INTELLIGENCE SUMMARY
(Erase heading not required.)

44th Div. Signal Coy. Vol 29

Place	Date	Hour	Summary of Events and Information	Remarks and references to Appendices
SAILLY LA BOURSE	1 Nov 1917		Re-organisation of existing signal lines at Div. Hqrs. begun. Separate Telephone Exchange room prepared and test made outdoors.	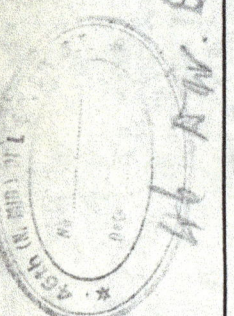
	2		Digging begun on cable trench W. of LOOS to connect existing cable lead to Right Battalion of 137 Bde. (H.L.79) 450 men of Devonshires employed.	
	3		Work done on cable trench enquired by 1st Cay. and A.D. Signals Maps. Tunnel entrances in old trench system W. of LOOS reconnoitred by Capt. Johnston with view of installing Triangle Fd. Central Communication.	
	4		Above cable trench was worked on by 450 men of training Bn. in vicinity of same. Classes for battalion signalling officers & men begun at Divl. Signal School. — Exam on West end Class, end course of 18 months.	
	5		Party of 350 men of Training Batt. dug in above Cable Trench to depth average 5ft 6in. Trench inspected and not approved by A.D. Signals Maps.	
	6		350 men of Training Batt. dug on cable trench from HYTHE ALLEY finished along west of NELSON trench to join cable lead in right flank of divl hand front. Trench regained to cross up 5ft 6in. O.P. and company.	
	7		450 men dug cable trench (unoccupied on 5th Div.) from crossing Town road on by O.E. navy trench South ALDRICH, and sht. depth of except 100 yds Cable Refer at North end of trench.	

Army Form C. 2118.

WAR DIARY
or
INTELLIGENCE SUMMARY.
(Erase heading not required.)

Place	Date	Hour	Summary of Events and Information	Remarks and references to Appendices
SAILLY LA BOURSE	November 1917 8		Remaining length of Cable laid on track completed yesterday by NZ party with party from Signal School under Lieut. HADRIOTT. Connect up at 12 noon unwound 100 CCS. to French dug-out near Dump. Q 4 a.350 and then trench to corner of Dump Qft. NELSON TRENCH.	
	9.		Found work on HILL 70 perfected by O.C. Signals. Cable laying in trench possible to NELSON TRENCH (HILL 70 — Z of LOOS) completed.	
	10		Cable trench broken through on several apparently by "Duds" on our side. In fact complete to repair system.	
	11.		Cable in above trench found to be broken. Fill in open trench	
	12.		Broken Cable in open trench on HILL 70 repaired by Capt. WILLIAMS' party into the found shelters in LOOS which completely knee out cable system. Major H.A. LEWIS, DSO proceeded to MAROEUIL (Signal Depôt Arr Base) for 7 days Course on Wireless.	
	13		Nil	

WAR DIARY
INTELLIGENCE SUMMARY

Army Form C. 2118.

40 DIV. SIGNAL Co RE

Place	Date	Hour	Summary of Events and Information	Remarks and references to Appendices
SAILLY LAbOURSE	14th Nov 18		Normal.	
	15	19/5	The G.O.C. Div. Maj. Gen. W. THWAITES CB inspected this Signal School	
	16		Normal.	
	17		Normal.	
	18		Normal. Major EASTWS returns from French Course at ABBEVILLE	
	19		Recless Gulet Patrol demonstration & kept personnel of Div Signal School, 22 Div, Gordon Andrews + 5 DIGNELL	
	20		Aeroplane Contact Patrol demonstration to recruits of Signal School.	
	21		Normal	
	22		Enemy raided HILL 70 (Left Sector) E. of LENS. Communication to Brig. down. S.O.S. received by wires only. Power Buzzer in Centre Coy of Left Battalion through ok but not used. G.S. Signals advised Inf. that buried route to Coy's in Advanced to ABOUSED & route communications were O.K. etc.	2" Corner of Inf Signal Setup Closed

WAR DIARY or INTELLIGENCE SUMMARY

Army Form C. 2118.

46 DIV. SIGNAL CO. R.E.

Place	Date	Hour	Summary of Events and Information	Remarks and references to Appendices
SAILLY LA BOURSE	23rd November 1917.		Staff mistrust that immediate steps be taken to recomplete mileage of immediate to front line of left battalion. HILL 70 Relief. CAPT JOHNSTON & Lieut LEWIS reconnoitred a tape out route from Cable Head via alignment line to CAMERON L. left battn 138 Btn in front line. 138 Bde Tel. over HILL 70 R.O.R. from 139 Bde. also took over ST ELIE Sector.	
	24.		Staff approve scheme on tried out with additions of connecting Centre Coy to left Coy by laying 3ft below bottom of front line trench. AD Signals McCafe made by O.C. Signal & T.S.O.! All above schemes. AD Sigs approves. Order 21189/8 01 C. received stating too many incoming calls for daytime on nights 24/25th and 25/26 Novr Lieut LEWIS & Sergt MORICH supervised digging front trench and recorded depth of 4 feet.	
	25.		Arrangements made with G. Staff & C.R.E. to lay cable on night of 26/27th with half of 1 Monmouth Regt. to fill in trench after 6 Yorkshire Regt. digging continued.	

WAR DIARY or INTELLIGENCE SUMMARY

Army Form C. 2118.

46 DIV SIGNAL CO. RE

Place	Date	Hour	Summary of Events and Information	Remarks and references to Appendices
SAILLY LA BOURSE	26 November 1917		Cable bench to front line HILL 70 left sub-sector was duy to average depth 5 ft trenches overnight. Party of MONMOUTH REGT. (200 men) detailed for laying cable & filling in trench cut in road to deepen trench to 6ft 6 in. 3rd Canadian Div Signal School opened. 100 students from battalions, RFA batteries, Trench Mortar batteries and Machine Gun Coys taught.	G.W.
	27.		32nd Inf. Bde. (11th Div) take over Hill 70 Right sub-sector from 138 Bde. 2 NCOs of the Coy. assisted 11th Div. Signals to Coy in carrying out cable tests.	G.W.
	28.		Normal.	G.W.
	29		Normal.	G.W.
	30		Normal.	G.W.

Army Form C. 2118.

WAR DIARY
or
INTELLIGENCE SUMMARY.
(Erase heading not required.)

Instructions regarding War Diaries and Intelligence Summaries are contained in F. S. Regs., Part II. and the Staff Manual respectively. Title pages will be prepared in manuscript.

46D Signals

Place	Date	Hour	Summary of Events and Information	Remarks and references to Appendices
SAILLY LA BOURSE	Dec 1 1916		Artillery carried out harassing fire on enemy supports onto trench dump. All communications found OK	
	2		Church parades	
	3		O.C. Inspection. Divisional Signal School	
	4		Ladies Inspection Stores transferred to workshops by SDDVS Company Section taken over from 25th Div. by 18 BM. Communications all complete	
	5		Normal	
	6		Normal	
	7		CO Inspecting Company also 10.2 batt stations. Horses turned over to train by re-equipping kits in covers by total of 4 Co's lost water cart to cooker taken from 10 Co	
	8		Saturday parade. Inspection of horses by O.C. Company	

Army Form C. 2118.

WAR DIARY
~~or~~ INTELLIGENCE SUMMARY.
(Erase heading not required.)

Instructions regarding War Diaries and Intelligence Summaries are contained in F. S. Regs., Part II. and the Staff Manual respectively. Title pages will be prepared in manuscript.

Place	Date 1917	Hour	Summary of Events and Information	Remarks and references to Appendices
SAILLY LA BOURSE	Dec 9		Church parade	
	10		O.C. visited 137 R.E. front	Seb
	11		Daylight raid carried out by 139 Bde. All communications worked satisfactorily	Seb
	12		Gas operations carried out on CAMBRIN front (138 & 139 Bde) All communications worked well	Seb
	13		Spent day inspected by GOC Division very satisfactory result	Seb
	14		Normal. Lieut H.E.C. LEWIS proceeds on leave	Seb
	15		C.O. inspected Company on parade. Dismounted. Lieut F. STEGGALL proceeds on leave	

A 5834 Wt. W4973/M687 750,000 8/16 D. D. & L. Ltd. Forms/C.2118/13

Army Form C. 2118.

WAR DIARY
~~INTELLIGENCE~~ SUMMARY.
(Erase heading not required.)

Instructions regarding War Diaries and Intelligence Summaries are contained in F.S. Regs., Part II. and the Staff Manual respectively. Title pages will be prepared in manuscript.

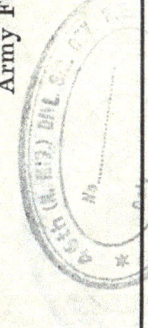

Place	Date 1917	Hour	Summary of Events and Information	Remarks and references to Appendices
SAILLY LA BOURSE	Dec 16		Church parade. Two radios sent for wireless course at Army Signalling School.	Sgt
	17		O.C. visited 139 Bde front.	Sgt
	18		O.C. visited Left Bde (Artillery) in commemoration Inspected offices &c.	Sgt
	19		Normal	Sgt
	20		Instrumental wireless Company of the wireless course at Signal Depot.	Sgt
	21		Divisional School examinees by D.C.	Sgt
	22		Normal. Captain A. McK. JOHNSTON proceeds on leave.	Sgt

Army Form C. 2118.

WAR DIARY
INTELLIGENCE SUMMARY.
(Erase heading not required.)

Instructions regarding War Diaries and Intelligence Summaries are contained in F. S. Regs., Part II. and the Staff Manual respectively. Title pages will be prepared in manuscript.

Place	Date	Hour	Summary of Events and Information	Remarks and references to Appendices
SAILLY to BOURSE	23		Church parade	Sgd
	24		Gas bombardment on Divisional front by four Special Coy. All communications maintained well	Sgd
	25		Xmas Day Church parade &c	Sgd
	26		Normal	Sgd
	27		OC visited 138 Bde front	Sgd
	28		GSO1 visited Divine Signal School with OC	Sgd
	29		Company inspected (Armaments) by 2nd Lieut H.C. LEWIS attached from Army MT	Sgd
	30		Church parade	Sgd
	31		OC explains Signal arrangements of Division to US Army Staff	Sgd

THE NAME OF THE UNIT IS **NOT** TO BE WRITTEN ON THIS MEMO.

To Lt C A Majurne

Reference O.O. No. 33, d/d 29-10-17, para 14.

The following code will be used:-

Succession of A's — 1st objective gained.
    "   "   B's — 2nd   -do-
    "   "   C's — 3rd   -do-
    "   "   D's — Resistance slight.
    "   "   E's — Resistance heavy.
    "   "   F's — Prisoners Captured.
    "   "   G's — Withdrawal commenced.
    "   "   H's — Station closing down.

James R Weeks 2/Lt
Signalling Officer.

30-10-1917.

WAR DIARY

INTELLIGENCE SUMMARY.

Army Form C. 2118.

46 D S

Place	Date 1916	Hour	Summary of Events and Information	Remarks and references to Appendices
SAILLY LA BOURSE	Jan 1		O.C. unit left section to report to communications	
	2		General PLUMMER U.S. Army visits Hyndfuhton O.C. Coro power Burger Dinnington Capt: G.G. ROBERTS proceeds on leave	
	3		Normal	
	4		Normal Wireless Intercept Station established at CAMBRIN to pick up enemy code calls and messages, which are forwarded to "Intelligence" O.C. visits 137 Bde fost any inspects communication	
	5			
	6		Church parade Warning received of impending relief of Aus sie by 11 Div	
	7		NORMAL Lieut. C.A. MAGUIRE awarded Military Cross in New Year Honours list	

Army Form C. 2118.

WAR DIARY
or
INTELLIGENCE SUMMARY.
(Erase heading not required.)

46 DIV. Signal Coy. R.E.

Instructions regarding War Diaries and Intelligence Summaries are contained in F.S. Regs., Part II. and the Staff Manual respectively. Title pages will be prepared in manuscript.

Place	Date	Hour	Summary of Events and Information	Remarks and references to Appendices
SAILLY LABOURSE	1918 Jany. 8		Enemy artillery active on CAMBRIN. Communication unbroken. Major E.A. LEWIS, D.S.O. proceeded on leave to ENGLAND.	
	9		NORMAL	
	10		do	
	11		do	
	12		Movement Order. Received from Div. Staff.	
	13		Wireless intercept station withdrawn from LOOS.	
	14		Capt. Johnts and Lieut. Lewis proceed to BUSNES to arrange accommodation for Div. Signal Coy. (with Schools concentrated) and for Div. Signal School when Division shall be relieved and withdrawn from the line. Div. Order issued for assembly of units course of Div. Signal School at BUSNES on 18th Jany.	
	15		Advance party moved to billets at BUSNES. G.O.C. 11th Div. visited Hqrs. to inspect dispositions of lines and personnel.	

Army Form C. 2118.

WAR DIARY
INTELLIGENCE SUMMARY

(Erase heading not required.)

46 DIV. SIGNAL Coy.

Instructions regarding War Diaries and Intelligence Summaries are contained in F.S. Regs., Part II. and the Staff Manual respectively. Title pages will be prepared in manuscript.

Place	Date	Hour	Summary of Events and Information	Remarks and references to Appendices
SAILLY LA BOURSE	JANY 16 1918		Move precautions ordered. Move to rest area postponed till further orders. O.C. 11th Div. Signals visited Brigade Group hqrs.	
	17.		Normal	
	18.		Capt. G.G. Roberts MC. reported from leave. 2/Lieut W.H. Alcock proceeded on leave to England.	
	19.		O.C. Signal 11th Div. visited right brigade area and inspected Signal Office of battalions and Coys.	
	20.		Normal.	
	21.		Normal.	
	22.		O.C. Signals 11th Div. visited centre brigade area. Interchange of 11th Div. Signals installed in place of Divl Signal office commenced.	
LABEUVRIERE	23.		Company moved to LABEUVRIERE. Arrived on arrival at 10 a.m. Sector handed over to O.C. 11th Div.	
	24.		O.C. Signal inspected billets and took over of new area. Hire of waters to movement Hqrs. arranged. Arrangements for signal school etc. Cav. drill. Reconnaissance party	
	25.		Training commenced. Infantry drill.	
	26.		Normal Training	

Army Form C. 2118.

WAR DIARY
or
INTELLIGENCE SUMMARY.

(Erase heading not required.)

Instructions regarding War Diaries and Intelligence Summaries are contained in F.S. Regs., Part II and the Staff Manual respectively. Title pages will be prepared in manuscript.

Place	Date	Hour	Summary of Events and Information	Remarks and references to Appendices
LA EUVRIERE	27 January 1918		Training continued.	
	28.		Divi. Signal School assembles. 3 men per battalion to Divi. Artillery. 1st School of instruction by Major LAZENUS D.S.O. 137th, 138th and 139th Infantry Brigade Sections conducted at LA EUVRIERE and arms collected.	
	29.		230 Bde R.F.A. Air Section arrived. Complete concentration of 231 Bde R.F.A. Pack Radio remains in the line at MAZINGARBE.	
	30.		O.C. Signals inspects Complete Coy. Training commenced as per attached programme.	
	31.		Training continued (as per programme).	

WAR DIARY

INTELLIGENCE SUMMARY

Army Form C. 2118.

Place	Date	Hour	Summary of Events and Information	Remarks and references to Appendices
LABEUVRIÈRE	FEBRUARY 1918. 1st		Training of concentrated Company: Equitation drill. Infantry, Run, and Rifle.	
	2		do. Route march.	
	3		do. Church Parade.	
	4		do. Equitation drill, Infantry & run drill	
	5		do. do.	
	6		do. O.C.'s Inspection of full marching order — Route march — Rifle and Run section to rejoin their respective Sqns.	
	7		do. Equitation & run drill	
	8		do. Cartridge drill: Smoke (testing of) & run Company	
	9		Sn. Hqrs. move to BOMY. Sn. office shut down at LABEUVRIÈRE 10am & open at BOMY same hour. Hqrs. & Hqrs. sect. were on road to REDINGHELLE and carried "scheme" Hqrs. of Div. 13th 1914 in front by Cable wagon, arrived 138 Pole Cable carry out Brit. post scheme. Commencement three-fifth diff up M.R. Anglesea Contact patrols. W.T. worked unsuccessful owing to soft and Carrying the cones fast sinking ground.	

Army Form C. 2118.

WAR DIARY
INTELLIGENCE SUMMARY.
(Erase heading not required.)

Instructions regarding War Diaries and Intelligence Summaries are contained in F. S. Regs., Part II. and the Staff Manual respectively. Title pages will be prepared in manuscript.

468th (W. RID.) FIELD. COY. R.E.

Place	Date	Hour	Summary of Events and Information	Remarks and references to Appendices
BONY.	1918 Feb		Outpost scheme in finished. March returned to BONY, where Hqrs April No. 11 Section billeted. 139 Bde Sect. billeted at CAPELLE and 4/5. 139 Old Sect. at ERNY ST JULIEN. 138 Bde Sect. billeted at R.E. at VERCHIN.	
	10			
	11		Interior Economy.	
	12		do	
	13		Training Resumed. Cadre loving. Wooden hut erection. Wired supplied	
	14		Training Continued	
	15		do	
	16		do	
	17		do	
	18		do	
	19		do	
	20		do	

WAR DIARY

INTELLIGENCE SUMMARY.

(Erase heading not required.)

Army Form C. 2118.

Ho DIV SIGNAL COY RE

Place	Date	Hour	Summary of Events and Information	Remarks and references to Appendices
BONY	1918 Feb. 21		Training Continued. Cable, wireless, visual signalling	do
	22		do	do
	23		do	do
	24		do	Musketry — do
	25		do. Div Warning Order (G.176A) received. Div T commence move to the line on March 12th	do
	26		do	do
	27		Quiets-attack scheme carried out by 138 Bry. Bn. Communications by cable, Power Buzzer – Amplifier, wireless no aeroplane	
	28		Counter attack scheme by 138 Bry. Bn. Communications in progress all day. Div. Order 276 B. received, with march table for 1st and 2nd march of T's move. G 137 & 139 Art. Orders. Aircraft the his train	

Army Form C. 2118.

WAR DIARY
or
INTELLIGENCE SUMMARY.
(Erase heading not required.)

Instructions regarding War Diaries and Intelligence Summaries are contained in F.S. Regs., Part II. and the Staff Manual respectively. Title pages will be prepared in manuscript.

Place	Date	Hour	Summary of Events and Information	Remarks and references to Appendices
BRUAY	MARCH 1		138 Inf. Bde. took over from 17 Inf Bde. at BEAUDONNE & NOEPHEN BELLEVUE	
	2		138 Inf Bde. opened office at BRUAY in ACTON BURNES	
	3		R.E. Office closed at BRUAY and opened at PRIERE ST PRY, FOUQUIERES. Chief transport moved to FOUQUIERES. Water supply arrangement. Lt MAGUIRE Mc. took over the R.E. Stores & Depôt at FOUQUIERES	
FOUQUIERES	4		46 Div. Sig. Office closed at VERCHIN & opened at FOUQUIERES. 137 Inf. Bde. moved to the line taking over GUINCHY sector from 57th Div Sig. Bn.	
			139 opened BEUVRY	
			138 Inf Bde moved to the line HOHENZOLLERN. B/E relieving Bde 9th Div	
			Hqrs opened SAILLY LA BOURSE station	
			137 Bde in reserve at BEUVRY & relieved at GUINCHY	
			Local units & spheres held by Div. broken up.	
	5		Normal	
	6			
	7		Open lines to BEUVRY - SAILLY good. Cut to Brom Fm.	
	8	9.32pm	"POISON" GAS BELT NORTH. Spread from 137 Brigade, the Germans opened fire	
			Normal	

A5834 Wt. W4973/M687 750,000 8/16 D. D. & L. Ltd. Forms/C.2118/13

WAR DIARY
INTELLIGENCE SUMMARY
(Erase heading not required.)

Army Form C. 2118.

H.Q. 46 Div. Signal Coy R.E.

Place	Date	Hour	Summary of Events and Information	Remarks and references to Appendices
FOUQUEREUIL	March 9	11 p.m.	Summer time instituted. Worked as arranged on Signals.	Intd.
	10		Normal	Intd.
	11	3.15 pm 4.15 pm	Lines b 737 & A. Bde down owing to shell fire. All lines restored to normal.	Intd.
	12		Lines Killed down between Div. Art. & all Inf Bdes. Sta LOCKET at 138 Bde Sch. wrecked in bed.	Intd.
	13		Lines b 737 & 138 Inf. Bde broken by shell fire in BETHUNE & SAILLY LABOURSE Rnd.	Intd.
	14		Contact patrol Rocket carried out in CUINCHY Sector. 139 Bde. moved into line between 137 & 137 Bde. Bde HQ at ANNEQUIN FOSSE 9. Thrown in airline. 3 Coles run from Junction Pole between BETHUNE & BEUVRY to SAILLY CHATEAU if necessary.	Intd.
	15		Normal	Intd.
	16		Art. Signal School closed at DOUY (Australian) instructors staying at NOEUX CHELLES, instructed to report	Intd.

Army Form C. 2118.

WAR DIARY
or
INTELLIGENCE SUMMARY.
(Erase heading not required.)

Instructions regarding War Diaries and Intelligence Summaries are contained in F. S. Regs., Part II. and the Staff Manual respectively. Title pages will be prepared in manuscript.

Place	Date	Hour	Summary of Events and Information	Remarks and references to Appendices
FOUQUIRES	1918 March 17		Naval Commercial teb arranged daily between Alfred Lecointe in Div. Arta and french arty	Enc.
	18.		Proposal submitted to SXO for direct routes Fer: 137 Inf. Bde. and 231 R.F.A. Bde. at ANNEQUIN. Buzfk 80s Ygo. 20 pair Enamel cable.	Enc.
	19.		Normal	Enc.
	20.		Lines to 139 Bde. put through in new trench cable route SAILLY LABOURSE and FOSSE 9 ANNEQUIN.	Enc.
	21.		Normal	Enc.
	22.		Raid on CAMBRIN & HOHENZOLLERN Sectors by enemy. Forward trench lines K Coys all broken but SOS signals repaired. 13. Attack recap. met 12.18 am.	Enc.
	23.		Major Gen. THWAITES CRMG D.M.I. Confiscated men on duty in Signal Office on their way through road Withdrew.	Enc.
	24.		Working fork of 400 men employed digging cable trench for route by road 18th March. 1st AUCHY. 4/137 Bde dugout experimental.	Enc.

Lieut. R.E. WILLS M.M. R.E. for OC. March this coy. from RE army signals.

A5834 Wt. W4973/M687 750,000 8/16 D. D. & L. Ltd. Forms/C.2118/13

Army Form C. 2118.

WAR DIARY
INTELLIGENCE SUMMARY.
(Erase heading not required.)

Instructions regarding War Diaries and Intelligence Summaries are contained in F. S. Regs., Part II. and the Staff Manual respectively. Title pages will be prepared in manuscript.

Place	Date 1918	Hour	Summary of Events and Information	Remarks and references to Appendices
FOUQUIRES	March 25		Rain fell through & ALBATROSES OH for G. off.	
			Lt Synd. 11th Canadian Div. visited 6C Lights Refe. Wef. Lt	Enr
	26		Normal.	Enr
	27		Div. 2 front taken over by 1st & 55th Divs.	Enr
	28		All Bdes. move with the Divd. 137 Bde. LENS Sek. Sqm DIEVIN 138 Bde. to PRESTES 145 139 Bde. ST PIERRE	Enr
	29		Divl office closed PRISNE 5-TPM. opened at BRACQUEMONT	Enr
	30		Normal.	Enr
	31		Normal.	Enr

46th Divisional Engineers

46th (NORTH MUDLAND) SIGNAL COMPANY R. E.

APRIL 1918.

Army Form C. 2118.

WAR DIARY
or
INTELLIGENCE SUMMARY.
(Erase heading not required.)

Instructions regarding War Diaries and Intelligence Summaries are contained in F. S. Regs., Part II. and the Staff Manual respectively. Title pages will be prepared in manuscript.

Place	Date	Hour	Summary of Events and Information	Remarks and references to Appendices
BRACQUEMONT	1/8/16		Signal Coy detailed to train mounted infantry order in despatch riding. Brigade	
	2		Normal	
	3		Buried cable route prospected from Brigade Hqrs to LIEVEN forward to test Batts. 4500 yds.	
	4/8		Existing cable and buried (?) reviewed. Wireless Station erected at Bde Hqrs in the line. Visual communication established from Bos(?) to Boles and Bde to Bn Hqrs	
	9		Wireless messages received at AWs during Eng Army Corps from SS-K Bn Sos and other Stations north of LA BASSÉE Canal during attack by enemy against our troads(?) and HILL 70 S. PIERRE sector	
			Heavy gas-shelling by enemy on PHILOSOPHE - LENS road. Despatch riders made (?) to pieces left at Bgade HQrs of group B gas shells 2(?). Heavy traffic on Bn HQ Sig J office. AB RC messages totd 937 Msg calls 773	
	10/11		Normal	
	12		138 Bde relieved in HILL 70 sector by 6th Bde. 139 Bde clear area of S. PIERRE. Relieved by Can S. Bde.	

Army Form C. 2118.

WAR DIARY
INTELLIGENCE SUMMARY.
(Erase heading not required.)

Instructions regarding War Diaries and Intelligence Summaries are contained in F. S. Regs., Part II. and the Staff Manual respectively. Title pages will be prepared in manuscript.

Place	Date 1918	Hour	Summary of Events and Information	Remarks and references to Appendices
BRUAY	Ap 13		Div Hdqrs moved from BRACQUEMONT to BRUAY scheme training for open warfare commenced.	Inh
	14 15 16		Normal — Division in rest — Training for open warfare	Inh
	17		Wired + Wireless scheme completed by 2/2 MILLS & Signals 139 Bde in event of Brigade manning defended locality of BETHUNE – BEUVRY, SAILLY – on – NOYELLES	Inh
	18		SAILLY LA BOURSE defended locality manned by 139 Inf Bde	Inh
	19		Normal	Inh
	20 21 22		Normal Training for open warfare	Inh

WAR DIARY

INTELLIGENCE SUMMARY.

(Erase heading not required.)

Army Form C. 2118.

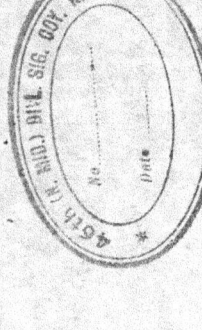

Place	Date	Hour	Summary of Events and Information	Remarks and references to Appendices
BRUAY	Apl 23		Morning order No 109 received referred postings of men to be taken over in ESSARS and GORRE Sectors from 137 & 138 Divisional Signal Coy. O.S.C Sigs. 1st Div. & 55th Div. interviewed.	SM
GOSNAY	24		Div. Hdqrs at Chateau CHARMEUX GOSNAY (A.A.M.G.) Cable wagon laid air pair from FOUQUIERES to left Bde rear Parson BETHUNE	SM
	25		ESSARS Section. 137 Inf Bde relieved 166 Inf Bde. Forward communications consisted of one open line to each battalion. GORRE Section. 139 Inf Bde relieved S & JBde Communications forward Batn. Hqrs consisted of one cable pair to each Batn. 138 Bde. moved to Div. reserve Hqrs Chateau S.PRY FOUQUIERES)	SM
	26		ROUTE A KEEP (Gosnay Sector) attacked & captured by enemy	SM
	27		Normal	SM
	28		"Route A Keep" regained by 137 & 139 Bde. Very heavy artillery fire brought down forward communications. Spr CRATCHLEY recommended for MM for repairing lines after he had been gassed & was almost blind	SM

Army Form C. 2118.

WAR DIARY
INTELLIGENCE SUMMARY.
(Erase heading not required.)

Place	Date 1918	Hour	Summary of Events and Information	Remarks and references to Appendices
GOSNAY	29	Normal	2/L Smith Sparkling recommended for MM for repairing lines under shell fire on nights of 25/26, 26/27	
	30	Normal	Sgt H Thomas 139 Pte recommended for MM repairing lines at ESSARS between 24 & 28 Cyt	

Army Form C. 2118.

Vol 35
46 Div Signal Co. RE

WAR DIARY
or
INTELLIGENCE SUMMARY.
(Erase heading not required.)

Instructions regarding War Diaries and Intelligence Summaries are contained in F.S. Regs., Part II. and the Staff Manual respectively. Title pages will be prepared in manuscript.

Place	Date 1918	Hour	Summary of Events and Information	Remarks and references to Appendices
GUINAY	May 1		Spr. MULROONEY and 5 men, No 2 Sect, admitted hospital suffering from shell gas poisoning	Sgh
	2		Cable line to Brigade cut by shell fire reported.	Sgh
	3		Armoured cable laid in RT BLANCHE river from GUINAY to BETHUNE (Air 18 to Left Bde HQ.) Spr. BATES wounded in fact while on this work.	Sgh
	4		Scheme (attached marked "A") submitted to CE Branch, for the burying of cables to Brigade HQrs approved. B: letter 3083/30/9 received, detailing brigades to supply labour for this work	Sgh
	5		Work begun on cable trench LA BASSEE CANAL to GORE CHATEAU; 80 men of 138th Bde. dug 160 yds. to Sept 4'6". Width encountered all from 3'-4' depth. 2/Lieut WILLS R.E. supervised. Anchor conto at FOUQUIERES shelled down in 5 tops. Cable suspected by NCO NICKSONS Signals.	Sgh
	6		O.C. Signals arranged with Bde. Major 137 Sig. Co. for supply of 200 men nightly in two parties for digging cable trench. Bde. Major of Batt. HQ at LE HAMEL. Labour arranged and cable carried from Corp.t Continued cable trench to GORE CHATEAU. 489339 Spr. HENDAN 91 and 492176 Spr. HA HONAS were awarded the Military Medal this day	Sgh

A5834. Wt.W4973/M687 750,000 8/16 D.D. & L. Ltd. Forms/C.2118/13

WAR DIARY
or
INTELLIGENCE SUMMARY.

Army Form C. 2118.

Place	Date 1918	Hour	Summary of Events and Information	Remarks and references to Appendices
(10 MAY)	May 7		O.C. Signal and 3rd Army Coms. visited BETHUNE forward with C.R.E. of 46th Div and 3rd Canadian Div with a view to establishing forward combined Army Hqrs. lines. O.C. 170 Tunnelling Co. reconnoitred mining sewers and underground passages in BETHUNE for laying safe cable lines. Three digging parties of 50 men 30 and 100 men respectively continued cable trench to GORE working party of 50 men commenced cable trench from railway to LE HAMEL by	SM
	8	1am	Second party of 60 men from 137 Bde. continued work on cable trench at LE HAMEL. Work executed at depths of 2'6" to 4'. 200 yards at 4' deep + 100 yds. Working parties recouped and tools and cable served.	SM
		6pm	Parties of 100, 100, 60, 100, worked on Cable trench to GORE CHATEAU, 600 yds. completed — Cable laid & trench filled in work done.	SM
	9	4am	150 yds shallow trench dug.	
			150 men from 1st Batt. of 137 Inf Bde. Completed Trench from Railway to LE HAMEL Batt. Hqrs. Cpls. BIRLEY and WILLIAMS found 2 pour announces alive in trackway — connecting they marched to LOISNE CHATEAU. Signal Officer in Case of Enemy attack warned (attached)	SM
	10		No working parties available. Hqr. 078 Spr. A. CRITCHLEY was awarded the Military Medal (chg B/15/U). Hqrs. 1414 L/Cpl. Wt. JOYNSON and 149015 Spr J. BEECH were wounded yesterday near BEUVRY — the former to hospital — the latter at duty.	SM
	11		No working parties available. W/Cpl. WILES took out proposed Cable trench from BET point in Railway Cutting — (BEUVRY — BETHUNE to proposed new Left Bde Hqrs. 150 yards.	SM
	12		100 men from A.W.E. Details dug trench from point yesterday to S.H. depth. 200 men from A.W.E. Details arrived yesterday. BEUVRY — BETHUNE and 4 m worked 9.5.30 pm. Enemy shell fire drove us. Details part delayed procedure to work on GORE turned Levels until 9.30 pm. Second part of 100 yds. completed work on this trench. Cable laid & total. Spr. CARD, RAE, and MURISON were wounded of BETHUNE.	SM

Army Form C. 2118.

WAR DIARY
or
INTELLIGENCE SUMMARY.
(Erase heading not required.)

Instructions regarding War Diaries and Intelligence Summaries are contained in F. S. Regs., Part II. and the Staff Manual respectively. Title pages will be prepared in manuscript.

Place	Date 1918	Hour	Summary of Events and Information	Remarks and references to Appendices
BDS MAY	May 13		Connecting route from new left Bde. Hqrs. near railway cutting BEUVRY - BETHUNE road. Completed by parties of 100 men from 3rd details - 8 ft deep French. 2/Lt. WETHORNS joined company from 1st Army depot.	SW
	14		Two parties of 50 men dug connecting cable trench from Rl. Bde. HQ to test point on main buried route across BEUVRY - BETHUNE road. 1 depth 8 feet. Lt. JONES R.E. supervised. 75 men under supervision of 2/Lt. WILES continued trench from BEUVRY test point towards VERQUIN.	SW
	15		Work continued on cable route BEUVRY - VERQUIN	SW
	16		Cable trench dug between new Rifle Bde. AM. HQ. (Rly-crossing BEUVRY - BETHUNE road) and new left group R.F.A. Hqrs. 175 yards. Two parties of 110 men worked on BEUVRY - VERQUIN cable trench. One length of 25 pair lead core cable laid in trench in 5 ft deep trench.	SW
	17		Work on cable trench continued.	
		10.30AM	Telegraph test rod used as instrument wire at wireless station (Aus. H.Q.) was hived. Cause unknown.	SW
	18		Work continued on BEUVRY - VERQUIN cable trench by parties of 150 men	SW

Army Form C. 2118.

WAR DIARY
or
INTELLIGENCE SUMMARY.
(Erase heading not required.)

Place	Date	Hour	Summary of Events and Information	Remarks and references to Appendices
GOSNAY	May 1918 19		BERRY - VERQUIN C.O.'s visit. 2nd Lt. Gee additional Foot [Inspected] G. D. of K. f. & 8 Sect. in training. Tent filled in.	[initials]
	20		No new Construction work on above front. Artificers reserve of [Huts] from [Bruilen] personnel of Sec. CRATCHLEY AIM.	[initials]
	21		[Pvt?] [T?] [J?] [Bunted] in BERRY - VERQUIN Burnt Cable kept under by/Lt WILLS R.E.	[initials]
	22		Cpl. WILLIAM S.H. wounded whilst laying Airline Left Division Left Corps near LAWE CANAL.	[initials]
	23		Personnel of Signal Coy arrived at funeral of Lieut. CRE HACH WALTHEW MC. Capt HINTON MC at FOUQUIERES.	[initials]
	24		Telephone traffic throughout 46 Div. except in case of medical emergency not necessarily maintenance. Orders issued by O.C. 46 Div. Signal Co (attached).	[initials]

Army Form C. 2118.

WAR DIARY
or
INTELLIGENCE SUMMARY.
(Erase heading not required.)

Instructions regarding War Diaries and Intelligence Summaries are contained in F.S. Regs., Part II. and the Staff Manual respectively. Title pages will be prepared in manuscript.

A6 Tar Signal C.R.E.

Place	Date 1918 May	Hour	Summary of Events and Information	Remarks and references to Appendices
GOSNAY	25		Report submitted to H.Qrs. Ref. non-Telephone Army (yesterday) instructions	
	26		New airline route via VAUDRICOURT used to supply additional communication to Right Brigade	
	27		Spr. CAMERON wounded at Batty Hqrs. on LA BASSÉE canal.	
	28		Hqrs TANDY wounded - all lines to Right Brigade on BETHUNE - BEUVRY rd kept active fire. 2/Lt. THOMAS took Right brigade Interim Comm. Officer.	
	29		Wires Right Bde. Hqrs. Kept shelled. H. JONES Kd. Harburg when home let. & 5529 shed against	
	30		OSBORNE wounded by shell fire in HESDIGNEUIL. Normal	
	31		Normal	

WAR DIARY 'A'

46th Division Signal Communications
Estimate of work required to render lines to Battns safe.

Item	From	To	No of pairs	Distance	Remarks
E Spt. Bde	Beuvry Bethune Rd near Rt Bde HQ	La Bassée Canal F 7 a 3.9	20	1500 yds.	Dig new trench
D Rt Bde (1)	Drawbridge I3 C 5.4	Spt. Bn HQ Rt. Bde.	6	200 "	Probable date of completion 13-5-18
(2)	"	Rt Bn HQ Gorre	6	800 "	
A Rt Bde	Point on Canal X 28 a 2.3	Left Bn HQ Loisne	6	400 "	
B Left Bde	Point on Canal le Hamel X 21 C 6.5	Rt Bn HQ Left Bde.	6	600 "	
C Left Bde	Point on Lawe Canal X 13 d 4.0	Left Bn HQ Left Bde.	6	600 "	

Labour 4100 yds = 4100 tasks to dig, put in cable and fill in

Work to be done in alphabetical order as noted in Column 1.

Cable required :- Ropes of 6 prs. 2600 yds
                         " 20 " 1500 "

Action in case of Attack.
Signal Arrangements

On receipt of code word "NETTLE" from O.C Divisional Signals, the following orders will immediately come into operation.

GENERAL
(1) Every available means of communication will be manned continuously, also Aeroplane dropping grounds.

LINES
(2) Linemen will be clearly instructed by the responsible Signal officer as to the particular tactical lines, on the maintenance of which they must concentrate

(3) Operators on duty on telegraph, wireless or visual, must be reminded of the necessity of immediately reporting any breakdown of the communications and the Superintendent on duty will be responsible that every available means of communication is attempted in order to get messages through.

PIGEONS
(4) Additional birds may be obtained, if required by Bdes on application through Divl Hdqrs Signals

MOVES OF H.Q.
(5) Remember always to report any impending, and completed change of your hdqrs to all units with which you are in communication, front, rear, or flank.

(6) Inf. Bdes and Artillery Bde officers must ensure that all alternative means of communication are made known to the officers commanding units especially Battery, Battalion & Company commanders.

The various means of communication are :—

1. Telephone & Telegraph   4. Runners
2. Visual   5. Despatch riders (horse or cycle)
3. Wireless (including Power buzzer & Amplifier)   6. Pigeons.

(7) Contact Aeroplane.

P.T.O.

Issued
7 pm
9/5/18

Copy N° 10

[signature]
Major R.E.
Divisional Signal Co. R.E.

Signal Orders.

1. From 8 am 24th inst. to 8 am 25th inst. no telephone will be used except those required for the maintenance of Signal lines or in case of tactical urgency.

2. This will not apply to urgent medical messages.

3. All telephone calls passed under the provision of para 2 will be recorded and reported to O.C. Div Signals by 1 pm 25th inst.

4. All other available means of communication may be used — telegraph — runners — visual — wireless — pigeons etc but no telephonic speech.

5. O's C Sigs Nos 2, 3, 4, 5, RA (including sub sections) will be responsible that the restriction is strictly carried out, to ensure a reasonable test of battle conditions.

6. The following officers will be on duty in the Divl Signal offices at the times named and will be personally responsible that the test is thoroughly made

   24th inst
   - 8 am – 12 noon — Capt Johnston
   - 12 noon – 4 pm — Lieut Boone
   - 4 pm – 8 pm — " Lowe
   - 8 – 12 midnt — " Thomas
   - 12 midnt – 4 am — " Wills
   - 4 am – 8 am — Major Lewis ASO.

7. A report will be rendered to OC Div Signal Coy by 2 pm 25th inst by all officers of the Coy, containing their observations on the working of the day's communications.

War Diary

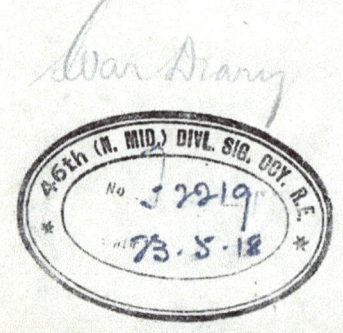

Major R.E. (T)
46th Divisional Signal Co. R.E.

Head qrs.
46th Divn.

Reference 46th Divn. G 588

The suspension of telephone calls for the 24 hours ending 8 am 25th inst. caused no inconvenience to Brigade & Battn Staffs

Other means of communication were used and proved satisfactory and expeditious.

Wireless and power-buzzer were successful.

Visual — So forward work was used successfully.

Pigeons were flown but, owing to the boisterous weather the service was rather slow.

Runners & Despatch riders were not increased, the normal number proving sufficient for the traffic.

The telegraph traffic through the Divisional Signal Office was very much below the average and at R.A. Inf. Bdes M.G. H.Q & Battns. only a slight increase took place

There was an increase of 35% in the number of registered despatches carried by despatch riders.

The advantages of a stringent limitation of telephone conversations would be

(a) Greater efficiency of signal service with much less strain to personnel.

(b) Excellent training for occasions when telephones may not be available.

(c) Accurate records of all transmitted orders

orders, instructions &c.

(d) Inadvertent any Reduction in the number of telephones to be maintained and transported

(e) More scope for alternative methods of communication

(f) Less danger of overhearing by enemy

25/8/17

R.A. Lewis
Major

…

WAR DIARY

INTELLIGENCE SUMMARY

Army Form C. 2118.

Place	Date	Hour	Summary of Events and Information	Remarks and references to Appendices
CITADEL LES CHARLIEUX	1918 JUNE 1		Normal	
	2		Shuttless day throughout 1st Corps – No telephone used. 6th Class Div Sigs School assembled at LEVENTIE ander over hi	
GOSNAY	3		Normal	
	4		Demonstration given to 139 Inf Bde with mersys carrying rockets	
	5		Our cable in AUBIGEE Cutted broken by Shell fire	
	6		Normal	
	7		Normal	
	9		Optical day from BETHUNE – BEDUNY had constantly Op front to Gro 2-4. with Reneby lined rocks	
	10		Demonstration to 139 Inf Bde with message carrying Rockets	
			BETHUNE proven & cable's of cemetery by Collin Kirby Sewell Bryer	
	11		Sub found cable cut at junction of LAGORGEE and LAVE cavados	
	12		Work continued in BETHUNE Cemetery. Cleared from junction of LA BASSEE Road. Div Spare phone moved from LEVENTIE to BRAY Ent newdreme	

Army Form C. 2118.

WAR DIARY
INTELLIGENCE SUMMARY
(Erase heading not required.)

Instructions regarding War Diaries and Intelligence Summaries are contained in F. S. Regs., Part II. and the Staff Manual respectively. Title pages will be prepared in manuscript.

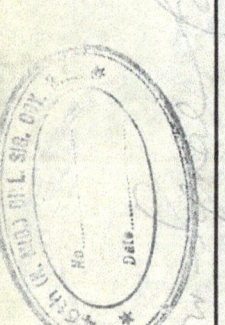

Place	Date	Hour	Summary of Events and Information	Remarks and references to Appendices
GOSNAY.	June 1918 13		Cable trench dug across PRISON road BETHUNE connecting nord & north of Fleet sewer. 8 foot deep bury near BOUVRY. Cut 6 sheet pull supply repairing.	
	14		Buried Cable completed in from road BETHUNE & Belmont Cellar. Cables field through sewer in street to LA BRETTE river.	
	15.		Forward line held up during attack by E.3.2 Div on left. Right	
	16. 17 18		Normal.	
	19		OC reconnoitred BETHUNE sewers with a view to further installation for cable route.	
	20.		Brig General NOBLE. U.S army inspected repairs of division & visited Signal School.	

Army Form C. 2118.

WAR DIARY
or
INTELLIGENCE SUMMARY.
(Erase heading not required.)

Place	Date	Hour	Summary of Events and Information	Remarks and references to Appendices
GIVENCHY	June 20		Line in LA BLANCHE river to Left Bdy. Fairly quiet except for shell fire near BETHUNE.	
	21		Normal	
	22			
	23			
	24			
	25		Line as above (LABLANCHE river) to Left Bdy.	
	26		Normal. Work completed in forming new Battalion Left Bdy. to Right Bdy. at RAILWAY CUTTING BETHUNE-BETHUNE Line moved from	
	27		New Bdy. of Left Bdy. extends to L. 13F Bdy. MINX to Bn HQ	
	28		Bn. transferred from 12 to 13th Corps. Line arranged now Coys OC	
	29		Various arrangements to connect new Left Bdy HQ complete. Bn at HESDIGNEUL	
	30		Normal	

Army Form C. 2118.

WAR DIARY
or
INTELLIGENCE SUMMARY.
(Erase heading not required.)

Instructions regarding War Diaries and Intelligence Summaries are contained in F. S. Regs., Part II. and the Staff Manual respectively. Title pages will be prepared in manuscript.

Place	Date	Hour	Summary of Events and Information	Remarks and references to Appendices
GORRAY	JULY 1918			
	1		Normal maintenance.	
	2		Normal.	
	3		Normal.	
	4		O.C. visited 5th M.A. Bde. re arrangement of communications.	
	5		138 Coy. lines down. Maintenance party sent to repair.	
	6		Normal.	
	7		do.	
	8		Enemy aeroplane had to with 137 W. Div. Sigs. Spade. POWER had new W/T.	
	9		Road messages.	
	10		O.C. Sigs. attended R. Div. Sigs. School on "Communication".	
	11		Normal maintenance.	
			Scheme drawn up and approved by A.A. Sgds. 13th Div. and "G" Branch Div. Staff for being existing Civil Civilian and telephone System in BÉTHUNE and burying cable to PRISON and to Railway Crossing BÉTHUNE–BEUVRY Catund road to Farm	

A5834 Wt. W4973/M687 750,000 8/16 D. D. & L. Ltd. Forms/C.2118/13

Army Form C. 2118.

WAR DIARY
or
INTELLIGENCE SUMMARY.
(Erase heading not required.)

46 DIV SIGNAL COY R.E.

Place	Date 1918	Hour	Summary of Events and Information	Remarks and references to Appendices
GOSNAY	JULY 12		Cable and tote dumped in BETHUNE for burying cable route Cemetery Gosnay with civil system. 137 Inf. Bde. moved supply.	
	13		170 men completed work of digging 5ft deep trench between TRIBUNAL and PRISON BETHUNE. Pair cable lightly covered. 4+ pairs in & rewired and bare - shotted cable laid & tested. Trench filled in & slates of SETT 200 men dug trench 4'6" deep - slates & slates on N. side of STREET from PLACE ST ELOI towards BEUVRY. 350 yds long. Cable (1 pair) laid, tested, and trench filled in.	MM
	14		139 Inf. Bde. asked to supply 100 men on 17th & 18th for cable work on lateral burried route from BETHUNE towards BEUVRY. (A17/8). also 500 men for the repair of R.R.3 and R.S. Rly. & Dieweissued lines Ext. scheme in forward area. By BASSEE CANAL IS ENDBURIED SET	MM
	15		Normal.	MM
	16		Forward portion of burried route (see A11/2) taped out.	MM

WAR DIARY
or
INTELLIGENCE SUMMARY.

(Erase heading not required.)

Army Form C. 2118.

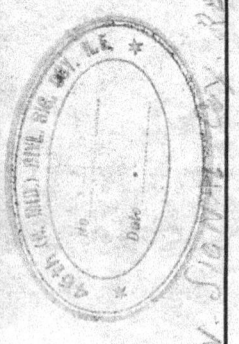

46 DIV SIGNAL 1918

Place	Date	Hour	Summary of Events and Information	Remarks and references to Appendices
GOSNAY	JULY 1918 17		Party of 550 men Completed Cable trench for N-Cet of BETHUNE - BEUVRY road. Cables (41 pairs) laid in trench and tested. Length of trench 1200 yds = length of trench.	
	18		Sinking of above trench commenced. Work commenced on buried route - FL LES QUATIGNES 440 men Coy 1. 6 ft deep. Cable laid & trench filled in.	
	19.		30 men employed digging new rotary cutting & OD test point on BETHUNE - BEUVRY road. Cabling & filling in completed. 360 men continued cable trench towards ESSARS from LES QUATIGNES. RUE DU BOIS reached, cables laid & trench filled in.	
	20		Sinking of new buried route proceeding	
	21.		G. 17/12 recd detailing 138 Inf. Bde. Frontage. 580 men for arrears target. Pouts in each night 23rd, 24th and 25th July.	
	22		Work began out for buried routes in continuation of equating and Inspection of Corps transport by G.O.C. followed by visit to visit Menin M/F	

WAR DIARY or INTELLIGENCE SUMMARY

Army Form C. 2118.

Place	Date 1918	Hour	Summary of Events and Information	Remarks and references to Appendices
GOSNAY	JULY 23		Party of 300 men for burying cable laid out through area on Light Railway. 460 yds trench dug to depth of 3 feet. Left spare of Signal Centre to Group offices at GW Depot on Communications.	
	24		450 men employed. Portion of trench made off unfinished yesterday, and remainder spun up. Support Bays WR. 5 CARS. Lieut W. ALDRICH wounded.	
	25		Cable route continued towards LA MOTTE. 450 yds 6 trench dug. Cable laid in, tested, and route filled in.	
	26		Normal	
	27		C4S	
	28		New work. Tape'd in forward buried route.	
	29		Party of 450 men. Continued work on Rear trench Trunk to LA MOTTE. Heavy shelling by enemy. Trench not completed. Cables however shell dug. Any hit. 800 yds.	
	30		450 men completed above trench + 350 yards new work. Cable laid & tested to LAMOTTE - CANAL Road	

Army Form C. 2118.

WAR DIARY
or
INTELLIGENCE SUMMARY.
(Erase heading not required.)

Instructions regarding War Diaries and Intelligence Summaries are contained in F. S. Regs., Part II. and the Staff Manual respectively. Title pages will be prepared in manuscript.

Place	Date	Hour	Summary of Events and Information	Remarks and references to Appendices
GODNAY	1918 July 31.		350 men Completed C.T. trench to B.A.BATTEE Canal. 100 men dug spur into new batt. Gun war E5d.a.m. Cooking & feeding Complete	

Army Form C. 2118.

WAR DIARY
INTELLIGENCE SUMMARY
(Erase heading not required.)

Instructions regarding War Diaries and Intelligence Summaries are contained in F.S. Regs., Part II. and the Staff Manual respectively. Title pages will be prepared in manuscript.

146 Div. Signal Co. R.E. (T.F.)

Place	Date 1918	Hour	Summary of Events and Information	Remarks and references to Appendices
GASMAY	1		Normal Maintenance	
"	2		Divisional Sports were held at G & O officer on the ground	
"	3		Telephone lines were put out to the [Bde?] Do not laid 3 7pr & 9 9pr & 2 lines extended to a distance of 40 yards. Machine Gun: 3 special loops & jacks in use at M & S2 Cat points. The company is trunk to Corps: The cable crossing the Canal to 3 special loops & ? at Fd.0.6 & Cat was done a little north of the canal at Fd.0.6 & Lat was done a little north of the canal	
"	4		440 rest supplied from the E.b. to Swomh 9/E 129 Bde standard at Le Plumet Relay Stn — Standard at Sissons X25 Central at (knee) 40 points, then 400 yards between X19 d.55.60 and X19 6.0.30. Cable used was 3 x 7pr armoured. 9 9pr armoured. 2Iron Covered. Total 41 points. The 7 pr armoured Cable goes a lot of trouble in falling out during laying. Recrerebuing a joint X19 c.25.05. Working party entrained at 3 a.m.	

WAR DIARY
INTELLIGENCE SUMMARY

Army Form C. 2118.

HQ 46th Div Signal Coy (E)

Place	Date	Hour	Summary of Events and Information	Remarks and references to Appendices
GOSNAY	5		350 km fm S.6.b.8. Blanc...d laid 350 yards trunk cable fm X.19.b.10.30 to Road. 9 Horse Coal at X.19.a.7.8. Cable laid was 3 × 7pr Brass sheet - 1 yard ground. 9 ton ground. Depth 6". Ditch crossing reqrs strengthening with railway lath. Considerable enemy shelling. 1 cat wounded.	
	6		Buried cable party cancelled but a supporting pf 12 cont up & dug but 15 yards reopen cable dropped into the canal. Enemy aeroplanes down right of S.17. Water very calm & cable spread low. Chaps SS Bn & 4FC rocks to L Cpl Ash.	
	7		Sig Hors to Mazingarbe. Fuels attendance.	
	8		10 km fm 1st Mazingarbe repairs to OP line for jointing.	
	9		Normal working.	

Army Form C. 2118.

WAR DIARY
INTELLIGENCE SUMMARY.
(Erase heading not required.)

Place	Date	Hour	Summary of Events and Information	Remarks and references to Appendices
GOSNAY	10		Machine Gunners moved from Verdrel and Wood to Hesdigneul. Pour greatly cut up from here to Rear H.Q. head quarters. Coys Winters Officer went round sector with a view to putting in a listening set. No suitable places found.	
	11.		N party of 450 men of the 1/5 Lincolns started to dig 41 foxes avoiding of 3'×7' by bores plank. 9 yards apart. 2 teams about from X19d56 to X20c2535. The party worked badly very slowly. Full depth of 6' not obtained. Trench left open. Battalion ordered in consequence by G.O.C. Div. to turn out again at 12.¹ᵘ—	
	12/		Same working party as on 11ᵗʰ completed trench to depth 4/6', weather fair & trench fires in. A.D. Signals & O.C. Sigs. offices at H.Q. between Beaury Church & GORRE brewery. Weather fine dry by the Pakiques labour party.	

Army Form C. 2118.

WAR DIARY
INTELLIGENCE SUMMARY.
(Erase heading not required.)

Instructions regarding War Diaries and Intelligence Summaries are contained in F. S. Regs., Part II. and the Staff Manual respectively. Title pages will be prepared in manuscript.

H⁴ 6th Divl Signal Co. 18/4/17

Place	Date	Hour	Summary of Events and Information	Remarks and references to Appendices
GOSNAY	13		Demonstration. A/Corp. set out to 138 Bde by 2. Lt Poore.	
	14		O.C. Signals went on leave to England & Lt Sheppard returned & took charge of 138 Bde. Sigs.	
	15		Portuguese (400) dug from Fd. A. no 10 Quincy chateau including in chateau approx 400 yards dug. Cable laid & filled in. 5 Casualties including 2 R.E. sappers. 41 pairs laid. The Coyfield two mile in cable laid & filled in. 5 Casualties including 2 R.E. sappers. 41 pairs laid. Ead was to appear to do 2 miles dig & 2 miles deep. La Pauline road crossed. from GORRE Bde to Bruay.	
	16		400 Portuguese Coys continued laying cable from Gor Bde to Bruay. 41 pairs. 8th Queens Relief to F.d. 8.0. for 400 yds in town put in trench ———— Work done between 8 am & 2 pm supervised by Lt Sheldon.	
	17		Portuguese & 8th Queens 300 yds from Frameries Quincy chateau undug trench completed. Cable laid & trench filled in to last covt.	

Army Form C. 2118.

WAR DIARY
or
INTELLIGENCE SUMMARY.
(Erase heading not required.)

Instructions regarding War Diaries and Intelligence Summaries are contained in F. S. Regs. Part II. and the Staff Manual respectively. Title pages will be prepared in manuscript.

H.Q. 1st Div Signal Co RE (TF)

Place	Date	Hour	Summary of Events and Information	Remarks and references to Appendices
GOSNAY	18		Pothynn reckd Bevry Church	
	19			
	20		2.00 Pothynn swimming at 1 pm (3 hour late) at F.3.b.5 (firm ground) + dig 400 yds of trent on North bank of canal to F.3.c.3.6. + 1 room consists of 3 7pr brass desk. 9 gas courses + 2 W.N. courses too heavy + failed in. 22nd R.G. with RE were in charge of the dig. Work is to extend from GORRE Brewery to B2 (F.d.60.00) + run along the railway embankment	

Army Form C. 2118.

WAR DIARY
INTELLIGENCE SUMMARY.
(Erase heading not required.)

Instructions regarding War Diaries and Intelligence Summaries are contained in F. S. Regs., Part II. and the Staff Manual respectively. Title pages will be prepared in manuscript.

4/6th Div Signal Coy NZEF

Place	Date	Hour	Summary of Events and Information	Remarks and references to Appendices
GOSNAY	21		175 Polhynier arrived at Mushroom Spur (F13 central) at 8.45 am by light railway from Mazingarbe. Stales went being cable at 9.20 to cross the Canal at 3 places by F3 C.3.6 & at 25 yds interval on other side. They lay by from F3e36 along railway embankment to F2 d.40.45 a distance of 350 yards. A dry out lie by at F3 c.25.47. Everything filled in st h 1.30 p.m.	
	22		200 Polhynier lay from F2 d.70.45 to F2 c.95.27 a distance of approx 350 yds. Cable laid & filled in	

WAR DIARY
INTELLIGENCE SUMMARY.
(Erase heading not required.)

Army Form C. 2118.

Place	Date	Hour	Summary of Events and Information	Remarks and references to Appendices
GOSNAY	23		350 Polygons dug from F,15.c.9.2.7 to F,15.d.60.00 & between 9/600 yds. Also two test dy ads 8'x8'xg' at F,15.c.0.45 & F,15.d.00.15. Cable laid right in to BD dug out (at F,15.d.60.00). One set of 9,41 pr joints made. Diggin throughout was difficult owing to 4' of chalk above the ordinary substratum.	
	24		Work done on dy outs in above lining; as the Boards appeared to be many both a Wooden station was put at Essen & worked back to a station at Bowvy; Beyonds & Invaneds were used for those Surveying. Several M Buds sending stations cand to work so as to give to Board the agreement. Totals forward have been taking place.	
	25		Lines between district lining & test strips were found up at BF + BG dug outs. 3 good 3 Boards in 1 test.	
	26		Dis could between P joint box & BD test box , from being opened. Local forces of local strips continued. roles dy ads. (unable to get 41 pr P+S boards.)	

46th (N. MIDL) DIV. L SIG. COY. R.E.
HQ & Div. Signal Co. RE (TF)

Army Form C. 2118.

WAR DIARY
INTELLIGENCE SUMMARY.
(Erase heading not required.)

HQ # Div Lg Sig bn RE (F)

Place	Date	Hour	Summary of Events and Information	Remarks and references to Appendices
GOSNAY	27		Threat opened 300 yards right of BD Coft box. Dis between Tr front + BD Dis centrally (outs) is fibre at BD. Pairs put through. Rate clear. Still awaiting 41 pr fifty worked loads.	
	28		Carried test on BV. BdS rest. Telly line between BV + BU. 7 apps is cabot. Faults discovered is joint from Battalion Bown road — badly made joint. Faults cleand out & retested.	
	29		Tests between BV + BU — OK. Testing from BU to BS. There was difficulty at first owing to linemen also could load at BdS Telly & short required on pair. All line proved clear.	

Army Form C. 2118.

WAR DIARY
INTELLIGENCE SUMMARY.
(Erase heading not required.)

Instructions regarding War Diaries and Intelligence Summaries are contained in F. S. Regs., Part II. and the Staff Manual respectively. Title pages will be prepared in manuscript.

Place	Date	Hour	Summary of Events and Information	Remarks and references to Appendices
GOSNAY.	30		Orders local war. fixed up at B.G. Observation of One Centigrade now (could fixed up at Bn. G. take appts & lines. (20 pour) team spirit. Runts have been slight Brown Club a 20 for believers. be to h. edded. (originals only). Letting at extends at Lowse.	
	31		Constructing reinforced cellar at O.R. fitting in Cooks Dugout. 9 guards bar been at 6 furnos. Sept. & 9 ants & Junds to energeth. to to Ant. Concurrent fitting Cellars in BDN—EB rads. Above cellars covered Shellos.	

WAR DIARY or INTELLIGENCE SUMMARY.

Army Form C. 2118.

Place	Date	Hour	Summary of Events and Information	Remarks and references to Appendices
GOSNAY	6/9/18		Handed over system of Communication to the 19th Division.	
"	13/9/18		Company entrained at CHOCQUES and proceeded to BEAUCOURT to S/HQ Reserve.	
BEAUCOURT	18/9/18		Moved from BEAUCOURT to CAUVIGNY FARM near TERTRY. Still in S/HQ Reserve.	
CAUVIGNY FM	19/9/18			
VRAIGNES	21/9/18		Company moved into the line at VRAIGNES, taking over from Right Bde of 1st Division and Left brigade of 4th Australian Division. Central communication Route Vraill-et-four VRAIGNES – HANCOURT – BERNES – VENDELLE with exchange at each of them. System of communication except attachment of W/T Set to BDO to whom HQ telephone was also run – revived established. A mean operation carried out by the division. All lines held up except line to BDO due to hill on line. Vraul & Winkes used to a limited extent and kept total through throughput. No wireless available.	
VRAIGNES	24/9/18		Advanced HQ moved to this place.	
VENDELLE	29/9/18		46 Division advanced across the S Quentin Canal and broke through the Hindenburg Line. Communication was carried out as per attack's instructions. Visual A ground, buried wires until late in the day because of intense mist. Wireless functioned to the D.O.O. throughout the day and to 137 Bde & 1157 Bde towards the close of the day.	
	29/9/18		Line burst impossible to maintain between CC 9+1 1pm the Col Hindenburg Line could be said principally established.	

WAR DIARY or INTELLIGENCE SUMMARY

Place	Date	Hour	Summary of Events and Information	Remarks and references to Appendices
VENDELLE	29/9/18 29/30/9/18		Lines back worked O.K. throughout & traffic was successfully dealt with. Action continued by 136 & 139 Bdes until lines objectives were reached when 32 Division passed through. Comm. Posts 136 & Bn H.Q. established & lines laid S. of Le Catelet by Wireless but Vimes not functioning forward of our original front line owing to the beng in the hollow and out of sight. Sufficient personnel for manning Decoeny transmitting stations not available.	

46th: DIVISIONAL SIGNAL COMPANY.

GENERAL INSTRUCTIONS FOR COMMUNICATION IN BATTLE.

The following instructions should be read in conjunction with 46th: Division General Staff instructions for operations (46th: Division G.56/17 of 14/9/18). They are intended to outline a General Scheme which will form the basis on which modifications will be superinposed according to the special circumstances of the operations in which the Division is engaged.

Economy in both cable and personnel is of the first importance and with this in view all efforts will be concentrated on the maintenance of one central Trunk Route of cable reinforced by all possible supplementary means of communication. So far as possible the Headquarters of Units to which communication during battle with superior, subordinate or lateral formations is essential will be situated on or near this main route. In cases, which are bound to arise, where this is impossible, the Headquarters of Units which are off the main route will be joined to it by means of spurs <u>run by them</u> to the nearest exchange on the main route.

GENERAL SCHEME OF COMMUNICATIONS

1. The general scheme of communication involves as already stated one main trunk cable route with exchanges at points suitable for the near establishment of Formations and Unit Headquarters. The sites of communication centres above mentioned will be chosen by the Divisional Staff in consultation with O.C. Signals.

2. This route will be reinforced between Division and Brigade by Visual D.R., Mounted Orderly and Spark Wireless Routes and between Brigade and Battalion and forward of Battalion by Visual, Loop Set, Power Buzzer-Amplifier and Runner Routes and Rockets.

3. Wherever possible Headquarters of Formations and Units will be actually at Forward Exchanges on the main cable route but when this is impossible short spurs will be run and maintained from the Formation or Unit Headquarters to the Forward Exchanges on the main route. Such spurs to be run and labelled by the Formation or Unit concerned.

4. The main route will be maintained by Division and will be run from rear Divisional Headquarters, Through advanced Division H.Q. to suitable Communication Centres central to both the Headquarters. If the situation demands it further communication centres will be chosen and the main route may be extended forward by Divisional personnel.

5. Normally routes forward of Bde. H.Q. will be laid and maintained by Brigade personnel.

6. When Brigade Headquarters move forward the Division will take over all routes in rear of the new Brigade Headquarters and will run forward the central route (preferably along one of the former Brigade - Battalion routes) to a further forward exchange situated in as close relation as possible to the new Brigade Headquarters.

7. Where it proves possible to locate Brigades at the same Headquarters or at Headquarters very close to each other, Brigade Section Officers will keep close liaison and in the former case will arrange to economise personnel by running a common Signal Office for both Brigades. In either case they will arrange their routes forward as close as possible to each other and if possible lead them into a common forward exchange at the next stepping-up place so as to facilitate as much as possible the running & forward of the main communication route after their own Headquarters has moved on.

8. In all cases where sufficient cable and labour are available the main Divisional route will be of three pairs laid on two alternative routes between exchanges; these routes to be kept as far apart as possible and looped into the exchanges. One pair will be run away from main roads and tracks which are likely to be marked on the map. Such a route is less likely to suffer seriously from shell fire and this method of procedure should therefore be persevered with even in face of considerable natural difficulties likely to delay the laying of the line.

9. In cases where speed of laying of the line is essential every effort will be made to get one straight route of two pairs to the next forward exchange completed as early as possible but if there is any likelihood of difficulty in maintaining this route a third pair by a safe if more roundabout route will be run as soon afterwards as the labour and cable become available.

2 Continued.

10. Possible arrangements of communications on the main Divisional Route are shown on Diagrams 1 and 2 attached.

11. Even when Headquarters of Formations and Units are situated at Communication Centres it will be laid down as a rule that Signal Offices shall not be established in the same dug-out or shelter as the Communication Centre though in exceptional circumstances Infantry Bdes may be allowed to have their exchanges there.

12. There will be be no separate Artillery Signal System. Artillery Staff extensions at Divisional H.Q. will run into the Divisional exchange and Artillery personnel will be pooled with Divisional personnel. The Artillery will thus share the use of the Trunk system.

13. Artillery Brigades will run telephone pairs into Communications Centres and will attach orderlies to the nearest Infantry Bde to deliver messages received by telegraph unless the distance is too great in which case special arrangements will be made.

14. Lateral communication with flank Divisions will be through their Divisional H.Q. exchange, lateral communication with flank Bdes will be through the Bde Communication Centre.

15. Lateral maintenance will be from right to left. Officers concerned will settle this debatable point with flank Officers immediately the Division take over the sector in which it is going to fight.

SUPPLEMENTARY METHODS OF COMMUNICATION.

1. **WIRELESS.**

One Wilson set and three Trench sets are available for the main Divisional Route and normally these will be disposed as follows:-

(a) Wilson set. At advanced Divisional H.Q. Keeping constant watch: controlling forward communications; and acting as a transmitting and receiving station to and from the Bde stations and the station allotted to the Divisional Observation Officer. It will also endeavour to get into communication with the Corps Directing Station and so act as a supplementary means of communication back to rear Divisional H.Q. via Corps H.Q.

(b) One trench set at or near the Brigade communication centre or in a central position with regard to Brigade Headquarters and will form supplementary means of communication at Brigade and will keep communication both with Wilson Set at A.D.H.Q. and with the Trench Set assigned to the D.O.O..

(c) One Trench Set with means of transport will be assigned to the D.O.O. This Set will be erected in a naturally concealed position as near his H.Q. as possible and will be available to dispose of the hourly pieces of information referred to in Divisional letter M....... D......... If possible this set will communicate direct with the Wilson Set at A.D.H.Q., but if range is too great will relay through the Brigade Trench Set.

(d) The third Trench Set will be in reserve at A.D.H.Q.

(e) All sets will be kept erected and tested through, whether they are kept in constant use or not.

(f) Loop sets, Power Buzzer and Aplifier will be available for communication forward of Brigade Headquarters and will be allotted by the Wireless Officer under orders of O.C. Signal Company as the situation demands.

2. **VISUAL**

(1) The general principle to be aimed at for the Divisional visualisation is a reliable supplementary means of communication between rear Divisional H.Q., forward Divisional H.Q. and Brigades.

(2) This will probably be best achieved by means of a central visual station (CVS) at a suitable point as close as possible consistent with safety to the A.D.H.Q. Communication centre, this CVS to be connected with the communication centre by telephone

(3) This CVS will work back to a terminal at rear D.H.Q. and forward to terminal Bde.Stations; transmitting stations being used where necessary.

3. **MOUNTED ORDERLIES**

6 mounted orderlies will be attached to the signal service for A.D.H.Q. under arrangements to be made by the Camp Commandant. These men will be used to provide a service between advanced D.H.Q. and Brigades or Divisional Units.

3. continued.

4. **DESPATCH RIDERS.**
Despatch Riders will be divided as required between rear and advanced Divisional Headquarters.

5. **PIGEONS.**
Pigeons will be issued under Corps arrangements to Division and will be allotted to Brigades and Battalions and to the Artillery for the use of F.O.O's as required.

6. **MESSAGE ROCKETS.**
A supply of message rockets will be available and a proportion will be issued to Brigades before they go into the line. A further supply will be kept at the forward Dump of Signal Stores at A.D.H.Q. and may be had on application to O.C. Signals.

7. **AEROPLANE SIGNALLING.**
(1) All units entitled Popham Panels will select a suitable ground station near their Headquarters, and will arrange that Panels are manned, and a good aeroplane watch kept.
(2) Dropping grounds will be selected at Brigade, Advanced Division and Rear Division H.Q., and ground strips put out; a continual watch being kept from sunrise to sunset.
(3) Brigade-Section Officers will notify O.C. Signals of the Map References of their dropping grounds and these together with those at advanced and rear Divisional H.Q. will be notified by O.C. Signals to the Squadron providing the Contact Planes co-operating with the Infantry of the Division.

****

The above general instructions are issued for the information of all concerned. Technical instructions dealing with particular phases of the system of communications are also being issued to Officers and personnel of the Divisional Signal Company.

****

SIGNAL INSTRUCTIONS

Lines.

A combined Divisional Scheme of Communications will be arranged as under:— (Diagram A attached)

(1) The 32nd A D H Q will be at R9 central and the 46th D at R8b central

(2) Forward of these Headquarters two main routes of overland cable will be laid, with Communication Centres and laterals between the latter.

(3) From 46th Division H Q three pairs by two alter-native routes will be laid forward to HUDSONS POST (HP) at R8a6,5. Here a Communication Centre will be established with a ten line cordless and a four plus three buzzer exchange. Personnel and stores will be found by 46 Div

(4) Two or if possible three pairs will be laid

(4) Two or if possible three pairs will be laid forward of this point (HP) to the position in the OLD HINDENBURG LINE (approximately G 27 d 0,5) which will be occupied on Z day by 137 Bde H Q.

(5) At this point O H a similar Communication Centre will be established. Stores will be found and the Centre manned by 137 Bde Section.

(6) The above route will be maintained by 46 Sig Coy.

(1) B From 32nd Div H Q at R9 b central three pairs will be laid forward to COLLINS COPSE (CC) at L 36 b 7,5. At this point a Communication Centre will be installed as in paragraphs 3 and 5 above. Personnel and stores for the Centre to be found by 32 Sig Coy.

(2) Forward of here two or if possible three pairs will be laid to G 21 c 5.1 which will become the next ADHQ for 32 Div. Here a similar Communication Centre will be installed as soon as circumstances permit by 32nd Div.

(3) Laterals from G 27 d D.5 to G21 c 5.1 will be run by the linesmen at the former position. At least two pairs will be laid.

LATERAL COMMUNICATIONS WITH FLANK DIVISIONS

(1) A lateral pair to the H Q 30th American Division will be run from 46 Div A D H Q at R8 b central and will be maintained by 46 Division.

(2) A Brigade lateral from CC to the Right Bde of the 30th American Division will be run and maintained by 32nd Division.

(3) Forward of this laterals will be run according to circumstances as the situation develops.

(4) Arrangements are being made with the O C Signals 1st British Division to lay and maintain laterals to 32nd Division Advance H Q at R9 central and HUDSONS POST as required.

(5) Five pairs will be run under arrangements made by 46 division to connect up the Advanced H Q of the 32nd Division at R9 b central with the 46th Advanced H Q at R9 b central

---

The Scheme outlined above is the general Divisional scheme of line communication and will be maintained as fully as possible throughout the operations. Brigades and groups will lay spurs to the nearest of the above Communication Centres and will be expected to maintain these spurs with their own Signal personnel.

VISUAL

A combined Divisional Visual Scheme will be in operation as under:— (DIAGRAM "B" attached)

(1) Visual Stations will be established at the following points
  (A) R 8 c 6.5   Central Visual Station. Personnel and instruments supplied by 32 Sig Coy. The station to be connected by telephone with YCB at R 9 central.
  (B) R 8 a 7.5   Central Visual Station. Personnel and instruments supplied by 46 Div Sig Coy. Communication with HP by Orderly.
  (C) Neighbourhood of ASCENSION FARM (G 25 c)   Exact spot to be notified later. Central Visual Station. Personnel and instruments to be found by 46 Div Sig Coy.
  (D) Neighbourhood of OH exchange (G 27 d 0.5)   Exact spot to be notified later. Personnel and instruments to be found by 46 Div Sig Coy.
  (E) Neighbourhood of YCBR (G21 c 3.1)   Central Visual Station. Personnel and instruments to be found by 32 Div Sig Coy. Exact spot to be notified later.
  (F) Neighbourhood of G 30 c.   Central Visual Station. Will be established by 32 Div Sig Coy as soon as the situation permits.

Brigades and Groups will get into communication with these stations as soon as possible.

WIRELESS

46 Div Sig Coy

(1) Wilson Set will be installed near ADHQ at R 8 c 3.3. This set will be connected with ADHQ by telephone and Orderly.
(2) One Trench Set will be installed at HUDSONS POST (R8 a 6.8) serving 138 and 139 Headquarters.
(3) A further Trench Set will be installed at or as near as possible to OH exchange at G 27 d 0.5.
(4) One Trench Set will be held in reserve complete with stores and personnel at HUDSONS POST and will be used as occasion directs either for stepping up or to replace casualty.
(5) The fourth Trench Set will be placed at the disposal of the D.C.O as part of a special system of communications for his use dealt with in other instructions.
(6) The forward accumulator-charging set will be at R 8 c 3.3 and the Wireless Officer will be responsible for the charging and distribution of accumulators. For this purpose a box car and limber will be placed at his disposal.

32 Div Sig Coy

(1) One Trench Set will accompany each Bde.
(2) One Trench Set will be erected at D H Q at R9 b central
(3) Wilson Set will be erected at G 21 c as soon as circumstances permit.
(4) Forward charging set to be sent to G 21 c.
(5) One Loop Set will be allotted to 14 and 97 Bdes to work under Bde arrangements.

MESSAGE ROCKETS

Ten Message Rockets will be issued to 137 Bde and five to 138 Bde and 139 Bde. They will be used under Bde arrangements.

PIGEONS

20 pigeons per day will be allotted to the 32nd Division. None are available for 46 Division.

MOUNTED ORDERLIES

Two Mounted Orderlies will be attached to each Brigade of the 46 Division.

DESPATCH RIDERS

The normal Despatch Rider service to Brigades will not run. Specials will be run to and from Bdes as occasion arises.

AEROPLANE SIGNALLING

All Brigade Signal Officers will notify Divisional Signal Company H Q of the positions of their Aeroplane Dropping Grounds immediately their Headquarters is selected. Ground Strips and Popham Panels will be laid out and a constant watch kept at Divisional and Brigade Dropping Grounds from daylight until dusk by men specially detailed for the purpose.

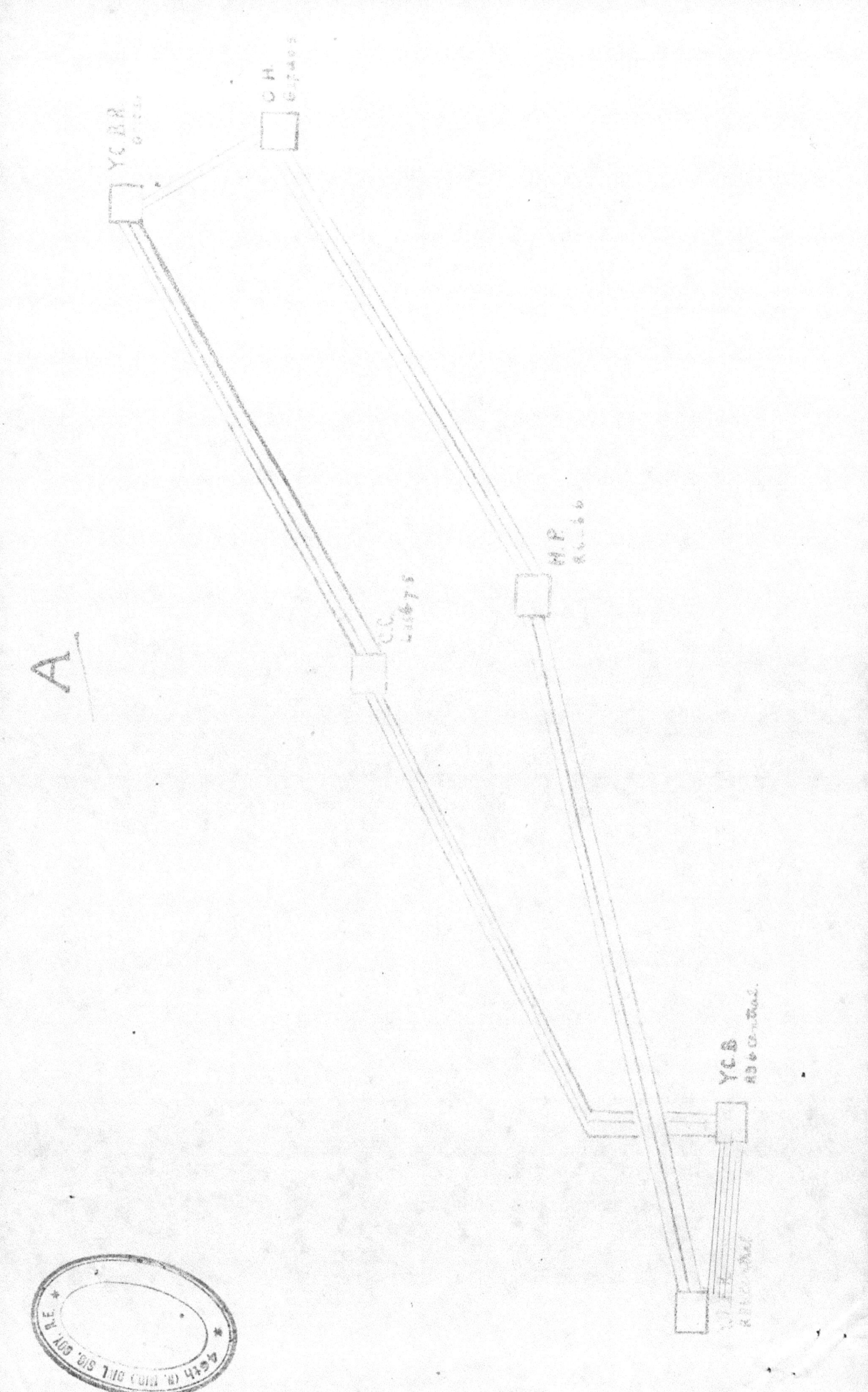

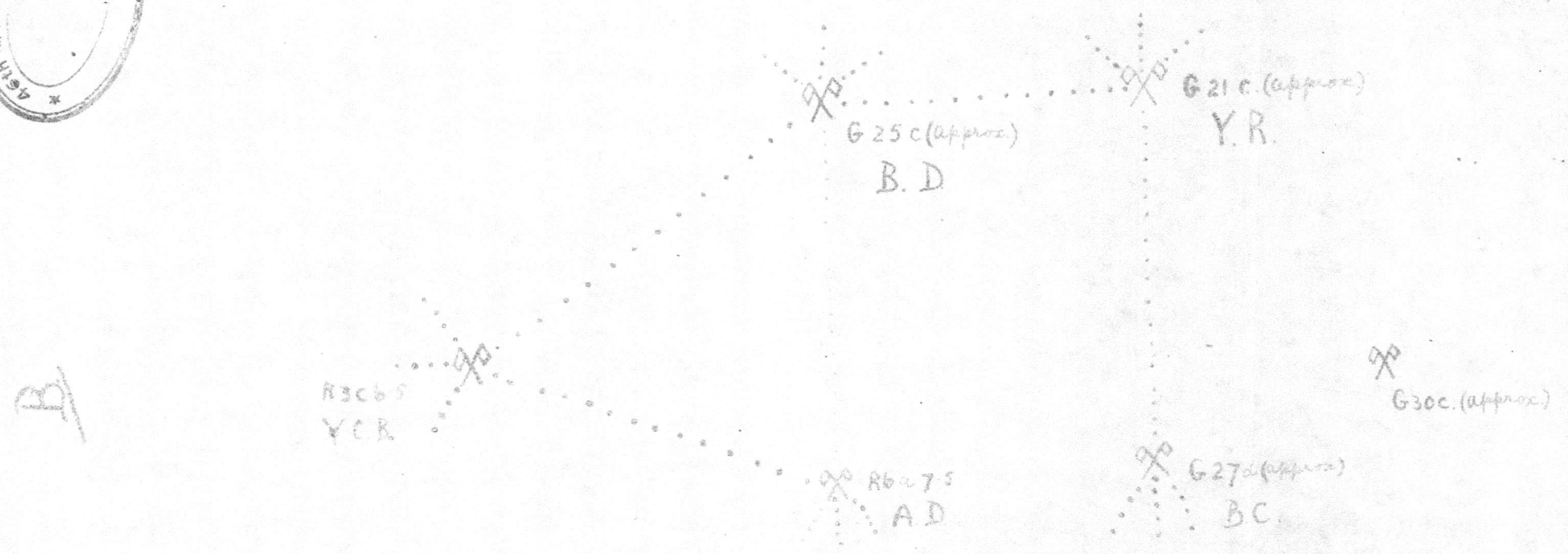
B
R3c6.5
Y.C.R.
G25c (approx)
B.D
G21c (approx)
Y.R.
R6a7.5
A.D
G27d (approx)
B.C.
G30c (approx)

Army Form C. 2118.

WAR DIARY
or
INTELLIGENCE SUMMARY.
(Erase heading not required.)

Instructions regarding War Diaries and Intelligence Summaries are contained in F. S. Regs., Part II. and the Staff Manual respectively. Title pages will be prepared in manuscript.

Place	Date	Hour	Summary of Events and Information	Remarks and references to Appendices
VENDELLES	1/10/18		Advd Report Centre established east of Vendelles canal at S.29.d.9.0. Lines laid out to all Bde HQs. Three cable detachments and personnel in charge of a linesman. Advd cable dump established at same place.	
LA BARAQUE	2/10/18 3/10/18	9 p.m.	We were informed at 9pm tonight that the Division was to fight again at 0600 on 3/10/18. All night was spent arranging lines/wireless & Visual Ground to the Bdes, Corps & Flank Divisions. The Cdn Corps — that is to the outburst Division on our left — came through at 0500 on 3/10. All comms held up throughout the battle, & the Divisional Staff was in touch by Telephone with all formations throughout. Wireless functioned throughout the Divisional & brigade networks but was only used for occasional situation reports once the line to Cavalry had started. MMK & Visual Scheme was arranged to commence from Zero — but the MMK the M.M. could not be called on to reach and was used with the rest of the troops following.	
LA BARAQUE	4/10/18		Wireless concentrates on own system & managing Visual to reach all Bdes. The whole of the Company now concentrated at LA BARAQUE	
MAGNY LA FOSSE	5/10/18 6th		Division moved to MAGNY from VENDELLE where it had been in rest previously. Report Centre opened at MAGNY in the Y.M.	
FRESNOY LE GRAND	10/10/18		Division moved forward again. Usual system of communication.	O Appd Centre

Army Form C. 2118.

WAR DIARY
or
INTELLIGENCE SUMMARY.
(Erase heading not required.)

46 Divisional Signal Company

Place	Date	Hour	Summary of Events and Information	Remarks and references to Appendices
FRESNOY LE GRAND	9/10/Y		A Report Centre was opened at BEAUREGARD FARM on this day but was reorganised according to the move forward to FRESNOY. Personnel & instruments were withdrawn on the 11th. During the present arms month numerous cable attachments & movements attached to the Infantry Bde — to supplement & maintaining comm. between Divan HQ & the Bde.	
	14/10/18		Div HQ Lins comm. satisfactory. Visual & Wireless left unless desirable. Instructions laid down in attached appendices A + B. Wireless between a French & British Divisions no on long latus to our right & the French on 6 Corps on our right, attached appendices for letter. All Stations attached Bde. to supplement for comms. between letter Division & the British Division on our left & for comms. between Division & Corps.	A + B C
	17/10/18		In cooperation with French Corps on our right & 6th + 1st Division on our left the 46 Division attacked this morning N of the Bro' a Regiments. All repetitions Arrangements early in the day. Comms. were so good or attached appendices C + time table of thruput the attack in spite of heavy shelling between YDFR behind Bde transport throughout to Bde, to on line of 13/Bde Visual HQ. Wireless worked throughout and morning when the 1st lady was imperative on the traffic was dealt with without delay throughout.	C

Army Form C. 2118.

WAR DIARY
or
INTELLIGENCE SUMMARY.
(Erase heading not required.)

Place	Date	Hour	Summary of Events and Information	Remarks and references to Appendices
FRESNOY LE GRAND	16/10/18		138 & 139 Bdes withdrawn to FRESNOY today. Divn HQ at REGNICOURT. 137 Bde remains with HQ in BOHAIN and Battalion at ANDIGNY LES FERMES. A cmph pair has been lent by Survey Co. to the latter place. Artillery shoot moved up to lines have been attended accordingly.	4 (D) Divn Signal Co.
"	31/10/18		Rest in FRESNOY. Wader & Vowel Training	

16 – 31/10/18

Alfgrnd Major R.E.
OC 46 Divisional Signal Company

WIRELESS.

(1) In future one trench set and personnel to work it will be allotted to each Infantry Brigade, the fourth set being either spare or in use by the Divisional Observation Officer.

(2) The Brigade Signal Officer will arrange to ration the three men who form the personnel of the set and will be responsible for the erection and working of the station serving their Headquarters. They will keep the Wireless Officer *early* informed of any repairs and spare parts required and will immediately report defects to him.

(3) The N.C.O. i/c the set or the Senior wireless operator will be responsible for the technical working of the set controlled by him and for the observation of wireless procedure.

(4) A trench mortar handcart is being attached to each Brigade Section for transport of the W/T set which will always accompany Brigade Headquarters.

(5) The Wireless Officer is responsible for the general supervision of the W/T sets and the personnel from the Technical point of view. He will inspect all Brigade sets at least once every two days and will see that they are correct in every detail of their equipment.

(6) When necessary he will withdraw sets requiring overhaul and repair and will then arrange to replace with a spare set if available or if the Brigade is in the line to replace set and personnel with that of the Reserve Brigade.

(7) He will be responsible for the changing of accumulators and their delivery to units and will at once report any cases where neglect or mishandling is apparent.

(8) By means of his directing station which will be erected at advanced Division H.Q. he will control procedure and see that touch is maintained with both flank divisions.

(9) He will report in writing to O.C., Signals on Sunday of each week that all sets have been inspected at least three times during the week and that all are complete and correct with specified exception.

(10) He will be responsible for the care and supervision of the set allotted to the D.O.O. and for its erection when required at the latters H.Q. He will detail personnel to stand by to man the set. When the set is out at rest he will take personnel and mules on his strength and will ration them through the Signal Co C.Q.M.S. This set will be overhauled and tested each time it comes out of action and will be inspected in detail before it is sent up the line again.

(11) Every effort should be made to dispose of as many messages as possible by wireless in normal times. If this is not done the sets cannot be expected to function properly in battle.

(12) All messages for the Brigade Wireless Station will be handed in at the Brigade Signal Office.

(13) The D.O.O. Station will be reserved for his work, the only *other* messages which will be dealt with at this station being urgent operation messages which have been submitted to him and franked by him.

2/10/18.

Major, R.E.
O.C., 46th Divisional Signal Co., R.E.

Office **B** VISUAL

1. Divisional Visual personnel will be utilised in future as under:—

2. At Divisional H.Q or on the nearest prominent point a terminal station will be provided working forward to Divisional Central Visual Station and to any units which may obtain direct communication with it.

3. This station will be connected with Divisional Signal office by telephone or Orderly according to the distance & will be manned night and day, using flags, lamp or helio as circumstances direct.

4. As far as personnel permits, Central Visual Stations will be established on prominent positions forward of Divisional H.Q, these positions being chosen with a view to obtaining visual communication with as many H.Q. of subordinate formations and units as possible.

5. Central Visual Stations will normally be provided with sufficient personnel and instruments to work three ways at once.

6. Their positions will be notified to Signal Officers Brigades & Groups & these in turn will be responsible for notifying responsible officers or N.C.O's of Signals of lesser formations & units.

7. The personnel of the stations will be instructed to keep a sharp look out for any units calling them but will pay special attention to traffic to and from Division, Brigades H.Q and Artillery Group H.Q.

8. Brigade & Group Signal officers will be held responsible for manning terminal stations at their H.Q to work back to the nearest of these Central Visual stations. Personnel for these Brigade & Group Stations will be found from the R.E. Sections, Subsections, or the Brigade Pool.

9. The O.C. Visual will submit to H.Q Div Sig Co a diagram with map references and calls of the stations in the Div' Visual scheme and will be responsible for notifying all changes.

10. Calls for Brigade & Group stations will be allotted from Div' Sig Coy H.Q.

11. H.Q Div' Sig Coy will be responsible for notifying Brigades & Groups of the positions & calls of the stations of the Divisional system.

12. O.C. Visual will be responsible for care of all visual stores belonging to H.Q & Sergt PURTON is detailed to act as Storekeeper under him.

13. Brigade & Group Signal officers will submit to H.Q copies of diagrams of their Visual schemes. This is especially important before any special operations in which the Division is taking part.

_____ Capt.,
for Major, 46th Div. Sig. Co., R.E.

SIGNAL INSTRUCTIONS.
****

1. **LINES.** (See Diagram A).

   (a) <u>Main Routes</u>. (i) An Advanced Div'l Exchange will be installed at present H.Q of 137th Inf: Bde (D 21 a 9.0). This will be connected to Divisional and Div'l Artillery Exchanges at FRESNOY by a trunk route of 3 pairs.

   (ii) A forward exchange will be installed at combined 138th, 139th Bde H.Q at D 11 b 5.0. This will be connected to Adv. Div'l Exchange (D 21 a 9.0) by two pairs.

   (b) <u>Artillery Lines</u>. (i) One pair will be laid from the Adv. Div'l Exchange to each Artillery Group.

   (ii) A lateral will be laid between the Right and Left Group.

   (iii) Sub-Groups will lay lines from their H.Q to those of their Groups.

   (iv) Liaison Lines between Infantry and Artillery Brigades will be laid by the Artillery Groups.

   (v) One line between Adv. Bde H.Q, Group H.Q and Division will be kept clear as far as possible for R.A work.

   (c) <u>Laterals</u>. (i) Two pairs are already in existence between 46th Division H.Q exchange and the H.Q of both flank divisions.

   (ii) 138 Bde will be responsible for laying a lateral between the combined Adv. Bde H.Q at D 11 d 2.9 and the Brigade H.Q of the 6th Division at VAUX ANDIGNY (W 19 a central).

   (d) <u>Maintenance</u>. (i) Div'l H.Q linemen and one cable detachment will be responsible for the maintenance of the Div'l laterals, Locals and the main trunk route to the Adv. Div'l Exchange.

   (ii) One cable detachment will be stationed at the Adv. Div'l Exchange to maintain the main trunk route to Division and the two pairs to Adv. Bde exchange.

   (iii) One cable detachment will be stationed at the Adv. Div'l Exchange to maintain all artillery group communications.

   (iv) One cable detachment will be stationed at Adv. Bde Exchange to maintain the two pairs back to Adv. Div'l Exchange and to assist in maintaining the inter-divisional Brigade lateral.

   (v) Artillery Sub-Groups will be responsible for maintenance of lines to Groups.

   (vi) Artillery Groups will arrange with Inf: Bdes for the mutual maintenance of liaison lines.

   (vii) Inf: Bdes will be responsible for maintenance of all lines forward of Bde H.Q.

2. **WIRELESS.** (See Diagram B).

   (a) <u>Spark Sets</u>. (i) One trench set will be established at DHQ.

   (ii) The Directing Sets will be erected near Adv. Div: Exchange.

P.T.O.

(iii) One trench set will be at Adv. Bde H.Q (D 11 d 2.9).

(iv) One trench set will be held in reserve at Adv. Bde H.Q to be used forward as required.

(v) One trench set will accompany the D.O.C and act under his orders.

(vi) One loop set complete with two operators will be issued to OC, Signals, 139 Bde, and will be used at his discretion.

(b) C.W. Sets. (1) Two C.W. Sets have been issued to 231 Bde, RFA: these will be used for communication between FOO and Group HQ. The Group Set will in addition work to Div'l directing Set.

(ii) Liaison with the French division will be established by C.W. Sets in addition.

Sets will be in positions on Y Day, but will not be tested through until after Zero hour, when communication will be established as quickly as possible.

"In clear" messages may be sent at the discretion of officers concerned from Zero to Zero plus 12 hours.

After this hour, all messages, unless specially franked "By wireless in Clear" by a Staff Officer will be sent in cipher.

3. VISUAL. (See Diagram C).

Visual Stations will be established as follows :-

Type of Station.	Map Reference.	Call.	Line Connections.
Terminal Station.	I 12 d 3.4.	DF	Phone to DHQ.
" "	D 21 c 2.1	AD	Phone to Adv. Div. Ex.
Central V Station.	D 26 d 0.4.	BD	
" " "	D 23 a 2.7.	OD	
" " "	D 11 c 5.0.	ED	Phone to Adv. Bde. Ex.

All above Stations will be worked under arrangements made by Div'l Signal Co.

Brigades and Artillery Groups will be responsible for providing sufficient Visual Stations to duplicate line communications forward.

Any station desiring to send messages by Visual will get into touch with the nearest of these stations.

4. PIGEONS. Eight pigeons will be issued to each Brigade on Y Day.

5. MOTOR CYCLES. (1) Two motor cyclists will be detailed for duty at Adv. Div. Exchange.

(ii) The remainder will remain at Div. H.Q.

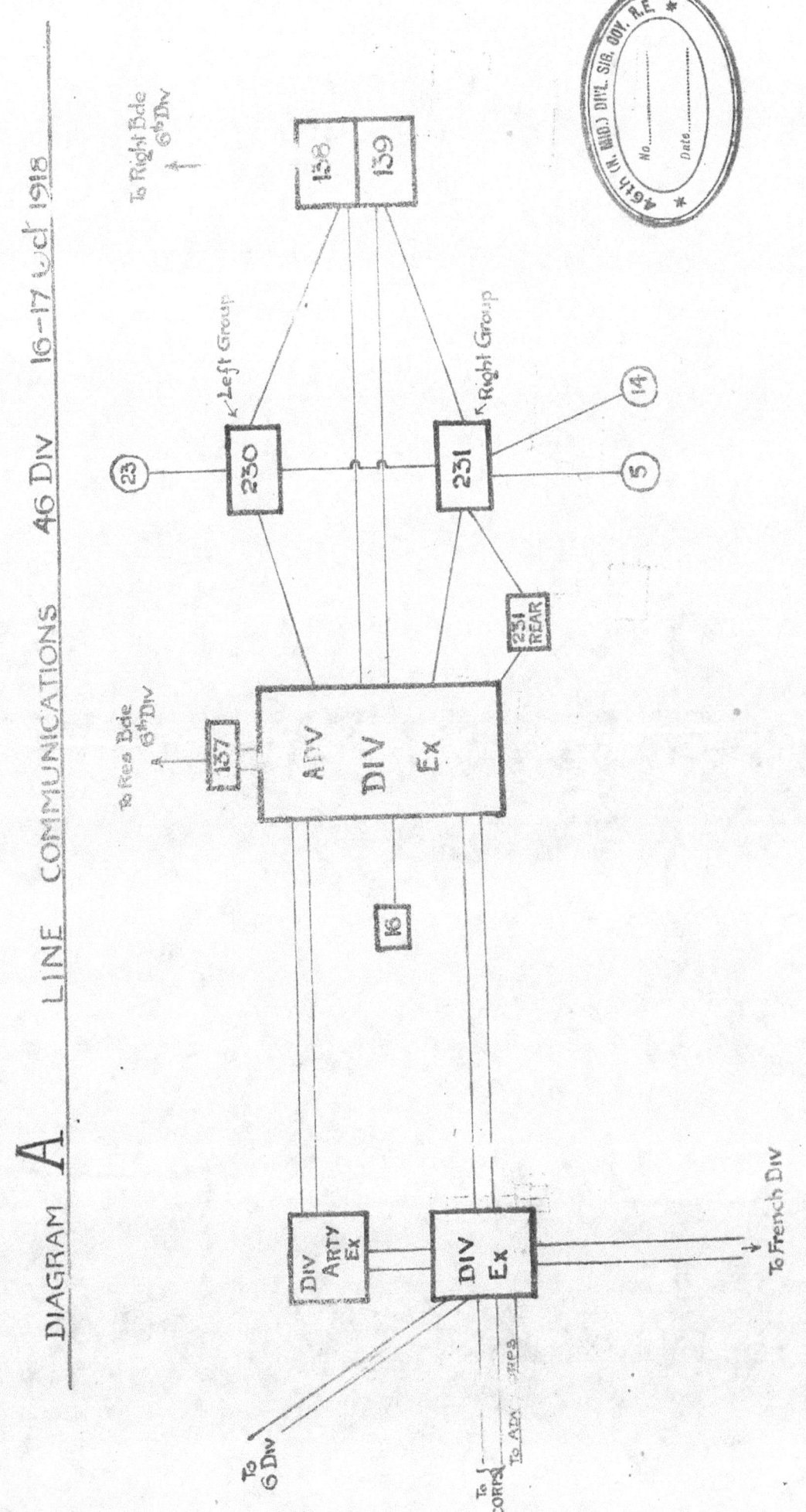

DIAGRAM B — WIRELESS COMMUNICATIONS 46 Div 16-17 Oct 1918

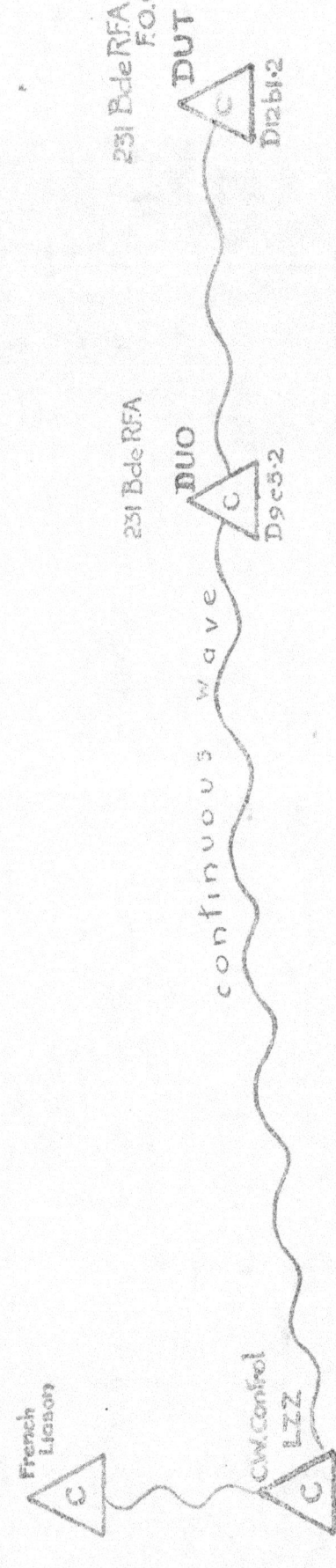
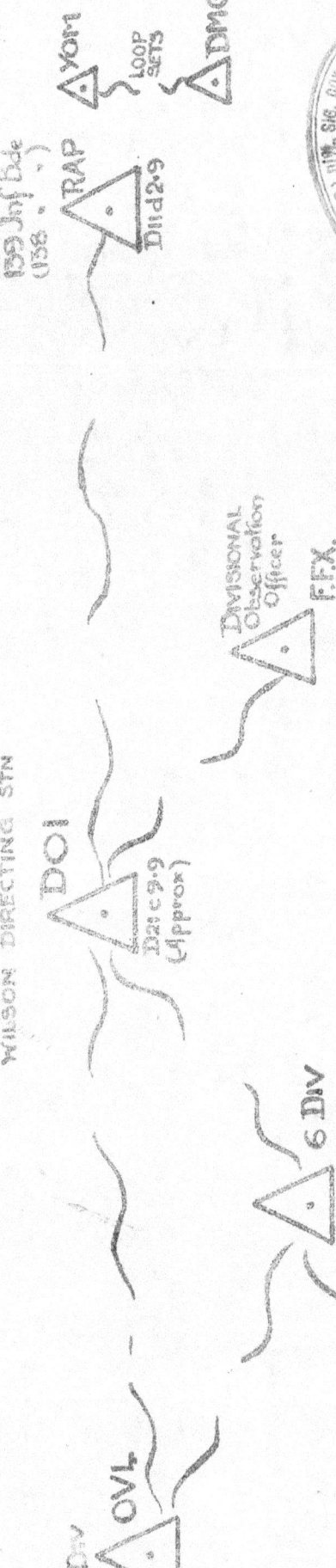

DIAGRAM C

VISUAL COMMUNICATIONS - 46 Div 16-17/10/18

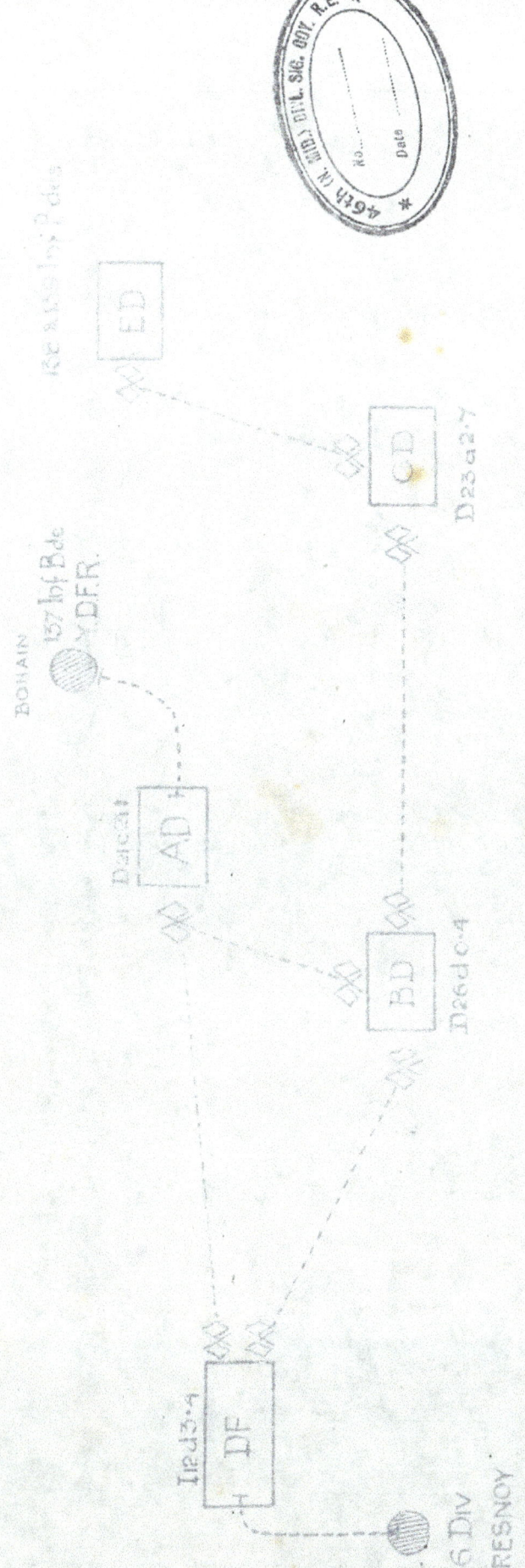

N.B.- Map reference of "ED" to be notified by WIRE later.

WAR DIARY
INTELLIGENCE SUMMARY

Army Form C. 2118.

Place	Date November	Hour	Summary of Events and Information	Remarks and references to Appendices
BOHAIN/pt	4th		On rest.	
MOLAIN	5th		Moving up in support of 1st Division	
L'ARBRE DE GUISE			Took over from 1st Division after their crossing of the OISE - SAMBRE Canal	
CATILLON	6th		Following up the retreating enemy troops. Officers out all forward reconnoitring Back permanent route. 3 Cable wagons with Advanced Party under Lieut Milne engaged in	
PRISCHES	8th		Carrying forward the Divisional Trunk Line in anticipation of move of Sigh HQ.	
CARTIGNIES	9th		Two Para Cirard and maintained throughout and attained forward of Sigh Battn	
SAINS DU NORD	11th		& Companies. Wireless stepped up as required by move of Wlar o Third R.W.I. Bas & Wad Div HQ. Bah set up but not just used. DOB's worked set and throughout the advance all Bde & forward Sets in touch without interruption. No Visual used. Special TK lines to regiment Communication Despatch Throughput	
LANDRECIES	14th 6.30ft		Armistice signed on November 11th. Division moved back to LANDRECIES on a 14th. Time opens devoted to relaying & clearing up. Signal Company complete to establishment & surplus stores returned to Corps.	

4/12/18

M Prentz Capt R.E.
for O.C. 46 Signal Cy

Army Form C. 2118.

WAR DIARY
or
INTELLIGENCE SUMMARY.
(Erase heading not required.)

46 D Signal

WR 42

Place	Date	Hour	Summary of Events and Information	Remarks and references to Appendices
LANDRECIES	DEC 1–31		In Rest. Time devoted to Salvage of cable in the Divisional area & the cleaning up of LANDRECIES. Order 165 mls of Cable were salved and Over 4 tons 3 cwts 2.2 qr lbs of Various gauges of copper wire salved – the G.L. wire being much when not salving the time was devoted to cleaning up of Lorries, Wagons &c. A Divisional School was opened on the 2 Dec – and closed on the 28 Dec. for the Xmas Vacation. Classes for Motor-cycle Repairs, Electric lighting, Wireless and Telegraphy & Telephony were taken. The Students being drawn from the various units in the Divn & from the signal Company as well.	[signature] Major R.E. Cmdg 46 Divnl Sig Coy RE

Army Form C. 2118.

WAR DIARY
or
INTELLIGENCE SUMMARY.
(Erase heading not required.)

Place	Date	Hour	Summary of Events and Information	Remarks and references to Appendices
LANDRECIES	JAN 1st–9th		At Rest.	
LE CATEAU	JAN 9th–31st		Time devoted to Salvage of Signal Stores and Cable in the Divisional Area. Le CATEAU Area Telephone Exchange taken over by this Coy on Jan 10th from XIII Corps Signals. The Divisional Signal School reopened on January 16th and courses started for Motor Cycle, Visual, Lantern Lighting, Wireless Telegraphy and Telephony. The Students coming from various Units in the Division. Fifteen moves were demobilised on the 27th and Eighteen on the 31st of January.	

Silvers
Major R.E.
Comdg 46th Divl Signal Coy R.E.

Army Form C. 2118.

WAR DIARY
of
INTELLIGENCE SUMMARY.
(Erase heading not required.)

Instructions regarding War Diaries and Intelligence Summaries are contained in F. S. Regs., Part II. and the Staff Manual respectively. Title pages will be prepared in manuscript.

Place	Date	Hour	Summary of Events and Information	Remarks and references to Appendices
LE CATEAU	February 1st – 28th		Company employed in taking the area of cattle. Signal Coy School of Motorcycling, Wireless and Telegraph Operating closed of 15th. Company proceeded with demobilisation of men and horses. Artillery Bde Subsections withdrawn to Coy Hdqrs during the month.	

WAR DIARY or INTELLIGENCE SUMMARY

Army Form C. 2118.

Place	Date	Hour	Summary of Events and Information	Remarks and references to Appendices
Le Cateau	1/3/19 to 31/3/19		Company proceeded with demobilisation of men and animals. The Brigade Schools and Inspections were concentrated with Head Quarters of Company. Telephonic Communication was gradually reduced and all cable lines reeled up. Major E.A. Lewis R.E. R.E. appointed acting C.S.O. XIII Corps on the 19th and Capt. C. Empsone M.C. R.E. took over Command of the Company. Divisional H.Qrs. moved to CAUDRY on the 25th and were put in communication with the CAULDRY Area Exchange. The Signal Company running at Le Cateau owing to scarcity of billets at CAUDRY.	

Army Form C. 2118.

WAR DIARY
~~INTELLIGENCE SUMMARY.~~
(Erase heading not required.)

Instructions regarding War Diaries and Intelligence Summaries are contained in F. S. Regs., Part II. and the Staff Manual respectively. Title pages will be prepared in manuscript.

Place	Date	Hour	Summary of Events and Information	Remarks and references to Appendices
LE CATEAU	April 1st/2nd		Company moved to CAUDRY on 2nd inst	WWW
CAUDRY	April 2nd/30th		Normal situation of men and horses was completed during the month.	

WAR DIARY
INTELLIGENCE SUMMARY.
(Erase heading not required.)

Army Form C.-2118.

Place	Date	Hour	Summary of Events and Information	Remarks and references to Appendices
CAUDRY	1st MAY – 31st MAY.		Stores and Equipment of the Company were checked and cleaned during the month. Several batches of returnable men were despatched to No. 3 Area Signal Coy and to the Rhine.	

O. Musgrave, Capt.
R.E. (T)
46th Divisional Signal Co. R.E.

WAR DIARY or INTELLIGENCE SUMMARY

Army Form C. 2118.

Place	Date	Hour	Summary of Events and Information	Remarks and references to Appendices
CAUDRY	1st JUNE to 30 JUNE		During the month the remainder of the retainable men were despatched either to the Rhine or to the Area Signal Companies. The Cadre was despatched to England for demobilisation on June 28th, leaving an advanced Guard of 2 Officers and 20 O.R. on the Cross and Wagons.	CMV

Carnagnere Capt RE
for Major R.E. (T)
46th Divisional Signal Co. R.E.